AMERICAN WITCHES

AMERICAN WITCHES

A Broomstick Tour through Four Centuries

SUSAN FAIR

Skyhorse Publishing

Skyhorse Publishing books may be purchased in bulk at special discounts for sales promotion, corporate gifts, fund-raising, or educational purposes. Special editions can also be created to specifications. For details, contact the Special Sales Department, Skyhorse Publishing, 307 West 36th Street, 11th Floor, New York, NY 10018 or info@skyhorsepublishing.com.

Skyhorse® and Skyhorse Publishing® are registered trademarks of Skyhorse Publishing, Inc.®, a Delaware corporation.

Visit our website at www.skyhorsepublishing.com.

10 9 8 7 6 5 4 3 2 1

Library of Congress Cataloging-in-Publication Data is available on file.

Cover design by Rain Saukas

Print ISBN: 978-1-5107-0380-3
Ebook ISBN: 978-1-5107-0381-0

Printed in the United States of America

Blame not witches, blame not wizards, magicians, sorcerers, or evil spirits, you are self-witched, infatuated, depraved.

—A Debate Proposed in the Temple Patrick Society, 1788

Contents

Preface

I was once accused of being a witch. I was ten years old.
Blame it on my proclivity for dressing up as a witch on
Halloween. Blame it on my well-known interest in "spooky"
things, or on a child's overactive imagination, or a bad dream.
At the time, all I knew was that my very large, very intimidating
next-door neighbor Mr. K* was at our door, and he was looking
for me. He entered the house; from behind him came the sound
of muffled sobs, and then the cute but tear-streaked face of his
five-year-old daughter Becky peeked out fearfully from behind
his pants leg. When she caught sight of me, she screamed. She
tried to run out the door, but her dad caught her.

"Noooo!" she wailed, flailing in her father's arms. It turned
out that my adorable little neighbor had dreamed the night
before that I was a witch. The nightmare had been so real she
could not be convinced that her neighborhood buddy, the shy
and timid Susan, was not the sinister fiend she had seen in her
dream. Becky had woken up early, Mr. K explained, screaming
"Susan's a witch!" and had remained semi-hysterical, disrupting
her family's morning until finally her father said, "Okay, let's go
over and see Sue. You'll see she's not a witch." Then he pretty
much had to drag her kicking and screaming over to our house.

Now he stood behind her in our kitchen, his hands braced on her shoulders, trying to get her to look at me. "See? It's just Sue! She's not a witch. She's just Sue! It was just a bad dream," he kept telling her. Becky kept clinging to him, giving me a five-year-old's version of the evil eye. My parents snickered as they passed in and out of the room, getting ready for church. Finally, Mr. K suggested that I dig out the witch hat I had worn that past Halloween, the one with the hot pink tissue paper fringe—a hallmark of a fake witch if ever there was one. Becky's wailing subsided to whimpering and sniffling at this proposal, though she was still staring at me with a look that was part fear and part disgust. But what I felt most was her *suspicion.* Suddenly, it was up to me to prove that I was not a witch. For a moment I wondered if maybe I really *was* a witch. Something that was pretty close to fear knotted my stomach.

I ran down into our basement, yanked a large, mildewed box marked "H'Ween" down from a dusty shelf, and, heart pounding, started rummaging through the semi-spooky debris of Halloweens past: a plastic red devil-head window light (dang, I wish I still had that!), cardboard cutouts of hissing cats, and bits and pieces of unidentifiable orange and black. Spying the incongruous hot pink fringe and glow-in-the-dark stars, I snatched out the hat, smooshed and raggedy though it was, and dashed back upstairs. Becky regarded it dubiously from the safety of her father's arms. She wasn't 100 percent convinced that I wasn't a witch, but she was also getting kind of tired of the whole thing. If I *was* a witch, I was a pretty boring one. She sniffled and took a cookie my parents offered her. The Great Harrisville Road Witch Hunt was over.

It's startling today to realize that, during a certain time in American history, an incident as seemingly innocent as a little girl's scary dream could have resulted in someone being prosecuted—and even executed—as a witch.

But here's a confession: for a while when I was a little girl, I was a witch. At least I *tried* to be a witch. My subgenre of witchcraft consisted of wielding a little baggie of "pixie dust" (colored sugar left over from Christmas baking, in very un-witchlike shades of red and green) that I would sprinkle around to presumably "do magic." (In reality, I probably just managed to attract ants.) I also had a book of spells that my father had found on a bus and brought home to me, knowing I liked weird stuff and that I liked all books, period. I might have attempted some of the spells in that intriguing book if they didn't call for prohibitively hard-to-obtain ingredients, like bat blood and unpronounceable herbs; none of them called for my festive sugar pixie dust.

Okay, so I probably wasn't a witch, but what *is* a witch, anyway? You'll find out soon enough, and you'll also see that I got off pretty darn easy for my suspected witchery, because not so long ago simply having someone believe that you were a witch could transform your life into a living nightmare.

Notes

* Identities changed.

Introduction

What makes witches so fascinating—and so terrifying? Maybe it's all the stuff they've been accused of doing over the years: eating children, having sex with the devil, making someone's bread smell funny. Admittedly, some of their hijinks are more fascinating and terrifying than others, but it's undeniable that witches are a staple of nightmares, fairy tales . . . and American history. Yet few of us realize what a pervasive presence witches have been in America. This history is traditionally and perhaps justly defined by the Salem witch trials, but we do ourselves a disservice when we limit our awareness of American witches to the year 1692. The purpose of this book is to bring to light some of the extraordinary lesser-known stories from America's witch history.

You're about to undertake a strange and startling tour across four hundred years of witchcraft in America, and it's going to be way weirder than you can even imagine. Our Broomstick Tour will showcase America as you've never seen it. Here is a sneak peek at what we'll encounter along the way. Ready to take off?

Look—down there! On the deck of that storm-tossed ship on its way to the New World we see a mob of angry sailors about to hang an old lady; in a few moments, she'll be swinging above the deck from a makeshift gallows on the yardarm. And over there, in that seemingly normal Puritan household in New England—are those children *flying* around the room? And quick, over there at the hearth! Is something trying to pull that little girl into the fire? And what on earth is going on here? It's the eve of the Civil War; why is that man putting on a dress to go witch hunting in New York City?

You will read about these and many other strange events in American witch history. How do we know these things really happened? Because the witches and their accusers left some very detailed records, including court documents, town ledgers, journals, diaries, letters, and newspaper accounts from an amazing number of witchcraft cases. But it's those first-person narratives—the diaries and letters—that tell the most compelling tales.

When you write about history, you spend a lot of time alone communing with dead people. Sometimes they come through loud and clear, like those times when you're up late into the night reading the seventeenth-century diary of a man who cried over the deaths of his children, worried about the state of his eternal soul until he almost couldn't bear it—yet helped send innocent people to their deaths as witches. That man was the Reverend Cotton Mather, and he, above all others, has come to be considered the real villain in the Salem witch craze. How did this intelligent, Harvard-educated, painfully sensitive man come to believe in witches? Luckily, the very candid diary he kept for much of his life reveals the conflicted person behind the witch-hunter persona. And then there's the letter sent "from Salem Prison" by accused witch Abigail Falkner, then pregnant with her seventh child and begging the governor for her life.

The words left by these troubled souls and others like them reveal the many lived realities behind the word "witch."

Witches followed settlers to the New World, and witches were already here, waiting on the shores and in the forests. Witches lurk in the all the darkest corners of American history. They are hidden deep within the dry pages of town histories, courtroom archives, and musty newspapers. But they don't want to be buried; they want to rise up from their forlorn graves and tell us their stories.

So let's get started. We've got some witches to meet.

A Note on Spelling and Grammar

In the interest of clarity, some spellings, punctuation, etc., have been altered from that appearing in the original texts and documents quoted. In addition to being written in the often-perplexing Early Modern English, many of the documents and narratives from which these stories come are incomplete, and names and spellings of names often differ from one account to the other. I've done my best to piece together these tales accurately; however, in the interest of storytelling, some cases include thoughts attributed to persons or other details that are based on conjecture from my readings of historical accounts.

Part I

America's Starter Witches

CHAPTER 1

A Field Guide to the American Witch

Every old woman with a wrinkled face, a furrowed brow, a hairy lip, a gobber tooth, a squint eye, a squeaking voice or scolding tongue, having a rugged coat on her back, a skull-cap on her head, a spindle in her hand and a dog or cat by her side, is not only suspect but pronounced for a witch.

—John Gaule, seventeenth-century clergyman

Witches—what's their deal, anyway? What do they want, and why do they want it? How can you recognize one? And what the holy heck is a *teat*? Do we really even want to know?

If you think you've got a witch on your hands—well, first of all, good luck. But this quick guide may help you identify your American witch and provide some insider details that will come in handy as you read the rest of this book. Even if you're pretty certain you'll never meet a witch, it won't hurt to be prepared—after all, this is America, where anything is possible. And because sniffing out the American witch is the culmination of centuries of European witch detection and persecution, it's really frighteningly easy.

Meet the American Witch

You'll be happy to know that in America, the devil is an equal-opportunity employer. While it's traditional to refer to witches with feminine pronouns, the American witch can be, and often is, a man. A witch can also be a dog or a pig or . . . well, we'll get into all that later. Suffice it to say, America can feel good about diversity when it comes to witches.

And just what *is* a witch? Traditionally, a witch is someone who has made a pact with the devil. We may think of becoming a witch as an aspiration for power-hungry sociopath types, but in fact, it's often the more vulnerable members of society who are most tempted by the devil's promises. Fed up with being the lowly laundress for a family that hasn't bathed since last winter? Sick and tired of lying awake at night waiting for a band of angry Indians to come howling out of the woods behind your house? Good news! A deal with the devil can give you much-needed peace of mind. A witch may also be promised other tempting stuff: nice clothes, plenty of money, not starving to death. What the witch is actually going to get, however, is a small plot of land in Hell. The witch's job description, as prepared by the devil's human resources minions, consists largely of trying to recruit other witches to assist the devil in overthrowing God.

What a Witch Wants, What a Witch Needs

Once she has taken the plunge and signed a pact with the devil, just what does a witch want from you? When it comes to *you*, the American witch generally wants one of two things: recruitment or revenge. What she does *not* want: your ruby slippers.

At the top of the newly minted witch's to-do list: getting you to sign "The Book." What is The Book? Those who have seen it describe it as a thick, heavy ledger of sorts, where unspeakable covenants were spelled out in red, and where vulnerable souls were invited to literally sign their lives away. The Book is an official document straight from the devil, and when you sign it, that's it. It's a bit like signing a student loan document, or a cell phone contract: you're pretty much committed forever. It's not so much the witch herself who wants you to sign up; it's just that she's got this quota to fill for the Big Guy, or, you know, *else*.

Occasionally, the devil will appear in person, book in hand, and this is where the really good offers can come in. He wants to make you an offer you can't refuse; he'll "take care of you," if you know what he means. You'll be in the *family*, he says. Case in point: accused Salem witch, Abigail Hobbs. The twenty-two-year-old Abigail was the subject of much whispering by local busybodies, and what of it? A girl just wanted to have a little fun, even if it was a Puritan village in the 1600s. And that was where the devil seized the opportunity to approach her in the woods (a favorite hangout spot for both the devil and Abigail, according to Salem tales) and tempt her. "He said he would give me fine things," Abigail reported; this was followed up by offers of fine clothes—which, Abigail complained, she never received.

Revenge is another matter entirely. Now that she's got pre-ternatural powers, a witch might as well enjoy them, right? So if your nemesis has become a witch, expect payback. This will most likely be in the form of something really crummy happening to your hogs, but, if the witch is really a jerk, it could be happening to your kid instead. There are, as we'll see, many forms of witch revenge, ranging from the mundane (You know that bread you like to bake? Well, it's totally not going to turn out very good.) to the terrible (You didn't really want all those kids anyway, did you?).

A New World of Witches

In many ways, the American witch—in particular the colonial witch—is a whole different breed from her cousins in the Old World. The American witch seems to spend a lot more time bewitching people, animals, and inanimate objects than the European witch. Witches in the Old World were much more concerned with having lascivious parties, eating babies, and doing unspeakable things with/to Satan, while, for the most part, the American witch, spawn of a Puritan community, con-fined her scandalous behavior to stuff like suckling her familiar during church services.

Identifying the American Witch

It was discovered pretty early on that one of the most entertain-ing—er, efficient—ways of finding out if someone was a witch was to strip her and give her a good looking-over. This type of thorough search quickly revealed any incriminating witch's marks, teats, or other blemishes that (if you wanted them to) could confirm that you had a witch on your hands.

Teats are the most notorious physical hallmark of the American witch, and they're pretty much exactly what you're thinking they are, except smaller, less photogenic, and in unlikely places. And guess what, men? You, too, can have witch teats! You're welcome.

The purpose of a teat is to enable a witch to suckle a devil's familiar, and most often it's said that the creature is sucking blood, not milk, from its witch. Teats can turn up anywhere on a witch's body; one Salem witch was seen suckling a familiar from a teat between her fingers, and a male witch was seen suckling a familiar from a teat underneath his tongue (in church, no less!). But the most common place to find a teat (or at least the most common place to look for one) was in the witch's most private areas. For example, according to Salem-era court records, a free-for-all on the body of accused witch Bridget Bishop located a "preternatural excrescence of flesh between the pudendum and anus much like teats and not usual in women."

A witch mark, also called a devil's mark, is sometimes used to describe a teat, but it can also be something different entirely. Basically, any unusual mark on the skin—be it scar, pimple, wart, bruise, bug bite, birthmark, or something you just kind of think that you might see if you squint just right—can be a witch mark if you want it to be.

Frenchman Nicolas Remy, a respected advisor to the royal court and a go-to authority on witches in the sixteenth century, provides some useful background on witch marks. In his *Demonolatry*, a sinister 1595 textbook that was used as a handy how-to guide (as in "how to tell who's a witch so you can kill her" guide), the historian, lawyer, poet, and demonologist explains, "It is not enough for Demons to hold Men bound and fettered by a verbal oath: but they furthermore mark them with their talons as an enduring witness of the servitude to which they have subjected them." When examining a witch mark, Remy notes, it's important to keep in mind that it will be "entirely insensitive and devoid of feeling." So poke away—the sharper the object, the better!

"Ducking," also called "dunking" and sometimes termed "swimming," is one of the most picturesque ways of identifying a witch. Ducking a witch didn't usually involve those elaborate contraptions depicted in European artwork; American witch detection is much more efficient (or maybe lazy). It was found that simply tying your suspected witch hand to foot and then tossing her into the nearest body of water worked just as well as a fancy machine. And what are you looking for when you employ witch ducking? It's simple: if your suspect is really a witch, she will float, despite being bound, and you can save yourself the trouble of having a trial and get right to the good stuff: planning a hanging. (But now you've got an angry, wet witch on your hands, so, well—good luck with that one.) And if your accused witch *isn't* really a witch? She'll sink like a normal person and drown. Done! Now, wasn't that easy?

Witch Words

Aside from teats (you just can't say that word too many times), witch marks, and witch ducking, there are a few other terms you need to know when it comes to discussing the American witch.

Here is a quick rundown of some of the most important words and phrases you're likely to encounter:

Familiars. They may look familiar, but don't get the wrong idea; these close associates of witches are imps sent by the devil from the depths of Hell to assist witches in their mayhem. After all, a witch can't do it all, can she? Sometimes she has to delegate. That's where familiars come in. No time to terrorize that annoying neighbor yourself? Dispatch your familiar in the form of a foul-tempered hog to chase him into his house! Want to freak out that lady from church who's always super judgey? Send in your menacing black cat familiar to jump onto her bed in the middle of the night! Familiars can appear in the form of virtually any creature, but cats, dogs, birds, swine, turtles, and toads are favorites. Unfortunately, familiars usually seem to be ravenously hungry; this is where the teats of a witch come in. Familiars require a lot of suckling—*a lot* of suckling—of the blood of their favorite witch.

　❦　*Goody or Goodwife.* You will often hear witches referred to as "Goody Cole," "Goodwife Jones," etc. In colonial America, as in England, these terms were not witch-specific. They were similar to using "Mrs." except with more class consciousness. Someone who was called "Goodwife" was not a member of nobility, but they weren't (necessarily) white trash, either. And "Goody" was simply a variation of "Goodwife," although sometimes it was used as a more casual title. We can safely assume that when one was addressing a witch, "*Good*wife" or "*Goody*" was probably said with a sarcastic sneer.

Maleficium. This is a fancy Latin name, usually reserved for court proceedings and official documents, for witchcraft that is used to inflict physical harm.

Poppets. These primitive, doll-like objects work on pretty much the same principle as the better-known voodoo doll; the difference is that a poppet is often merely a piece of wax, a knotted rag, or some other rough stand-in for the person the witch wishes to harm. These will often be found hidden around an accused witch's home; for instance, that rolled-up rag stuffed into the witch's window sash that she says is meant to keep out drafts? That is totally a poppet. Believe it.

Witch cake. Even witches don't want to eat a witch cake. The witch cake's fifteen minutes of fame came at the onset of the Salem witch craze, when Tituba, the West Indian (or African, or Native American, depending on which version of events you believe) slave of a local minister baked a cake made of rye flour and the urine of the little girls who were thought to be bewitched. Tituba was accused of witchcraft for making the cake, since doing so was considered a form of magic. But witch cakes were a European folk magic practice, and, sure enough, a white neighbor admitted having instructed Tituba on how to make the witch cake. The belief was that when this cake was fed to a dog, the dog would reveal the identity of the witch, presumably by vomiting at his or her feet.

And on that note, we're as ready as we'll ever be. Let's step back in time and discover some American witches.

Chapter 2

Witches on a Ship

*This Deponent hearing these words (She is dead) ran
out and asked who was dead, and it was replied the
Witch.*

—Court deposition regarding some unpleasantness on
board the ship *Charity* bound for Maryland, 1654

The first colonists brought many useful things with them
from Europe to the New World: pigs, cows, sheep, even
honeybees. They brought trunkfuls of household supplies and
clothing. They also brought some things that would have been
better left behind, things like teeny-tiny microbes that mor-
phed into diseases that would kill millions in America over
the coming centuries. Another dangerous, albeit interesting,
thing they brought with them across the wide Atlantic was a
long-standing, deeply rooted belief in witchcraft. According
to some records, the early emigrants from England even inadvertently brought along a few actual witches on their ships. In
this chapter, we are going to check out a few really bad voyages

to America and meet some of these alleged stowaway witches; along the way, we'll see what might happen to someone whom fellow passengers suspect of being a witch.

Let's say you're an emigrant boarding a ship for America in the 1600s. It's a pretty safe bet that your transatlantic voyage will be a veritable festival of foul smells, bad food, and seasickness. Since the ship you're on had been designed for transporting cargo (also known as merchant ships, they were the only vessels at the time that were sturdy enough to make the trans-Atlantic voyage, and besides, no one had thought to invent the passenger ship yet), guess where you're going to be sleeping after a long day at sea? And as you fail to enjoy your damp, cramped spot in the cargo hold, you will nonetheless be thanking your lucky stars if your berth isn't anywhere close to the privy, because the stench is almost certain to make you gag. Speaking of gagging, once you get over your seasickness—if you get over your seasickness—you can expect to enjoy some of the finest dry foodstuffs that can be carried on a ship for two months without getting *too* moldy. Oh, and did we mention your trip is probably going to take about two months? And that's if you have a *good* voyage.

And what can you expect if you're a passenger on a bad voyage, of which there were really quite a lot? First of all, your ship will be blown off course, possibly for weeks. Some of your fellow passengers or crew members will almost definitely manage to fall overboard and drown, completely missing out on all the fun that ensues when the ship starts springing leaks. Oh, and eventually you may very well discover that the cause of your ship's misfortunes is that one of your fellow passengers is a witch.

You could hardly blame sailors and emigrants leaving England for the American colonies for expecting witches. Witchcraft was very real to the English—and very punishable by death, as per the witchcraft act passed by the Parliament in 1604. Sailors especially were well versed in what witches were capable of and what they could do to a ship, and it wasn't pretty. Their beloved King James I had an absolute witch obsession, and, expert that he was, he wrote a book about them. The book, *Daemonologie*, reads as if he were making it up as he went along, but *still*. And as for witches cursing ships? Don't even get him started: violent storms caused by witches had interfered with the monarch's long-distance romance with Anne of Denmark, and he held a king-sized grudge.

King James VI of Scotland, later James I, King of England, struck his subjects as kind of weird and awkward and the nobility as worryingly wimpy for a king. His subjects were nonetheless encouraged when it was announced that James would take a queen, as he hadn't shown any interest in girls or in creating heirs to the throne. But when James traveled to Denmark to become betrothed to Anne of Denmark, daughter of King Frederick II, he discovered something at least as tantalizing as his fourteen-year-old fiancée. Members of Anne's royal court informed him that Denmark was having quite the witch problem. Indeed, Denmark was in the throes of what would later be called a "witch mania"; terror reigned in Denmark as folks, beset with the notion that Satan had unleashed a horde of witches on that nation, enthusiastically accused one another of witchcraft.

Months later, when James and Anne married in Denmark, there was one little problem, and it wasn't witches. James didn't attend his wedding—he was back in Scotland. Someone else stood in for him while he waited at home in the comfort of his own castle. After this peculiar wedding, Anne set off on the ocean voyage to her new home and husband, but her ship was plagued by dangerous mechanical mishaps. When unrelenting storms forced the ship into port in Denmark, James was suddenly impatient to be with his new bride; he broke character and set off on his own ship to pick her up, only to find himself also in the midst of a really bad voyage. He persevered, however, and at last retrieved his very patient wife. But when their return trip to Scotland was also beset by treacherous seas and relentless storms, James came to the only logical conclusion: it was witches. Duh.

James was convinced that witches totally had it in for the royals. After all, witches were working for Satan in his plan to take over the world, so it stood to reason that kings and queens would be VIP targets. When at last James and Anne made it safely to Scotland, everyone breathed a sigh of relief (especially since he had declared a state of fasting and prayer until his safe return), and James celebrated his new marriage by kicking off a spree of witch hunting that resulted in years of torture and executions and a big embarrassing smudge on his resume.

After decades of witch hunting in Britain and especially after James's discourse in *Daemonologie* on witches and their fondness for messing around with ships, most people seemed to agree with the king that witches were the number-one cause of really bad ocean voyages. And a number of women immigrating to America found out just how bad a bad voyage could be. Because there was one thing even scarier and more dangerous than *having* a witch on board your ship: *being* the witch.

Mary Lee's Uncharitable Voyage and Other Really Bad Trips

❧ We know very little about the woman called Mary Lee who was on board the ship *Charity* (spoiler alert: witch-infested ships tend to be ironically named) bound from England to the Province of Maryland in 1654. We do know that she was very, very unfortunate thanks to two documents giving first-hand accounts of the incident. The first one of these is a complaint Maryland's governor, William Stone, received from a twenty-five-year-old concerned passenger named Henry Corbyne after the *Charity* docked. It alleged, "About a fortnight or three weeks before the Said Ships arrival in this Province of Maryland, or before A Rumour amongst the Seamen was very frequent, that one Mary Lee then aboard the Said Ship was a witch." The document went on to describe the events that had led to the discovery of said witch on board the *Charity*: stormy weather, treacherous crosswinds, and a ship that "daily grew more Leaky." That's Leaky with a capital "L," which had to have been pretty darn leaky.

The second account of the episode came from a Jesuit priest named Father Francis Fitzherbert (Fitzherbert used the pseudonym "Francis Darby" when traveling, as Jesuit priests teetered only about one step above witches in the colonists' hierarchy of intolerance),who happened to be on the ship as well. The clerical publication the *Jesuit Letter* described the Father's experience on board the *Charity* as the ship endured an exceptionally long spell of unrelenting bad weather. It reads, "The Tempest lasted, in all, two months, whence the opinion arose, that it was not on account of the violence of the ship or atmosphere, but was occasioned by the malevolence of witches."

Fitzherbert (still sticking to the pseudonym "Francis Darby") also gave an official deposition to the "Governour and Councell" in the Province of Maryland. The fact that the priest, who was trying to keep a low profile, felt compelled to report the incident to the authorities suggests that he felt uneasy about what had occurred. Fitzherbert's complaint recounted the progression of the witch incident. The sailors had quickly picked out the most likely (i.e., oldest and most vulnerable) candidate as the witch to blame for their ordeal: an elderly woman immigrating alone to America. The sailors defended their witch accusation with the classic ungentlemanly "she was really kinda asking for it" excuse: it had been "her own deportment and discourse" that caused them to believe she was a witch.

Corbyne described what happened after the sailors identified their witch: "The Seamen apprehended her without order and Searched her and found some Signall or Marke of a witch upon her." The sailors showed off their find to others on board, including Corbyne, who unfortunately didn't describe what he saw. The witch mark was most likely of the teat variety, though, because Corbyne noted that the next day "it was Shrunk into her body for the Most part."

With their aggressive strip search a success, the sailors chained Mary Lee up for the night. In the morning, the men again approached the terrified woman. Desperate, she gave them what she thought they wanted: Mary Lee confessed to being a witch.

The whole situation had made the *Charity*'s captain, John Bosworth, a tad uncomfortable, though not uncomfortable enough to interfere. He politely excused himself and disappeared into his cabin. By the time he finally came back out, Mary Lee had been hanged. The captain feigned surprise, although he was obviously relieved that the witch issue had been resolved. According to Darby, when Captain Bosworth heard that the "witch" had been hanged he "speaking with trouble in a high voice replied he knew not of it."

Apparently Father Fitzherbert himself displayed the same "well whaddya gonna do when the guys are determined to execute a little old lady?" attitude. As the *Jesuit Letter* insisted, "Needless to say, at such a time, it would have been useless for the priest to have made any interference."

And as far as the post-witch part of the voyage of the *Charity*, did the ship's luck improve? According to the Jesuit's report, after the hanging of Mary Lee, "the winds did not in consequence abate their violence, nor did the raging sea smooth its threatening billows. To the troubles of the storm sickness was added next, which attacked almost every person and carried off not a few." Sadly, the rest of Mary Lee's story—the part about what inspired a woman of advanced years to leave her homeland and set off for the new world—was, like her few paltry belongings that were dumped into the sea, lost forever.

Maryland's fledgling justice system eventually responded with a shrug as well. No one was ever tried for the death of Mary Lee, and the ship's safe arrival in port only served to reinforce the colonists' wariness of witches.

Four years after Mary Lee's interrupted emigration to America, another woman bound from England to Maryland met a similar fate. When the ship *Sarah Artch* docked in Maryland, one of the passengers filed a complaint in Maryland's provincial court charging that the ship's owner, Edward Prescott, had put a damper on the voyage from England when he "hanged a Witch in his ship."

The late so-called witch in question was a woman named Elizabeth Richardson. Interestingly, the complainant was one John Washington—great-grandfather of George Washington. Also of note was the fact that Josias Fendall, proprietary governor of Maryland, took the hanging of Elizabeth Richardson very seriously, although not so much because of the "witch" thing as because of the fact that the shipboard execution had been "extra-jurisdictional"; deciding to execute somebody as a witch was really a matter to be settled on dry land, said the courts. The governor had Prescott arrested and notified Washington of the trial date so he could come testify and, according to the letter, "make good your Charge."

But Washington's zeal for civic duty seemed to have cooled considerably by then, because he recused himself from the trial via a letter full of rambling excuses: "I am sorry that my extraordinary occasions will not permit me to be at the next Provincial Court Because then god willing I intend to get my young son baptized, all the Company & Gossips being already invited, besides in this short time Witnesses cannot be got to come over." Prescott's trial was held without benefit of Washington's testimony, and the captain's assertion that hey, he had objected to the hanging but the riled-up crew was threatening to mutiny, and besides, a guy named John Greene was *really* the one in charge of the voyage got him off the hook. In the end, no one was held accountable for the hanging; and again, the life story of the accused witch, Elizabeth Richardson, remains unknown.

Yet another person immigrating to America from England was hanged at sea in 1659. Katherine Grady, also a purported "old lady," was journeying toward a new life in Virginia when bad weather hit. Bad weather, as we have seen, was a very bad harbinger for old ladies on ships in the 1600s. The storms on this voyage were so relentless and brutal that the weary passengers and crew knew they could only mean one thing: there was a witch somewhere on the ship. A mob formed, as tends to happen when the word "witch" comes up on bad voyages, and Katherine Grady was quickly identified as the witch responsible for the ship's predicament. The captain, fearing both the witch and the angry mob, promptly had her hanged from the yardarm. Done and done.

On reaching port, the captain was summoned to appear before the General Court at Jamestown for exceeding his authority in authorizing the execution. Sadly, the record of Katherine Grady's very bad voyage ends there; court documents from 1659 were among those burned by Confederates just before the fall of Richmond in 1865.

The Wildest Witch Voyage Ever: The Atlantic Passage of the *Recovery*

Stirring up treacherous seas and causing ships to be "Leaky" are pretty good shenanigans, but one bewitched voyage takes the (witch) cake as the weirdest Atlantic crossing ever. In 1691, a London periodical called the *Athenian Mercury* (penned by a self-described "society of experts") published an extraordinary account of the strange happenings on board the ship *Recovery* as it sailed from England to Virginia in 1674.

According to the article, the *Recovery* seemed to be beset with bad luck and bad weather from the moment it left port.

The report related first-hand accounts from people on board
the ship and began with the captain's enumeration of the vessel's mishaps and misadventures—stuff like the topsail breaking (twice), anchors being lost, mizzen yards and foretops
and "spristsle" yards and any other old-time ship part you can
think of splitting, breaking, shattering, or washing overboard.
"What was mended one day would the next day be in pieces,"
he groused. A scheduled stopover in Portugal to pick up wine
for importation to America turned into a magnum opus of
Murphy's Law, the low point of which was the casks of wine
plummeting to the bottom of the sea.

And the *Recovery*'s bad luck was just getting warmed up. A
sailor tumbled from the mast, got tangled up in a sail on his way
down, plunged into the sea, and drowned. Then another man
toppled off the boat never to be seen again. By the time a crew
member—the ship's carpenter—announced that the *Recovery*
was bewitched, it seemed pretty plausible to everyone. To add
to the credibility of the accusation, the carpenter said that it had
been revealed to him by God. That was good enough for the
captain, crew, and most of the passengers. They wasted no time
in selecting their witch: Elizabeth Masters, a passenger who
had, for some reason, apparently just kind of rubbed everyone
the wrong way. When another passenger reported that he had
seen Masters behaving suspiciously (he had observed her praying alone on deck—go figure), everyone was satisfied that, yep,
Elizabeth Masters was the witch responsible for the seemingly
cursed voyage.

The passengers decided they had to put a barrier between
the witch and themselves. But once Masters had been seized and
chained to a large gun in steerage, things on board the *Recovery*

went from disastrous to *weird* and disastrous. The passengers began claiming that the witch was assuming the form of a black cat and sneaking around the ship, even leaving bloody scratches on one man. Then *more* cats appeared, and forget trying to slash them with your sword; they would totally just evaporate. Then, never mind the cats, because now there were huge, shaggy black dogs. Even more alarming, beer began mysteriously disappearing from sealed casks. Several men were startled to see a group of phantom sailors appear and then vanish on the deck. And though she was chained below deck, Masters made numerous appearances throughout the ship in the night—sometimes sitting right on top of passengers in their beds and imploring them to "join her gang" (i.e., Satan's posse).

One passenger, a young man named William Rennols, complained that Masters had appeared in his cabin in the middle of the night to discuss his mother back in England; it turned out Masters had actually *lived* with his mother, which, oddly, only further incriminated Masters. Rennols's mother may or may not have been a witch herself; Rennols was only too happy to assert that his mom "was a very Lewd Liver and kept a brothel house in Dog and Bitch Yard, London, and would often in the night go abroad, and come home very bloody."

As the *Recovery* continued to struggle across the Atlantic, things grew yet stranger and more outlandish. To wit: a woman named Mary Leare was "Dreadfully pinched at the small of her back, hips, and buttocks." The aforementioned areas of Mrs. Leare's body were dutifully examined and it was confirmed: those marks were the work of the witch, all right. (Years later it would be speculated these spots were flea bites, common on ships and pretty much everywhere else.)

Leare (who, keep in mind, was *not* accused of being a witch), asserted that smearing the witch's blood onto her sores would act as a healing charm, and so she paid the shackled woman a visit and helped herself. This reverse magic caught on, and soon others were visiting steerage to "prick" Masters for blood in the belief it would cure what ailed them.

Unfortunately, the *Athenian's* story abruptly ends here. The ultimate fate of Elizabeth Masters, purported witch, was not given, and no other records of the strange voyage seem to exist. It's speculated that Masters was put ashore somewhere other than America, but she may have been hanged.

Or it *could* be that the article, published the year before the Salem witch trials, was pure propaganda. Tales of witches had become big sellers, and conveniently the *Athenian's* authors professed to be rabid believers in witches. One of them, John Dunton, would go on to publish Cotton Mather's book on the incidents at Salem. But even the eggheads at the *Athenian* failed to address the pressing question of why a witch would want to jeopardize the passage of the very ship on which she was a passenger; after all, there is no known account of a cross-Atlantic trip by broomstick.

In Which Quakers Are Witches

In 1656, two women who sailed together for the New World also found themselves in dire witch-related straits and proved that old women traveling alone weren't the only gals subject to witch accusations: having an unpopular religion was also a risk factor. But on the plus side, Ann Austin and Mary Fisher made it as far as the Boston Harbor before they were accused of being witches.

❧ To get an idea of what awaited them in the Massachusetts Bay Colony, we can take a look at soldier-turned-Quaker-activist George Bishop's later complaint-in-book-form called *New England Judged by the Spirit of the Lord*. Bishop scolded the inhospitable residents of New England: "Two poor women arriving in your harbour, so shook ye, to the everlasting shame of you, and of your established peace and order, as if a formidable army had invaded your borders."

To be fair, the two ladies from England *had* made one crucial faux pas: they had the chutzpah to be Quakers. The colonists had already done some quick, convenient math that looked something like this: Quaker = blasphemous = witch.

Today, many associate the word "Quaker" with pleasant things, like peace and simplicity. After all, they are also known as the Society of Friends. But in the 1600s, Reverend John Higginson of Salem wasn't feeling so friendly when he described the Quakers as "A stinking Vapor from Hell." The General Court of Massachusetts helpfully chimed in that Quakers were a "Cursed sect of Heretics." To be fair, the Puritan colonists considered people of pretty much *any* other faith to be heretics. And these particular heretics, the Quakers—well, the colonists, just like most of England, found them perfectly insufferable. But there could have been another, more self-serving reason the good people of Massachusetts wanted to keep Quakers out: Quakers spoke out against the evils of slavery. In 1641, Massachusetts had been the first American colony to legalize slavery.

When they reached America in 1656, Ann and Mary were fresh from a six-month stay in Barbados, where their faith had been much more warmly received than it was to be in Boston.

But England, in fact, hadn't exactly been kind to the ladies, either. Mary Fisher, the younger of the two women, had been un-gainfully employed as a servant in Yorkshire when she discovered Quakerism. She wanted to share her faith with others and soon felt called to the ministry. This promptly landed her in prison for a year and a half, but she emerged undeterred. She and another Quakeress undertook a mission to spread the Good Word to the young gentlemen at Cambridge University. The students found the ladies and their message quite hilarious, but the local mayor was not amused. He ordered the women to be stripped to the waist and "whipped at the market cross till the blood ran down their bodies." Mary followed this up with another six-month prison stay. Of her first two years as a Quaker, Mary Fisher had spent all but six months behind bars. When she was released from prison a second time, Mary finally took the hint and decided to leave England. She linked her fortune with that of fellow Quaker Ann Austin and, wielding a stockpile of religious literature, the women hit the high seas.

Less is known about Ann Austin; history only records that she had lived in London, was the mother of five children, and finally, that she was "stricken in years." *Ouch.* Stricken in years or not, Ann arrived in Boston harbor with her friend Mary on board the ship *Swallow*, prepared to spread the Good Word to the colonies. But news of incoming Quakers had preceded them. Before Ann and Mary could even disembark, Deputy Governor Richard Bellingham, who had stood by as his own sister was hanged as a witch not long before, ordered them detained on the ship and had their belongings searched. A hundred books containing "corrupt, heretical, and blasphemous doctrines" were discovered in their baggage and promptly turned into a bonfire, which, for an extra flourish of menace, was ceremoniously lit by the local hangman.

Ann and Mary were led from the ship and taken straight to prison. The women were *charged* with "being Quakers"—not technically a crime in Massachusetts yet—but they were *accused* of being witches. The authorities wasted no time in having the missionaries stripped and examined for the ever-incriminating witch marks. The examiners, supposedly all midwives, proved to be persecutors of surprisingly little imagination compared to some of their peers; they reported that they found nothing on the bodies of the women that could be construed as witch marks. (Ann did wryly note later, however, that one of the "midwives" who conducted the strip search appeared to be a man in women's clothing.) This fruitless search probably saved Ann and Mary from being hanged as witches.

Details of the bad treatment of the Quaker women were indexed in our indignant friend George Bishop's *New England Judged*, in a series of accusatory "and did ye nots?" of which this was a highlight: "Did ye not order . . . Mary Fisher and Ann Austin to be stripped stark naked and to be searched and misused as is a shame to modesty to name; and with such barbarousness as one of them, a married woman and with five children suffered not the like in the bearing of any of them into the world?" For five weeks Ann and Mary were imprisoned in a dark, sweltering cell, where the accommodations included being starved and allowed no communication with the outside world (such as it was). Finally, they were hustled back to the ship and sent packing, just about the same time a ship bearing more Quakers arrived in port.

Despite their best efforts to be inhospitable, the colonists were unable to keep the Quakers out. And so the Society of Friends proceeded to annoy the colonists by preaching love, getting along with the Indians, and occasionally crashing church services naked. The colonists reacted by continuing to persecute—and at times even execute—the Quakers.

As for the two intrepid missionaries, Mary eventually returned to America, where she died in Charleston in 1698. But the unfortunate Ann ended up back in England where, despite her stricken years, she was unceremoniously imprisoned in yet another filthy, dank cell. There she stayed until 1665, when, true to form, she died of the plague.

The incidents of witch persecution of women en route to America were the early examples of the insidious escalation of witch paranoia that was on the horizon for the settlers of the strange New World. Before becoming a melting pot, America was a witch's cauldron of religious literalism, ignorance, dangerous superstition, and grim misfortune.

Chapter 3

First Offenders: Early Witchcraft Cases in the American Colonies

Sometimes when I look out into these dark forests and hear the hooting owls and feel the awe of our American wilderness and think of all the women around us bad enough to sell themselves to Satan I shudder.

—Seventeenth-century missionary
Francis Makemie, quoted in *The Days of Makemie* by Littleton Pernell Bowen

Jamestown, the first American colony, was settled in 1607. It took a good fifteen years before anyone in Virginia was accused of being a witch. When that first charge of witchcraft *did* emerge, the fledgling American court system responded with a resounding "meh," which was pretty darn amazing considering the nightmare witchcraft in America would become. But it was surprising for another reason, too: the witchcraft law

on the books in Virginia at that time set a mighty hefty punish- 🪶
ment for witchcraft: death.

This law was the same as the anti-witch law in the
merry olde England most of the colonists had recently left
behind. That law, passed by Parliament in 1604, was "An Acte
against Conjuration, Witchcrafte and dealing with evill and
wicked Spirits" that took three paragraphs of olde (technically Early Modern) English and a lot of "inchantment" this,
and "charme" that, and "wicked" this, and "town pillory" that
to basically get to point that witches should be sentenced
to death. It was actually a quite generous "two strikes and
you're out" deal: the first offense would only get you a year
of hard time, during which you would be trotted out every
three months, hauled to ye local market faire, and made to
stand upon the pillory for six hours, where you would tell
passers-by about the errors of your ways while they gnawed
on scraggly chicken legs and scratched themselves.

This same law also carried on about how it was illegal
to do a number of other "obviously a bad idea" things, like
digging up dead bodies, "feeding" evil spirits, and, oddly, not
revealing where any treasure may or may not be. (This last
provision could have been a sign that King James was pretty
sure there was valuable loot hidden around Britain and was
concerned that someone else would find and claim it.) The
fact that this law had been enacted in England just three years
before the founding of Jamestown shows that witchcraft was
still a very relevant issue in the seventeenth century.

Long before 2001, September 11 was already an infamous date in American history. It was on September 11, 1626,
that the General Court of Jamestown heard the first charges

of witchcraft in the American colonies. The alleged witch in question was one Joane Wright (also known as Goody or Goodwife Wright), a sometime midwife who had emigrated from England. She and her husband of sixteen years, Robert, had arrived on the ship *Swan* about 1608 and were well ensconced in the small community of Elizabeth City in Virginia. But judging by the nature of the witchcraft charges against Goody Wright, even in its infancy the would-be nation's gossip wheels were already efficiently at work churning up dangerous waters.

The first testimony against Joane Wright was presented by a Lieutenant Giles Allingtone, who reported that he had heard one Sergeant Booth say that Goody Wright had asked him to share a "piece of flesh"—or hunk of meat—of which he was the proud owner. When Booth denied her the delectable meat (he "would not or could not" share it with her, said the testimony), she put a curse on him that resulted in him becoming an embarrassingly bad shot; as a matter of fact, the poor guy hadn't been able to hit a single deer since. This was of course second-hand information, but, you know, Lt. Allingtone just thought he'd mention it.

He went on to say that he himself had hired Goody Wright to serve as a midwife when his wife had gone into labor with their latest youngster. But when Wright arrived, Mrs. Allingtone noticed with alarm that the midwife was left-handed—a very suspicious characteristic, especially for someone already rumored to be a witch. Mrs. Allingtone demanded a new midwife and—inexplicably not concerned that the new midwife's name was Goody Graves—threw Goody Wright out. The dismissed Wright went away from the house "very much discontented," Allingtone claimed. (In witchcraft allegations, leaving someone's home "discontented" usually meant the person was muttering to herself, often for very understandable reasons.) Not long after the birth of the little Allingtone tyke, Lt. Allingtone and his family began to feel the effects of what they were sure was a curse placed on them by rejected midwife and reputed witch Goody Wright. According to the court documents, soon Mrs. Allingtone's "breast grew dangerously sore"; this unfortunate malady continued for a torturous month. No sooner had she recovered than Lt. Allingtone himself got sick with an unnamed illness that hung on for three weeks. But worst of all, Allingtone's testimony said, their newborn baby "fell sick and so continued the space of two months, after which it recovered, and so did continue well for the space of a month, and afterwards fell into extreme pain the space of five weeks and so departed."

Sore breasts and dead babies aside, Goodwife Wright also displayed an unsettling propensity for predicting the deaths of her neighbors. Records show that she told a certain Rebecka Gray that her husband would die (no outcome mentioned), told a Mr. Sellgate that his wife would die (this "came to pass" the record says), accurately predicted the untimely expiration of the wife of a Mr. Harris, and so on. Then there was the complaint that a disagreement with a local servant girl over a piece of wood had ended with Goody Wright warning the girl "she would make her dance stark naked." Again, no confirmation of this coming to pass.

Robert Wright, Joane's beleaguered husband, took the stand and claimed to be in the dark about his wife's alleged witchcraft-related hobbies; the testimony states that he "Sayeth he hath been married to his wife sixteen years but knoweth nothing by her touching the crime she is accused of." But circumstantial accusations continued to pile up against Goody Wright.

Some of the stories were more than rumors. According to court records, the apparently guileless Goody Wright admitted that when she was living in Hull, England, she had been the servant of a woman who taught her how to perform magical spells. Goody Wright had used a spell to keep another woman's hand stuck inside a butter churn for several hours, and she had adeptly performed a magic spell that involved flinging a scalding horseshoe into her mistress's urine to temporarily sicken a rival witch. Once in Virginia, Goody Wright had continued to use a form of folk magic and wielded what little power she could by encouraging her neighbors' fears that she was a witch.

The colony of Virginia was easier on witches than other colonies would be, and in the end, the court gave Goody Wright a colonial slap on the wrist in the form of, at worst (records are sketchy), a petty fine—which must have seemed to her a pretty sweet deal considering that several years earlier she had been sentenced to be whipped for doing an unsatisfactory job of sewing a shirt. In 1627, the long-suffering Robert Wright, understandably wanting to get out of town, asked for and was granted rights to a plot of land called "Labour in Vain." But in the end, Robert just wasn't able to make a go of it in the New World. In addition to being saddled with a witch for a wife, he was repeatedly jailed for debt; he died in 1629. No further mention of America's starter witch, Joane Wright, was recorded.

There were also a number of trivial witch charges brought to court and casually dismissed in New England in the early and mid-1600s. Prosecution of witches was still quite a thing in the Old World; why, then, was the New World seemingly so easy on witches? Was it because the settlers were too busy building shelter and trying to obtain food to take each other to court for witchcraft? After all, the era affectionately known as "the Starving Time" was not long past. Or maybe it was that witches were traditionally female. Early on there were few enough ladies in the colonies; if they started winnowing out everyone who might be a witch—well, winter nights were cold enough as it was. Or perhaps it had something to do with the fact that the Puritans hadn't yet become so influential in the colonies. Once that religious element and its accompanying tough stance on all things Satan were established in the New World in the mid-1600s, times began to change. The hangman was about to catch up with America's witches.

America Kills Its First Witch

"One of Windsor arraigned and executed at Hartford for a Witch." On May 26, 1647, this brief notation in the journal of Puritan elder and statesman John Winthrop marked the first execution for witchcraft in the American colonies. This unnamed woman in Winthrop's journal was Alse Young of Windsor, Connecticut; she was hanged in the Meeting House Square in Hartford after being found guilty of witchcraft. Almost nothing is known about Young's case; there is speculation that she was blamed for a local epidemic, and some have suggested that she was accused of witchcraft because of an estate dispute.

But Alse Young definitely had something working against her that Virginia witch Joane Wright hadn't. The General Court of the Connecticut Colony had written its very own law against witchcraft in 1642. It was short and not very sweet: "If any man or woman be a witch (that is) hath or consulted with a familiar spirit, they shall be put to death. Ex 22.18: Lev. 20. 27: Deut. 18. 10, 11."

The Bible verses cited to support this edict were courtesy of the King James version, and basically asked, *What part of kill all the witches don't you understand?* To wit: "Thou shalt not suffer a witch to live; A man also or woman that hath a familiar spirit, or that is a wizard, shall surely be put to death: they shall stone them with stones: their blood (shall be) upon them." And the Deuteronomy verse expanded the definition of a witch: "There shall not be found among you anyone . . . that useth divination, or an observer of times, or an enchanter or a witch, or a charmer, or a consulter with familiar spirits, or a wizard, or a necromancer."

One by one, the New England colonies demonstrated that they were invested in dealing harshly with witches by writing their own death-to-witches laws, and then, with gathering speed, they began to enforce them. And as one might expect, it was America's early working poor who were the first to pay the ultimate price.

Witch's Work

Being a servant girl in the colonies in 1648 was a hard-luck life. In addition to the fact that you were probably fated to remain in servitude or a similar state pretty much forever, there was the day-to-day Cinderella-like drudgery of sweeping the hearth, emptying the ashes, doing the wash, shooing wayward pigs away from the crops, and taking care of the chamber pots—and let me tell you, you don't even want to *think* about the chamber pots. One such servant girl, Mary Johnson of Wethersfield, Connecticut, allegedly used too much innovation in getting out of her chores. While some might think she was ahead of her time by subcontracting out tiresome chores, her masters didn't appreciate her ingenuity. Maybe it was because they didn't approve of her general contractor: Satan.

The court record of the indictment against Mary Johnson stated, "The jury finds the bill of indictment against Mary Johnson that by her own confession she is guilty of familiarity with the devil." In *Memorable Providences, Relating to Witchcrafts and Possessions*, Puritan minister and hater of witches Cotton Mather explained how the servant girl had found herself in such bad company: "Her first familiarity with the devils came by discontent; and wishing the devil to take that and t'other thing and the devil to do this and that whereupon a devil appeared unto her tendering her the best service he could do for her." It isn't quite clear why the devil took such a personal interest in Mary, but it was a pretty sweet deal while it lasted; once the understanding with the horned one was established, he was only too happy to dispatch his devil-minions to lend the girl a hand with her odious tasks.

Rev. Mather also knew of a time when, after Mary was scolded by her master for not clearing the ashes from the hearth, a devil came and took care of the job for her. All in all, the whole goblin assistant thing was quite a perk and even offered the opportunity for some rare entertainment for the hard-working girl: "Her master sending her into the fields to drive out the hogs that used to break into it, a devil would scare them out, and make her laugh to see how he fazed 'em about." But maybe it wasn't *all* fun, games, and side-splitting hog chases: "She confessed that she was guilty of the murder of a child, and that she had been guilty of uncleanness with men and devils."

Samuel Stone, another important minister of the day, took a personal interest in the case and devoted himself to converting the witch girl to Christianity. It all ended happily enough, according to Rev. Mather's account of the witch-coaching: "She was by most observers judged very penitent, both before and at her Execution; and she went out of the world with many hopes of mercy. . . . And she died in a frame extremely to the satisfaction of them that were spectators of it." Mather cheerfully concluded, "Our God is a great forgiver."

The Devil in Goody Jones and Consider the Legg Vapours

John Hale was a New England minister who went from witch-believer to witch-sort-of-doubter. In his 1697 book, *A Modest Inquiry into the Nature of Witchcraft*, he recalled a memorable witch-related outing that took place when he was twelve years old: "The day of her execution I went in company of some neighbors, who took great pains to bring her to confession and repentance. . . . But she constantly professed herself innocent of that crime . . . and so she said unto her death."

The witch in question was Margaret Jones, the first witch executed in the Massachusetts Bay Colony. Goody Jones was hanged in Boston on June 15, 1648. John Winthrop, governor of the Massachusetts Bay Colony had been a member of the court that tried the witch, and he journaled the weird but apparently Puritan-plausible testimony:

> At this court, one Margaret Jones, of Charleston, was indicted and found guilty of Witchcraft and hanged for it. The evidence against her was: That she was found to have such a malignant touch that many persons, men, women, or children, who she stroked or touched with an affection or displeasure, or etc., were taken with deafness, or vomiting, or other violent pains or sickness. She practicing physic (medicine), and her medicines being such things as, by her own confession were harmless, as aniseseed, liquors, etc., yet had extraordinary violent effects. She would use to tell such as would not make use of her physic that they would never be healed; and accordingly their diseases and hurts continued. Some things which she foretold came to pass accordingly; other things she would tell of, as secret speeches, etc., which she had no ordinary means to come to the knowledge of. She had upon search an apparent teat in her secret parts, as fresh as if it had been newly sucked. . . . In the prison, in the clear daylight, there was seen in her arms . . . a little child, which ran from her into another room, and the officer following it, it was vanished.

Rev. Hale reported that the unrepentant witch had behaved very badly at her trial, "railing at the jury and witnesses," and that it was "in like distemper she died," even as the pious spectators witnessed to her about "God's punishment."

John Hale later became involved in the Salem witch trials, and some even accused him of being one of those responsible for the witch craze. Hale became considerably less fervid about prosecuting witches when his own wife Sarah was accused of witchcraft, and several years later he published *A Modest Inquiry Into the Nature of Witchcraft,* in which he stuck to his guns that there were witches but admitted some innocent people may have been executed because, well, it's just really hard to tell who's really a witch, what with Satan being so tricky and all. He pointed out that the weird stuff that can go down in a person's brain when he's sick with some seventeenth-century medical malady could be remarkably similar to what people who claimed to be bewitched experienced:

Yea persons not under such Diabolical impressions, may by some disease or sores and vapours thence ascending, have the Images of persons represented to their Imagination. Mr. John Phillips of Boston, told me, That be had a sore swelled Legg, and lying in the warm bed with Eyes open, he saw, as he thought, Women in silk cloathing come to his bed side, and spake to them: but a man that stood by said there were no Women; whereupon he suspected the man of Conjuring tricks; which moved him to send for a Physician three Miles off . . . and all the time the Messenger was gone, was he haunted with these Women, as they seemed to him. The Physian sent word, that the vapours ascending from his sore Legg had caused a water in his Eyes, and disturbance in his Braines, by means whereof he was troubled with such Visions; and sending an eye water to wash his eyes with, and a cordial to take inwardly; upon the use of these, this disturbance vanished in half a quarter of an hour. If a disease may do this, what may Satan working upon bodily distempers and vapours impose upon the Imaginations?

Hale goes on, throwing some serpents, frogs, blood, pharaohs—you name it—into the mix, but basically saying, "Hey, if a legitimate case of the legg vapours can make you hallucinate, just imagine what can happen in your braines if Satan starts messing with your vapours and distempers and whatnot." Toward the end, for those who made it that far, Hale finally admits: "We have been too fierce against supposed Malefick Witchcraft."

But before witch hunters could reflect awkwardly on their mistakes, the era of the witch craze would have to play out in full. With witchcraft on the minds of the colonists and capital punishment for witchcraft the accepted penalty, the stage was set for the second half of the seventeenth century, when the homes of New England filled with terrible wonders, and troupes of witches danced from the ends of nooses like macabre marionettes.

CHAPTER 4

Native Nightmares

The devil has come among us and we are killing one another.

—Delaware Indian Youth, 1806

C omparative mythology tells us that there are certain stories and themes that appear in cultures around the world—the story of a great flood, for instance. Something else that shows up in many cultures throughout history is the belief in witches, those dark but colorful recurrent characters whose close personal relationships with a supreme evil being score them awesome powers that they use to do crummy stuff. So when the first explorers and colonists wended their uninvited way to the New World with their stowaway witches, the witches of the indigenous cultures of America were already well entrenched and ready to meet them. More common than the witches themselves, however, were the fears, suspicions, and prejudices that often accompanied the belief in witches. Sometimes the Native Americans and the Europeans would seem to each other to be textbook cases of witches or devils—occasionally for very good ⟶ reason. And when the Europeans first came calling, the indigenous peoples of the Americas may well have been better off with actual devils.

The Taino, for instance, were a gentle people of the Caribbean who until the late fifteenth century were happily doing their own thing. They were skilled artisans, efficient farmers, and expert navigators who on the regular built ocean-going canoes so large they held one hundred or more rowers. They were so chill they invented the rubber ball and then spent every spare moment playing a super fun ball game that they also invented.

They made quite a favorable impression on Christopher Columbus, who was greeted by the Taino when he put medieval booties on ground in the New World for the very first time on what is now part of the Bahamas. He cheerily wrote home about his new friends:

> They were well-built, with good bodies and handsome features. . . . They do not bear arms, and do not know them, for I showed them a sword, they took it by the edge and cut themselves out of ignorance. They have no iron. Their spears are made of cane. . . . They would make fine servants. With fifty men we could subjugate them all and make them do whatever we want.

The Taino didn't have any experience with Europeans, or they probably would have attempted to convince Columbus and his crew that one of the island's many giant monsters had recently eaten up its entire supply of gold, and P.S., the Great Typhoon was due any second and would definitely last at least a good ten years. Oh, and by the way, don't let the door hit you on the aft end on your way back out of the harbor. But instead, the Taino were friendly and welcoming to the newcomers, not knowing what a bad day it was for them and other native peoples of the Americas. Thanks to Columbus and his ilk—slave-traders, opportunists, imperialists, treasure hunters, and other assorted riff-raff stopping by at all hours—a mere four years after Columbus's first visit, the Taino population was reduced by *two-thirds*. And by 1600 the population of the ball-playing, sea-going Taino was zero. That's a *zero*.

As the invaders moved north, they had pretty much the same effect on the rest of America's indigenous population. Between Columbus's arrival in 1492 and the era of the Salem witch trials, America's native populace was reduced by an astounding 90 percent as the Old World delivered a nightmare of fiery destruction, merciless subjugation, and deadly disease to the New World. The Indians who remained, however, would get to enjoy the effects of the other super-thoughtful gifts the Europeans brought from the Old World: firearms and alcohol.

These European newcomers tended to use several terms interchangeably when it came to witchcraft: *witches* worshipped the *devil*, but sometimes those associated with Satan were themselves called *devils*, and were said to practice *witchcraft*. And "devil" was a super convenient label to place on the group of people who inhabited the land that the settlers wanted for themselves. So it was no surprise that the colonists found themselves dealing with "devils" in the New World—devils who, of course, worshipped Satan and were to be held responsible for all sorts of misfortunes.

By the 1600s, those who were settling on the eastern sea-board found an additional use for the diminishing Indian pop-ulation besides enslaving them: scoring bonus points toward getting into heaven by converting the "devils" to Christianity. In the ironically titled *Good Newes from Virginia*, theologian Alexander Whitaker crafted an advertisement for the New World in the form of a sermon, which he then sent to England to try to encourage more immigration:

> Let the miserable condition of these naked slaves of the devil move you to compassion toward them. They acknowledge that there is a great good God, but know him not.... Wherefore they serve the devil for fear, after a most base manner sacrificing (as I have here heard) their own Children to him: I have sent one image of their god to the Counsell in England, which is painted upon one side of a toad-stool much like unto a deformed monster. Their priests are no other but such as our English Witches are.

The real "good Newes," Whitaker implied in his sermon, went something like this: "Hey, all you chumps in England, aren't you totally bored with dying of the plague and being persecuted for your religious beliefs? Wouldn't you like to be the ones doing the persecuting, er, saving for once? Come to America and help rehabilitate the witches!" And by the way, Whitaker added, everyone who comes over and helps to civilize the savages will be remembered as "the Apostles of Virginia."

For the native peoples of America, however, it was a "takes one to know one" type situation. With the arrival of the Europeans, bad luck had increasingly struck the Indians, not the least of which were brand new diseases that left entire villages decimated. The Indians knew cause and effect when they saw it. The effect: sick and dead Indians; the obvious cause: the new witches from the Old World. The word "witch," of course, meant different things to different tribes of America's native populations. But as is the case in other cultures, it involved using supernatural means to gain powers and usually doing bad things to others with these powers.

When a group of Jesuit missionaries arrived in America from France and invited themselves to save the Indians in northern New France (now upper New York and lower Canada), the natives would have much preferred to have been left alone. The Huron, the Jesuits' targeted converts, were pretty sure from the start that the Jesuits were witches; there just had to be a direct link between the newcomers and the plague of illnesses that seemed to have arrived with them. In June 1637, a Jesuit priest writing from Canada mentioned that after a recent measles outbreak, the Indians were giving them the side eye:

> They are still saying, almost as much as ever, that *we* are the cause of the malady. These reports are partly founded upon the fact that it is in this season much more fatal than it was during the severe cold of the winter, and consequently the greater part of those we baptize, die. Besides this, very recently a certain Algonquin captain has given our Hurons to understand that they were mistaken in thinking that the devils caused them to die. . . . This sorcerer added that we, even ourselves, meddle with sorcery; that for this purpose we employ the images of our saints.

One of the more stubborn of the Jesuit missionaries in New France was Isaac Jogues. He made the journey to and from France several times. The first half of Jogues's first mission in 1636 was a *bit* iffy, what with the seasickness, the all-corn diet, and the less-than-flattering nickname the Huron gave him: "Bird of Prey." And then there was the eerie uneasiness he and the others from his mission experienced that made the hair on the back of their holy necks stand up when they were around the natives. As fellow Jesuit Jerome Lalemont said, "These missionaries see themselves the abomination of those whose salvation they seek, at the peril of their own lives." Jogues and the other Jesuits stubbornly refused to take the hint from their potential converts. But then again, they probably didn't anticipate just how bad things would get.

In 1641, Jogues was traveling on the St. Lawrence River with a large group when they were ambushed by a group of Iroquois. The Iroquois not only were enemies of the Huron, they were also super disgusted with the way their enemies were fraternizing with the sanctimonious witches from France. Like the Huron, the Iroquois believed the newcomers kept causing illness and death, and in a way, their suspicions were correct: the Jesuits, like all the Europeans who came to the New World, brought with them the Old World scourges of diphtheria, small-pox, whooping cough, influenza, syphilis, and a little thing called the plague—all previously unknown to the Native Americans.

Letters from the Jesuits to their colleagues in France had reported the ominous rumbles that snowballed as the disease death toll mounted in the native communities. They refused to acknowledge responsibility, however. It was their old friend the devil who was, ironically, making the Indians think they were "sorcerers," Father Francois Le Mercier wrote. "He has recently stirred up new tempests against us. They are still saying, as much as ever, that we are the cause of the malady."

This attitude naturally did nothing to change the natives' minds. The ambush on the St. Lawrence River would be the start of a period of hell on earth for Jogues. The extended period of captivity and torture commenced with him having his fingers gnawed on and his fingernails pulled off; then he endured a beating that left him unconscious. Unfortunately for Jogues, he regained consciousness. He and his fellow captives were next introduced to the concept of "running the gauntlet," which involved being stripped naked and made to run up a steep hill through a crowd of stick- and club-wielding Iroquois, who competed with one another to see who had the best swing. Afterward the prisoners were shuffled off to another town and another gauntlet, this one featuring metal rods, courtesy of some Dutch traders who kept the Iroquois supplied with things they never knew they needed.

As Jogues's wounds—including a thumb that had been sawed off with a clamshell—festered with squirming worms, the Iroquois finally had to tend to some other non-witch-tormenting-related stuff. The priest's torture abated, but his captivity lasted another year. Jogues eventually escaped—minus a few fingers—and returned to France. But in 1644 he returned to New France, presumably the old adage about the futility of doing the same thing and expecting different results having not yet been on the books. There was a good news–bad news situation for the Jesuits in New France. The bad news, according to the Jesuits' correspondence, was as follows:

> The Algonquins and Hurons—and next the Hiroquois, at the solicitation of their captives—have had, and some

have still, a hatred and an extreme horror of our doctrine. They say that it causes them to die, and that it contains spells and charms which effect the destruction of their corn, and engender the contagious and general diseases wherewith the Hiroquois now begin to be afflicted. It is on this account that we have expected to be murdered, in all the places where we have been; and even now we are not without hope of one day possessing this happiness.

On the plus side, however, the madder the Indians became, the more likely the Jesuits were to succeed in one of their most heartfelt desires: becoming martyred.

Things might have gone a *bit* better for Jogues on this mission had he not pushed his luck and returned to the exact area where he had been taken captive the last time, and where the Indians were even more convinced than ever that the Jesuits were practitioners of sorcery. "They cast reproaches at him that he was a wizard; that his prayers were sorceries, which prevented the success of their hunting," a fellow Jesuit wrote. Nonetheless, the Indians gave Jogues the benefit of the doubt and tolerated him fairly well, until at last he was called away on other business. But he had made a classic traveler's mistake: he had over-packed. He asked his Indian hosts if they wouldn't mind storing a wooden box until he could get back to retrieve it. They acquiesced; it probably seemed a small price to pay to get rid of their pesky guest. But they soon began to second-guess their decision. The mysterious box was just the sort of thing to inflame suspicion; as nineteenth-century historian Francis Parkman wrote, the Indians were soon wondering if it "contained some secret mischief."

When the worst corn blight ever set in, courtesy of worms that even the mightiest warriors among them couldn't conquer, and starvation settled into their villages along with the already-rampant deadly diseases, the Indians put two and two together. This time Father Jogues had really done it: he had unleashed a box of demons in an attempt to destroy the Indians. In October 1646, the tirelessly naïve Isaac Jogues received a dinner invitation from a group of Mohawk peoples called the Bear Clan, which he happily accepted. Instead of a meal, he got a tomahawk to the scalp, after which his head was severed and set on a pike. The hapless priest had become a martyr, and the Indians were finally free from the witch they called Bird of Prey.

Prophetic Persecutions

Europeans weren't the only people America's natives called witches. Some aspects of human nature, both good and bad, are universal, and so the Indians would on occasion accuse *each other* of being witches—and why not? Native American legends, like those of peoples all over the world, were full of tales of witches who were perpetually up to no good.

The sinister witch of Native American tradition is very much like the stereotypical wicked witch of other cultures: evil, ugly, and prone to unnatural appetites. For example, the Pawnee (Indians of the Great Plains who, while rated "friendly" by the American government, were particularly hard on witches) portrayed witches in a "wicked witch from Hansel and Gretel building a gingerbread house to attract delicious children" kind of way. Yes, Pawnee witches were known to be totally into eating people, and while they preferred meals of children, they weren't totally opposed to having an adult for dinner on occasion. One notable Pawnee witch was known to send her son out to pick up carry-out for dinner, in this case by killing men and lugging them home for her to feast upon. Another witch had an especially crafty shtick that went something like this:

Witch: [*Spying an appetizing dude.*] Hey, tough guy, see that there lake? I'll bet you I can stay under the water longer than you can!

Man: Get back in your hut, you crazy old woman!

Witch: No, really. I'm dead serious, sonny-boy. See? [*Walks into lake.*]

Man: What are you doing, you old hag? You're going to drown!

Witch: [*Looking over her shoulder at him, long, tangled black-and-gray hair trailing behind her in the water.*] Oh, look at the little boy scared to come into the lake with an old lady! Poor baby! Do you want me to call your mama to come get you? Wah, wah, wah! [*Rubs her eyes with her fists in fake crying motion.*]

Man: Seriously? Are we doing this? [*Rolls eyes, sighs, and walks into lake.*]

Witch: [*Suppressing a cackle.*] Okay! You go under first, big guy, and I'll time you!

Man: You are totally going to be so embarrassed, lady! [*Takes deep breath and ducks under water.*]

Witch: [*Chuckling.*] One Mississippi . . . Two Mississippi . . . Three Mississippi . . . [*Dives under the water, where, with supernatural strength, she seizes the man, drags him into her secret underwater cave, and eats him.*]

Much like the white man's witch problems and persecutions, most of the Indians' witch problems and persecutions occurred under the guise of godliness. Throughout history, self-styled religious leaders who called themselves prophets and claimed to receive their edicts directly from their god or gods have proven to be particularly dangerous people. This was all too true for Indian prophets as well.

One early would-be witch hunter was Wangomend, a Munsee Indian living in what is now northern Pennsylvania who, despite his best efforts, just didn't have the knack for instigating witch hunts. John Heckewelder, an evangelist in the mid-1700s who spent many years among the Indians, was one contemporary who described Wangomend's ascension to power. Wangomend, he said, had started off with some pretty solid ideological elements, such as the following, which had been revealed to him in a vision:

He had been borne by unseen hands to where he had been permitted to take a peep into the heavens, of which there were three, one for the Indians, one for the negroes, and another for the white people. That of the Indians he observed to be the happiest of the three, and that of the whites the unhappiest; for they were under chastisement for their ill treatment of the Indians, and for possessing themselves of the land which God had given to them. They were also punished for making beasts of the negroes, by selling them as the Indians do their horses and dogs, and beating them unmercifully, although God had created them as well as the rest of mankind.

That all sounded pretty reasonable, but it lacked the kind of commercial appeal an aspiring prophet needed to keep things interesting and attract followers. (Actually, Wangomend's strict anti-firewater stance probably lost him more votes.) Hmm, what's something that's always guaranteed to get folks stirred up? Yes, it didn't take Wangomend long to announce that *witches* were the problem. Witches were to blame for the general downward spiral of his people (as opposed to the giant white elephant in the room), and Wangomend made a really big deal out of it. In 1775, he even secured a spot at a Delaware Indian council where he made a lot of noise about catching and killing witches. He was apparently a pretty persuasive speaker because the council was totally on board, but in the end Wangomend's plan backfired. After his initial success at the council pretty much everyone started randomly accusing everyone else of being witches, and chaos ensued. Eventually even Wangomend himself was accused of witchcraft. This, unsurprisingly, signaled the end of Wangomend's great witch hunt. A few decades later, however, two other Indian prophets would take up where he left off—with much more terrible success.

One of them was Handsome Lake, a Seneca Indian chief who had a weakness for what we today would call "partying." His teachings, now known as *The Code of Handsome Lake, the Seneca Prophet,* were documented by Seneca Chief Edward Cornplanter, half-brother of Handsome Lake, and include an account of Handsome Lake's early club kid years. His partying, of course, was courtesy of the alcohol brought to the New World by the Europeans, and according to the anthropologist Arthur C. Parker, who published *The Code,* Handsome Lake wasn't the only Seneca who overindulged. On one pivotal occasion, he and a group of Seneca went among the whites to trade furs for supplies and came out of negotiations with a great big barrel of alcohol. They began to indulge in earnest: "Now all the men become filled with strong drink. They yell and sing like demented people."

Sounds fun, but the party didn't end there; they kept it going when they got back to the village (it was a *barrel*, after all): "Now that the party is home they revel in strong drink and are very quarrelsome. Because of this the families become frightened and move away for safety. . . . The drunken men run yelling through the village and there is no one there except the drunken men. Now they are beastlike and run about without clothing and all have weapons to injure those whom they meet." Handsome Lake had hit rock bottom. As he lay prostrate in a cold hut, a supply of alcohol within arm's reach, he began to contemplate his life. Soon he began to formulate what would amount to a spiritual awakening—and his own one-person addiction recovery program. *The Code* tells us:

Now as he lies in sickness he meditates and longs that he might rise again and walk upon the earth. So he implores the Great Ruler to give him strength that he may walk upon this earth again. And then he thinks how evil and loathsome he is before the Great Ruler. He thinks how he has been evil ever since he had strength in this world and done evil ever since he had been able to work. But notwithstanding, he asks that he may again walk. . . . Now it comes to his mind that perchance evil has arisen because of strong drink and he resolves to use it nevermore. Now he continually thinks of this every day and every hour.

Yea, he continually thinks of this. Then a time comes and
he craves drink again for he thinks that he can not recover
his strength without it. Now two ways he thinks: what
once he did and whether he will ever recover.

Handsome Lake prays that he will live through the night. When
he does, he asks the Great Creator to help him live through
another day. In this way he proceeds *one day at a time* (sound
familiar?) out of his sickness. He begins to see visions and
receives messages from the Creator, but has no idea that during
his recovery and spiritual awakening *four years* have passed.
Handsome Lake's family has spent years gazing on the skeletal,
yellow body of the sick man, wondering when he will at last
succumb. One day, Handsome Lake gains consciousness and
strength enough to stagger out of his hut, where he makes a terrifying sight to the villagers. He then proceeds to collapse and
dies before their eyes.

Mourners spent the night sitting by the body of their
deceased friend, but when the sun rose, they found Handsome
Lake sitting up—and not in a rigor-mortis kind of way, but
in a "hey look at me I'm not dead anymore" kind of way. Not
only was Handsome Lake not dead, he felt better than he had
in years, and he had quite a story to tell. He had been to the
other side, he said, where he had made the acquaintance of a
certain group of VIPs who had appeared to him in the form of
Indians in old-time dress. Handsome Lake called these Indian
spirits the Messengers, and he said that they had given him
some very important directives. A lot of these were very cool
and helpful, like "don't hit women and children" and "don't imi-
tate the white man" and especially "don't poison yourselves by

drinking all that alcohol the white man is trying to kill you with." Handsome Lake's stunning resurrection and the insider info he now possessed granted him almost instant prophet status, and the messages from the other side were given great credence. But Handsome Lake's intel also included several messages from the Creator that would ultimately cause a lot of trouble for the Seneca. The subject line heading of these messages: witchcraft. One such message read, "Now we think that a time will come when a woman will be seen performing her witch spells in the daylight. Then will you know that the end is near. She will run through the neighborhood boasting how many she has slain by her sorcery."

It was these messages that eventually led to the bad thing that came to be known as the Seneca Witch Hunts. The Messengers showed Handsome Lake how a witch would be punished, and it wasn't exactly in keeping with the new progressive party line: she would be thrust into a boiling cauldron, pulled out, then put back in. Repeat as needed.

Witches had long been a fear and concern for the Seneca, and now with Handsome Lake's directives, the Seneca were ready to do something about them. With interest in witches mounting, Handsome Lake's visions began to include glimpses of specific witches, whom he quickly named. The result was deadly. For the most part, if Handsome Lake accused you of being a witch and you confessed and promised to repent, you were *pretty* unlikely to end up scalped or burned to death; on the other hand, if Handsome Lake suspected you of being an opponent to his prophet status as well as being a witch, you could pretty much count on meeting an unpleasant demise (and if you were a woman: bonus points toward getting executed).

Handsome Lake's tendency to accuse people he disliked, especially those he considered rivals—such as Seneca chief Red Jacket—ultimately doomed his witch hunting.

Just about the same time Handsome Lake was getting his vision-inspired witch hunt going, a Shawnee with a similar background had the same idea; he would become the most notorious Native American witch hunter, mostly because of the gruesomeness of the hunts and this prophet's high-profile brother. Tenskwatawa was a man with a reputation for too much drinking and too little bravery, but when he had a vision in 1805 and began preaching against Indians assuming the behaviors of white culture, his message resonated. It didn't hurt that he had an influential older brother, Tecumseh, who was a persuasive speaker, vehement opponent of letting the white man get away with things, and eventual author of the famous put-down of pudgy, incompetent War of 1812 Major General Henry Proctor: "You are unfit to command; go and put on petticoats."

And why was the prophet concerned with witches? Wiping out witches was of vital importance to the preservation of the Shawnee way, Tenskwatawa insisted, because Indians were using witchcraft to destroy each other. By amazing coincidence, Tenskwatawa happened to have a special ability to detect witches, and when a particularly bad fever epidemic swept through the villages of nearby Delaware Indians, they called in the self-appointed Shawnee witch finder to help.

When Tenskwatawa arrived, the villagers suspected of being witches were made to stand before him as he grandly pointed out each person who was a witch. These witches were then imprisoned until their accusers could get around to dealing with them. Finally, one by one, the witches were pulled from the prison and executed in hellishly overstated ways. Two missionaries living in the area recounted harrowing scenes like this one:

> We were overcome with terror and fright when all of a sudden we saw ten Indians with their faces painted black, some on foot, others on horseback, coming into our village with old Chief Tedpachsit. Soon after these barbarians built a large fire near our place, struck the old Chief on the head with the hatchet and threw him half alive into the fire. Meanwhile they stood near and rejoiced over the pitiful cries and movements of the unfortunate one. The plains south of our village and the woods caught fire so that our village was full of smoke and fumes.

The missionaries' anxieties increased immediately after this execution when "the monsters, quite wild, came into the house." The Indians demanded something to eat and some tobacco, which the missionaries quickly provided "to get rid of them." The Delaware then outdid the devil himself when they took four days to slow roast an old woman they accused of witchcraft, finally getting her to incriminate her own grandson.

Like those before him, Tenskwatawa had a strong tendency to accuse his opponents of witchcraft; this and his brutal executions led to grumbling and disillusionment among the Shawnee. When the prophet took a hard line on traditional Indian healing practices—he said they were nothing more than sorcery—folks were *really* rubbed the wrong way. But it is a fed-up young Indian brave who is credited with putting a halt to this particular witch hunt. A chief named Tatepocoshe had just been put to death, and now the chief's young wife, also accused of being a witch, waited hopelessly as the witch council prepared to execute her as well. Suddenly her brother walked calmly into their midst, took his sister by the hand, and led her from the council house as her would-be executioners stood stunned. Moments later the young man returned alone and declared, "The devil has come among us and we are killing one another." This simple statement, it is said, snapped the Delaware out of their witch-killing frenzy, and effectively ended the Delaware witch-hunting segment of Tenskwatawa's career as prophet/bigshot. But the prophet was not finished with witches.

When Tenskwatawa got word of a witch hunt being held by a group of Wyandot Indians living in Ohio, he was all over it. He made the rounds of the Wyandot villages in spring of 1806 and selected four women to accuse of being witches, condemning them to execution. Frustratingly for Tenskwatawa, the executions were stayed by the local tribal leaders. The Wyandot, however, ultimately caught the witch fever, and an outbreak of witch hunts and executions ensued. Finally, Indiana Territory Governor William Henry Harrison had to speak up, saying to the Wyandot, "I charge you to stop your bloody career. . . . Let your poor old men and women sleep in quietness, and banish from their minds the dreadful idea of being burnt alive by their own friends and countrymen."

As for troublemaker Tenskwatawa, Governor Harrison suggested the Indians put him to the test before putting so much stock in his witch claims. "If he really is a prophet," Harrison sarcastically suggested, "ask him to cause the sun to stand still, the moon to alter its course, the rivers to cease to flow, or the dead to arise from their graves. If he does these things, you may then believe that he has been sent from God."

No problemo, Tenskwatawa responded; he confidently announced that he would have his pal the Master of Life turn the sun from gold to black on June 16, 1806. In one of history's most "can't make this stuff up" occurrences and what was certainly Tenskwatawa's most satisfying moment, a total solar eclipse *did* occur on June 16, 1806. (Harrison would eventually one-up the prophet's coup in 1841 by becoming the ninth president of the United States, although this success would quickly be converted to the honor of becoming the United States president with the shortest term of office, when he died just thirty-two days into his presidency.) The feud between the prophet and the future president continued to fester; eventually, despite his impressive astrological skills, Tenskwatawa's witch-hunting contingency slowly lost interest. Instead of bowing out of public life, the prophet, possibly still holding a grudge against Harrison, re-invented himself. He joined forces with his brother Tecumseh in fighting the whites' encroachment of the Indian lands.

Because it was the early 1800s, a governor's duties were a little more hands-on than what they eventually would become. Instead of appearing at $500-a-plate fund-raisers and keeping up a fun but informative Twitter feed, governors were literally expected to lead their armies in war. And so in 1811 the former witch hunter and the future president were destined to meet on the battlefield.

At this time, a community known as Prophetstown had built up around the powerful figure of Tecumseh and served as home to the prophet and his movement. In November 1811, Tecumseh had left the village in the hands of his brother, with strict orders not to start any trouble while he was away on a diplomatic visit to another village. He probably should have known better. Governor Harrison, in response to the growing Indian population of Prophetstown and the corresponding alarm of the adjacent settlers, led his army to the village, stopping and making camp just a short distance away. When word of the approaching army reached him, Tenskwatawa sent emissaries to suggest a formal "let's talk about this like reasonable nemeses" meeting to Harrison's camp. They had no sooner left than he decided that, really, it would just save everybody a lot of trouble if the Indians went ahead and murdered Harrison and the other invaders while they slept. He also demonstrated just how thin the line between being a witch and a prophet was when he reassured his followers that they totally didn't need to worry. He had a very reliable magic spell that would ensure that the whites' bullets couldn't hurt them.

The Indians' attack on Harrison's camp on the shores of Tippecanoe River did not go well at all. After a bloody skirmish at the camp, the prophet's men—those who hadn't already been shot—were routed and fled back to their village, which in short order was burned to the ground by the whites. Many Shawnee were killed and the rest fled into the woods. The Indians' stores of food were destroyed, and the prophet, who had sat the battle out behind a hill, was heard muttering a lot of stuff about how his wife had screwed up his magic. When the fighting and burning were all done, each side put a nice little bow on the ugliness by digging up and desecrating the dead of the other army. Tecumseh returned home to find that he had no home, and his brother the prophet had officially become a liability.

Tenskwatawa's credibility was a thing of the past; Tecumseh, while fighting alongside the British in the War of 1812, proved to be the real prophet. He announced, "Brother warriors, we are about to enter an engagement from which I will not return," then was killed in the next day's battle. Tenskwatawa outlived his notoriety and died in 1836.

These Indian-on-Indian witch hunts occurred in the early nineteenth century—a little over a century *after* the 1692 witch hunts of Salem. The Christians, as we saw above, were quick to deride the Indians for doing something they too had done. Their hypocrisy didn't go unnoticed. In 1821, the Erie County Court in New York charged a Seneca Indian with murder after he executed a woman as a witch on behalf of his tribal council. Seneca chief Red Jacket, famous for his oratorical skills, was quick to call them out on it:

> What! Do you denounce us as fools and bigots, because we still believe that which you yourselves believed? Your blackcoats thundered this doctrine from the pulpit, your judges pronounced it from the bench, and sanctioned with it with the formalities of law. . . . Go to Salem! Look at the records of your own government. . . . What have our brothers done more than the rulers of your people have done?

❧ The courts in New York killed some time passing this particular accused witch killer around, trying to make the situation someone else's problem, then pretty much conveniently forgot about the whole thing. The defendant, who had admitted killing the alleged witch by slitting her throat, was released.

Red Jacket's story proved that the natives and the newer Americans had something in common after all: conveniently bad memories. In 1801, Red Jacket had been accused by our old friend Handsome Lake of being a witch. Had he not been such a persuasive speaker, he likely would have been among the other Indians executed for witchcraft. Instead, Red Jacket, ultimately a devotee of a different demon, died an alcoholic in 1830.

The European settlers and the Indians had met on the shores and in the forests of America as believers in witchcraft, each group convinced that the other held malevolent powers. In the end, however, it would be the white man's witchcraft that would prove more merciless, terrible, and enduring.

PART II

Witchcraft Takes Off

CHAPTER 5

Predatory Pigs, Phantom Puppies, and Other Sinister Sidekicks

If it can be proved that the party hath entertained a familiar spirit, and had conference with it, in the likeness of some visible creatures; here is evidence of witchcraft.

—William Perkins, *A Commentary Upon the Epistles of the Galatians*, 1604

It was the best of times, it was the worst of times ... to be a pig.

If you were a pig in colonial New England, you were a highly valued asset. You knew what it meant to be *appreciated*. You can bet that the person who owned you was darn happy to have you, and, if you didn't think too much about what he was eventually going to do with you (which, being a pig, you probably didn't), life was pretty much as good as it could get under the circumstances. Your esteemed pig ancestors, having survived a heroic voyage across the ocean, had probably arrived in America about the same time as your owner's ancestors in the early 1600s, making you, whether pilgrim or Puritan, a very notable pig indeed. A founding pig, if you will. At certain times of the year, your owners might have let you run about at will, the local woods being a popular place for a pig to see and be seen, to meet other pigs, to feed on this or that, and to luxuriate in the throes of an afternoon nap beneath some leafy bough. If you hit it off with some other pig, which you inevitably would, a nice time would ensue, which would very likely result in a large litter of little pigs.

Now, it should be noted, noble New England pig, that your swinish brethren to the south were the (delicious) embodiment of those embarrassing relatives we all have, coarse descendants of the forest pigs who were brought to America by inconsiderate Spanish scallywags, who left them to run wild in the New World, which they did with a vengeance. They munched such a path of destruction through the Native Americans' corn that they were an actual factor in the destruction of this people. But you, noble New England pig, were of a much classier lineage!

Pigs were at such a premium in colonial New England that whether you ate one, sold one, or bred one and then sold its piglets, being the owner of a pig was pretty much win-win. Their meat was easy to preserve, and there was always, always a market for it. And that, perhaps, is why pigs were so often the targets of spiteful witches; after all, what better way to get revenge on someone who had slighted you than to mess with their prized possession?

Preternatural Porkers

It was a dark and stormy night. The man shivered beneath his blankets as the wind howled outside. Suddenly, from downstairs came the eerie sound of . . . a pig?

No? Pigs aren't what you expect to find spooking folks in stories of witches and haunted houses. But in 1684, in his *Remarkable Providences,* a book designed to show folks what sorts of freaky things could happen if Satan was allowed to get the upper hand, New England minister Increase Mather shared the real-life woes of people whose houses were "vexed with evil spirits," including one about a fellow whose otherworldly tormentors found that saying it with swine was an excellent means to get one's point across. In 1679, Mather wrote, William Morse of Newberry in the Massachusetts Bay Colony was having a little problem with his house being haunted. More specifically, it was being "strangely disquieted by a demon." He described one incident:

> On December 3, in the night time, he and his Wife heard a noise upon the roof of their House, as if Sticks and Stones had been thrown against it with great violence; whereupon he rose out of his Bed, but could see nothing. Locking the Doors fast, he returned to Bed again. About midnight they heard a Hog making a great noise in the House, so that the Man rose again, and found a great Hog in the house, the door being shut, but upon the opening of the door it ran out.

Well, obviously, a skeptic might say, the man simply didn't notice the big hog in his house when he locked up for the night. Or perhaps he had been entertaining the hog in the parlor earlier in the evening and had simply forgotten he was there. There could be all sorts of explanations for a hog appearing in one's home in the middle of the night, but at a certain time in colonial New England, there was only one: bewitchment. Richard Morse definitely had a witch mad at him.

Pigs were also entered into court testimony in the Salem Witch Trials. A deposition against accused witch Martha Carrier in Salem included her former neighbor John Roger's reminiscence of some pretty great pigs he had—that is, until Martha Carrier bewitched them. It all started when Roger had a little falling out with Martha:

> There happening some difference betwixt us she gave forth several threatening words as she often used to do and in a short time after this deponent had two large lusty sows which frequented home daily which were lost and this deponent found one of them dead nigh the said Carriers house with both ears cut off and the other sow I never heard of to this day.

And it didn't even matter that this incident had taken place seven years before; when it came to large lusty sows, holding a grudge was to be expected (and when witch persecutors were determined to get their witch, old stories from disgruntled neighbors were just fine). And obviously, it was much more likely that the second sow had disappeared via bewitchment than that someone had, say, eaten her. Regardless of what had actually happened, it's poignant to picture Mr. Roger at the door of his abode, looking up and down the road, waiting and watching for the return of that large lusty sow.

Pigs figured in other testimony against accused witches as well. The Edwards family had problems with their piggies— at least that was what was entered as testimony against Rachel Clenton in her witchcraft trial at Salem. According to Mrs. Edwards, Clenton was annoyed that the family did not have work for her, and, despite the fact that Mrs. Edwards had grudgingly shared some yummy blood pudding with her, she had gone away muttering under her breath. Piggie problems ensued, and sick animals following a disagreement could only mean one thing in Salem: bewitchment. The Edwardses' brood of nine eight-week-old piggies was taken ill; five of them died. A few weeks after the untimely demise of the baby piggies, the Edwardses' yearling piggies came down with some sort of "fits" that oddly mirrored the fits displayed by many of the possessed girls of Salem. They jumped and roared, Mrs. Edwards testified, then tumbled down, one after the other. All of these unfortunate pig problems were directly attributed to a spell placed on the Edwards family—and their piggies—by Rachel Clenton.

A Salem couple called the Blys testified against Bridget Bishop (who would eventually be hanged as a witch), alleging that she had bewitched their sow following a sow-related argument. (Mr. Bly had bought a pig from the Bishops and they quarreled about the price.) The sow in question was taken with strange fits, during which she would foam at the mouth, smash her head into a wall, jump up in the air, and run "as if she were stark mad." After several fits of this sort, the pig recovered (or else was eaten; the record is not clear).

Familiar with Witches

Pigs weren't always victims when it came to witchcraft. A teat-suckling pig familiar made an appearance in a Salem witch trial testimony by a certain Susannah Sheldon. She swore that a whole gang of witches had gotten into the habit of paying her nocturnal visits, trying to get her to sign The Book, etc., etc. During one of these visits, one of the gang—Martha Corey—had "pulled out her breast and the black man gave her a thing like a black pig and she put it to her breast and gave it suck."

During another visit, after offering her money (which, of course, she turned down) to "sign the book," one of the witch gang members, John Willard, had proceeded to suckle the "apparition of two black pigs on his breasts." Another one, Elizabeth Colson, suckled a yellow bird, while a third person, an old man whom Sheldon did not recognize, suckled a long black snake. At this point the suckling fest was interrupted by the appearance of the devil, and the witches had to stop and kneel before him as the horrified Sheldon watched.

A witch also has the option to turn herself into an animal, and that witch-in-animal-form is sometimes called a familiar, too. And here the ever-versatile pigs make lots of appearances. The Salem court heard swine-related testimony against the elderly Mary Bradbury about an incident thirteen years earlier, wherein some neighbors with whom she had quarreled claimed that she turned herself into a blue boar. Once she had become the blue boar, she dashed outdoors and caused her neighbor's horse to stumble—but, thank heaven, no harm was done. But that, along with other testimony involving stuff like bewitched butter, got the sickly woman sentenced to death. Bizarrely,

Mary Bradbury did not use her witchcraft to turn herself into a blue boar and run away from her persecutors. Instead, she was helplessly led to prison. Her execution was fortuitously delayed, however, and she outlived the witch craze, dying in 1700.

In a similar incident, at the almost-dawn end of a night of drinking with accused witch Susannah Martin and some other goodtime gals, Joseph Ring, who said he had been forced to party with the witches against his will, witnessed Martin turn into a black hog and trot away. In Salem, it's not a party until somebody turns into a black hog. And we thought Puritans didn't have any fun . . .

Witches had other animal options besides the ever-popular pig persona, however. A traditional story from North Carolina tells of a witch who was famous for turning herself into a deer and teasing hounds and hunters alike. A South Carolina witch had a habit of turning himself into a bear; he liked to wake people up in the middle of the night by prowling around their bedrooms. Another male witch was known to turn himself into a turkey on occasion, and a little further north witches in the Allegany Mountains were said to keep pens of egg-laying toads, presumably as familiars to do their bidding.

In Salem, a familiar even appeared in insect form; accused witch Mary Barker claimed that a fly had spoken to her, telling her that she could afflict several of her neighbors by clenching and unclenching her fists. This activity would cause the nasty neighbors a lot of pain, the fly assured her. Mary admitted that she did indeed take the fly's advice, and that it worked. She also said that she was sorry that she had listened to the fly.

In the cutest familiar category, testimony against the aforementioned Susannah Martin also included an anecdote featuring some pretty adorable familiars. A man named John Kemball said he had a dispute with her over the selection of a puppy from a litter of Martin's dog. Kemball had argued with the alleged witch, saying she had not let him get the puppy he wanted. Martin had gone away muttering, "I'll give him puppies enough!" (which, by the way, has got to be the cutest curse ever uttered by a witch). Sure enough, several days later as Kemball made his way home along a local road, he was plagued by a series of terrifying phantom puppies—puppies that, he said, were most definitely Witch Martin's familiars, because they had been extremely aggressive. The first puppy, Kemball testified, "shot between my legs forward and backward."

Kemball's reaction to this was to swing his ax at the puppy, although he was quick to add that he had been "free from all fear." Fortunately, the ax had gone right through the phantom puppy. He then encountered another puppy, a little bigger than the first, and much more aggressive; this phantom puppy, he claimed, tried to tear out his belly and throat. Although he tried to fight the puppy off "a good while without fear," he was only human, and the terror of the phantom puppy attack got the best of him. He felt his heart sink, he said, and then became so terrified he thought the life would go out of him. He took off running, "calling upon God and naming the name of Jesus Christ." The mean little puppy finally disappeared.

As further proof that Susannah had sicked the puppy familiars on him, Kemball said that the next day Susannah inexplicably knew the details of the incident, despite the fact that he, for some reason, had not told anyone about the frightening phantom puppies. But somehow (okay, because she was a witch) Susannah Martin knew all about it; she said to Kemball's neighbor, "They say he was affrighted last night." When the neighbor asked with what, Susannah replied, "With puppies."

Menacing Monsters

There weren't only puppies, pigs, and buzzing insects assisting witches; some of the creatures associated with early American witches can be described as nothing short of straight-up monsters. In Salem, one man testified that he had a terrifying encounter that started with a pig but got considerably more dire. John Louder said he was home sick on a Sunday (i.e., taking a mental health day from prayer services). He had locked the door and was settling in for a quiet afternoon when he was startled by the unexpected sight of a big black hog coming across the room in what he apparently took to be a menacing manner. He bravely ran toward it and kicked at the beast, only to have it vanish before his eyes. But the pig was just the warm-up act.

Recovering from that inexplicable encounter, Louder had just settled himself comfortably back in his chair when he was startled anew by a terrifying visage at his window. It was a "black thing," he swore, that crawled right through the window into the room and stood face to face with him. Louder couldn't believe his eyes: "The body of it looked like a monkey, only the feet were like a cock's feet with claws and the face somewhat more like a man's than a monkey. And I being greatly affrighted not being able to speak by reason of fear I suppose so the thing spake to me."

The monkey-thing went on to tell Louder that he (the monkey-thing) was a "messenger" from the devil, and that Louder would "want for nothing" if he would only agree to become a devotee. Louder snapped out of his state of shock and sprang into action; he tried to grab the creature, shrieking, "You Devil, I will kill you!" but it got away and, being monkey-like, jumped back out through the window. Louder said he ran outside after it only to come upon not a monkey-thing, but well-known witch Bridget Bishop. True, she was just standing in her own yard, but it was suspicious just the same. A few days later, Louder saw it—or another creature like it—in the orchard. This time, he said, it was flying about, knocking apples off trees and generally being pretty reckless. Louder was "struck dumb and so continued for about three days" by this sight.

Strange, unidentifiable creatures became commonplace in Salem; William Allen, testifying against accused witch Sarah Good (she is one of the "two or three women" mentioned below), stated that

> He heard a strange noise not usually heard that so continued for many times so that he was affrighted, and coming nearer to it he there saw a strange and unusual beast lying on the ground so that going up to it the said beast vanished away and in its place straight up two or three women and flew from me not in the manner of other women but swiftly vanished away.

Another inhabitant of Salem, Elizabeth Wellman, reported that she saw accused witch Sarah Cole in the woods in the company of "a black thing of considerable bigness." (Blackness was associated with the sinister in the colonies. In witch accusations, Satan was sometimes described as "the black man"; colonists were also known to call Indians "black.")

Animals were an important part of life in colonial America, so it makes sense that they figured prominently in witch accusations. But talking flies, monkey-like monsters, and "black things"? Were these strange creatures testament to the wiliness of Satan? Or were they reflections of other subconscious fears of the colonists? If you were standing trial as a witch, it didn't really matter if these creatures came from the depths of Hell or your neighbor's imagination; they could still help get you killed.

Chapter 6

Hell Comes to Hartford: America's Starter Salem

Get the broad axe and cut off her head!

—Elizabeth Kelly, age eight

The town of Hartford in the Colony of Connecticut, early spring, 1662.

Beside a freshly dug grave, Dr. Bray Rossiter stood before the body of eight-year-old Elizabeth Kelly and, with the help of local schoolmaster William Pitkin and a not-very-clean knife, cut her open from throat to groin. Carefully, tentatively, he examined her womb and her bowels. The raw March air bit at his gloveless hands as, with a trembling finger, he stroked what seemed to be fresh blood out of the girl's opened throat. He instructed Pitkin to write, which the nervous man did, trying to control a tremor in his hand: "The gullet . . . was contracted like a hard fish bone that hardly a large pea could be forced through." Otherwise, Rossiter could find nothing wrong with the small body; if anything it seemed, at several days postmortem, oddly fresh. He noted, "The whole body, the muscular parts, nerves and joints were all pliable." Dr. Rossiter issued an invoice for 20 pounds—a considerable sum—and the first autopsy in the American colonies was on the records. The official cause of death? "Preternatural causes" (i.e., witchcraft).

It was Connecticut, not Salem, that broke the ground for witch persecution in New England. Although the first Hartford witch execution, that of Alse Young, had been barely a blip on the record books, witches would turn into such a problem for that town fifteen years later that it became New England's starter Salem, with witch persecutions less systematic but deadly just the same. Between 1662 and 1663, the time known as the Year of the Witch in Hartford, eight people would be accused of witchcraft, and four of these accused witches would be hanged. These cases would thrust fears of witchcraft deeper into the souls of godly New Englanders, with ungodly results.

At the side of the sad, open grave in Hartford, Rossiter—a respected physician from the town of Guilford some twenty miles away—had confirmed what the little girl's father, John Kelly, and local officials had suspected: Judith Ayres, a neighborhood nurse who had long been rumored to be a witch, had put a spell on the girl.

Judith Ayres, known as Goody Ayres, was an immigrant from England who hadn't done herself any favors by previously enthralling neighbors with colorful stories—like the one about the time that she had, back in London, stood the devil up for a date, making him so furious that he pulled the iron bars right off a fence. And she had another strike against

her: her husband, William, was a sometime thief with a stolen ox and a purloined pig on his rap sheet. Both the Ayreses
had been the subject of whispers and grumbles stemming
from their frequent quarrels with their neighbors and money
problems.

According to John Kelly's court testimony, one afternoon the week before, Goody Ayres had joined up with little Elizabeth—affectionately known as Betty—as she walked
home from her grandmother's house. Ayres had invited herself into the Kelly kitchen, where she ladled some "broth hot
out of the boiling pot" and insisted the girl share it. Despite
her parents' objections that it was too hot, Elizabeth had some
of the broth "out of the same vessel" as Goody Ayres. Almost
immediately the little girl was taken ill with terrible pains in
her stomach; by evening she was feverish, but the family tried
to sleep. Then, in the middle of the dark Hartford night, Betty
Kelly began screaming, "Goody Ayres chokes me!" This kicked
off five terrible days of suffering, and five days of the girl complaining of Goody Ayres choking her, pinching her, and sitting
on her stomach. "She will break my bowels!" the girl cried. She
begged her father to call the magistrate to arrest the witch and
force her to relieve her cruel suffering.

As the girl's fever escalated, so did her mania against
Goody Ayres. Thrashing feverishly in her sickbed, she desperately implored, "O Father, set on the great furnace and scald
her! Get the broad axe and cut off her head!" But, in one of
the strangest turns of any seventeenth-century witchcraft case,
John Kelly and his wife did *not* accuse Judith Ayres of witchcraft and demand that she be arrested—far from it. Instead,
Goody Ayres was brought in to help nurse the girl.

At first, Elizabeth, who was growing weaker, responded to Goody Ayres's presence with an odd, dazed calm and simply lapsed into sleep. But later that day the girl whispered to her father that while she had been left alone with Goody Ayres, the woman had threatened her, saying, "Betty why do you speak so much against me? I will be even with you before I die! But if you will say no more of me, I will give you a fine lace for your dressing." Betty failed to take the witch up on her generous offer, however; the following day, Elizabeth Kelly again cried out, "Goody Ayres chokes me!" then promptly fell back on her pillow dead.*

Everyone agreed that they had never seen an illness like Elizabeth's; combined with the babbling about witchcraft and the suddenness of her death, it made John Kelly suspicious of Goody Ayres. An impromptu Inquest Committee was quickly formed in Hartford, and the group of men gathered to investigate the death of Elizabeth Kelly—starting with an examination of the body, still in the Kelly's home. John Kelly, Goody Ayres, and others were also present. Afterward, the Inquest Committee prepared an official statement, describing the examination, complete with odd experimentation on the little body:

> We whose names are under written, were called forth and desired to take notes, of the dead child of John Kelly, do hereby testify, what we saw as followeth: the child was brought forth and laid upon a forme [bench], by the Goodwife Ayres and Goodwife Waples, and the face of it being uncovered good wife Ayres was desired, by John Kelly to come up to it and to handle it; the child having

purged a little at the mouth the Goodwife Ayres wiped the   ¡
corner of the child's mouth with a cloth.

But this was no time for kind gestures. Goody Ayres was then
told to take hold of the dead girl's sleeve and

> Turn up the sleeve of the arm and she did endeavor to do it,
> but the sleeve being somewhat straight, she could not well
> do it. Then John Kelly himself ripped up both the sleeves of
> the arms and upon the back side of both the arms, from the
> elbow to the top of the shoulders were black and blue, as if
> they had been bruised or beaten.

This dramatic turn of events seemed to show that the girl really
had been the victim of a brutal phantom attack. Goody Ayres
was sent out of the room. But the Inquest Committee wasn't
finished with Betty's body yet:

> After this the child was turned over upon the right side
> and set upon the belly, and then there came such a stench
> from the corpse, as that it caused some to depart the room.

Then, in a sort of ad hoc witch test, Goody Ayres was brought in
again to see what the effect might be upon the girl's body:

> The child being turned again, and laid into the coffin
> John Kelly desired them to come into the room again to
> see the child's face, and then we saw upon the right cheek
> of the child's face, a reddish tawny great spot, which cov-
> ered a great part of the cheek, it being on the side next to

Goodwife Ayres where she stood, this spot or blotch was not seen before the child was turned.

❧ The officials looked from the strange spot on the girl's face to Goody Ayres and then at each other. They were all pretty sure they had a witch on their hands. Despite this, something like reason still ruled the day and someone sent to Guilford for Dr. Rossiter, as there was no physician available in Hartford. By the time he arrived, Elizabeth Kelly had been dead for five days and lay in her coffin beside her newly dug grave. Up until this point, no physician had performed an official autopsy in America, and so Dr. Rossiter's postmortem of the girl was an unconventional undertaking. But the morbid curiosity of the witch-fearing citizens of Hartford was powerful; no one objected to this strange turn of events. And as soon as Rossiter issued his finding that Elizabeth Kelly had died by "preternatural" causes, officials turned their attention in earnest to the woman the dead girl had accused of being a witch—Judith Ayres. "This will take away my life!" Goody Ayres exclaimed when she was arraigned on formal charges of witchcraft.

❧ All the talk of witchcraft had the predictable result upon the townspeople, and a full-blown witch panic ensued. Before long, William Ayres was also accused of witchcraft—a common occurrence for spouses of supposed witches. But again the people of Hartford wanted to be extra, *extra* sure about the witchcraft thing. There was no lie detector test in the 1600s, or even incriminating Google search histories. But there was what amounted to witch profiling, and the Ayreses—poor, problematic to the community, a bit eccentric—fit the bill.

But still another official assessment of the situation was needed; the Inquest Committee and onlookers convened at a small pond, where the Ayreses were subjected to the classic water test. Effectively incapacitated by being bound hand to foot, they were each thrown into the pond. The good news was that they didn't drown. The bad news: they didn't drown. This confirmed that the Ayreses, bobbing on the water's surface like buoys, were indeed, as everyone had thought, witches. They were pulled from the water and taken, dripping and cold, back to jail.

The writing was on the wall for the Ayreses: as Judith had predicted, the witchcraft charge was about to be the death of her—and her husband. But the couple, it turned out, had at least a few friends in town who were willing to help, and, with the clock ticking down on a one-way trip to the gallows, Judith and William Ayres somehow pulled off an escape from the Hartford jail. It was not a moment too soon; by then two other witches at been executed in Hartford. Meanwhile the Ayreses disappeared into New England, leaving behind two little boys, ages five and eight.

Judith and William Ayres barely escaped a one-way visit to Hartford's Gallows Hill. Four other folks would not be so fortunate.

A Match Made in Hartford . . . or Hell?

They must have made quite a pair. As described by a local minister, the twice-widowed bride was "lewd, ignorant, and considerably aged in years." Her groom was runty, quarrelsome, and often in trouble with the law for stealing and lying. Nonetheless, they married their fortunes—such as they were—together, and, while Rebecca and Nathaniel Greensmith were decidedly unpopular with the neighbors, they were making a pretty decent go of it on their farm in Hartford. At least until that strange, strange spring of 1662 when they were dragged unmercifully into the narrative of the Hartford witch panic.

It was bad enough that the little Kelly girl had died allegedly as a result of witchcraft; now several young women of Hartford were displaying symptoms of having been bewitched. A special day of prayer and fasting was declared out of concern for the girls, and on that day many from the town gathered at the meeting house. But all the attention only made the devils behave like naughty children, and they brought on an extra-bad flare-up of fits in the girls, who commenced jerking about and making strange, guttural utterances as the startled congregation looked on in terror. The most afflicted of this tortured trio was Ann Cole, who, as the congregation prayed for her, contorted in such an unnatural way that one woman observer fainted dead away.

Ann was the daughter of John Cole, a highly regarded landowner of Hartford, and when she announced that there was a band of witches living in that town, people listened—even if she was thrashing around on the floor and speaking in what seemed to be the voice of a demon when she did so. There was one name that was prominently featured in the girl's witch rantings: Rebecca Greensmith.

Ann and her demons weren't the only ones who knew that Goody Greensmith was a witch. A local man named Robert Stern testified that he himself had seen Goody Greensmith and sundry other local witches dancing a devilish circle around two black creatures that he said looked like Indians, "but taller." The group also had been cooking something suspicious in a cauldron. The gig was up for Goody Greensmith. She was promptly arrested and locked in jail, where she waited helplessly as the witch persecution/prosecution ran its course.

Meanwhile, Ann Cole indignantly complained that the witches were carrying out an intricate plot against her to ruin her reputation in order to keep her from ever being married. This was an unusual claim against witches, who were normally all about getting someone to sign The Book and pledge themselves to Satan, or getting revenge for some small slight. But witches were witches, and as such were surely capable of any sort of devious mischief. As word spread of Ann's plight, many high-profile clergymen, including Rev. Samuel Stone, came to witness the devil in Miss Cole. The minister from Ann's own church, John Whiting, would later write a letter to renowned clergyman Increase Mather about the incident of Ann's bewitchment. Mather himself wrote about the case, adding credence to it by declaring that Ann Cole was "a person of real piety and integrity." Or so he had heard.

The devil—or devils—put on quite a show, having conversations with each other through the young woman. They apparently decided she was talking about them too much, and decided to complicate things further by actually saying this out loud through Ann. "Let us confound her language that she may tell no more tales," one of the devils next proposed, and sure enough Ann's speech became unintelligible. Then, when she spoke again it was with a thick Dutch accent that Rev. Whiting called "very awful and amazing." Rev. Stone was a big fan of this trick; he declared that the accent was so authentic there was totally no way she could be faking it. The gentlemen transcribed everything the devils said through Ann, then sent for the magistrate. The devils had spoken: Goody Greensmith was a witch.

When the accusations against Goody Greensmith were read to the old woman, she quickly confessed; her strategy seemed to be to fully cooperate with the court. She helpfully confirmed that the other local women implicated in Ann Cole's rants were indeed also witches, and attempted to redirect the prosecution's attention with titillating tales. Though she conceded that when she was first questioned by prosecutor Joseph Haines she would have liked to have "torn him to pieces," Goody Greensmith was now in a *much* more agreeable state of mind and was happy to tell all about her Satanic associations:

> She likewise declared that the devil first appeared to her in the form of a deer or fawn, skipping about her, wherewith she was not much affrighted, and that by degrees he became very familiar, and at last would talk with her, moreover she said that the devil frequently had carnal knowledge of her body, and that the witches had meetings at a place not far from her house and that some appeared in one shape, and others in another, and one came flying amongst them in the shape of a crow.

As if these fantastic tales about witch meetings and sex with the devil weren't enough, there was someone else Goody Greensmith was ready to implicate: Mr. Greensmith. Despite the fact that he visited his wife in prison and begged her not to implicate him in her testimony, she eagerly pointed out some very suspicious things about her husband—for instance, just how was a man of such teensy physique able to perform such feats of strength as her husband was known to do? There just *had* to be witchcraft involved, right? According to notes taken during the proceedings, Goody Greensmith stated,

> I do now testify that formerly when my husband hath told me of his great travail and labor, I wondered at it how he did it; this he did before I was married, and when I was married I asked him how he did it, and he answered me, he had help that I knew not of.

Superhuman strength was one thing, but then things got considerably spookier:

> About three years ago, as I think it, my husband and I were in the woods several miles from home, and were looking for a sow that we lost, and I saw a creature, a red creature, following my husband, and when I came to him I asked him what it was that was with him, and he told me it was a fox.

And Mr. Greensmith had offered the old "don't worry, honey; that creepy thing in the woods was just a fox" explanation on another occasion:

> Another time when he and I drove our hogs into the woods beyond the pond that was to keep young cattle, several miles off, I went before the hogs to call them, and looking back I saw two creatures like dogs, one a little blacker than the other; they came after my husband pretty close to him, and one did seem to me to touch him. I asked him what they were, he told me he thought foxes.

Then Goody Greensmith casually dropped a comment that added an extra layer of insinuation: "I was still afraid when I saw anything, because I heard so much of him before I married him."

And then it was back to "how does such a little dude pick up such heavy stuff, anyway?"

> I have seen logs that my husband hath brought home in his cart that I wondered at it that he could get them into the cart, being a man of little body and weak to my apprehension; and the logs were such that I thought two men such as he could not have done it.

She really hated to have to say such things about her husband, but she was just trying to do the right thing, the brave old woman insisted:

> I speak all of this out of love to my husband's soul, and it is much against my will that I am now necessitated to speak against my husband. I desire that the Lord would open his heart to own and speak the truth.

But Goody Greensmith wasn't finished; she had more beans to spill regarding the other ladies in her witch gang and some of their shameless shenanigans:

> I also testify, that I being in the woods at a meeting, there was with me Goody Seager, Goodwife Sanford and Goodwife Ayres. And at another time there was a meeting under a tree in the green by our house, and there was

James Walkley, Peter Grant's wife, Goodwife Ayres, and
Henry Palmer's wife, of Wethersfield, and Goody Seager;
and there we danced and had a bottle of sack.

But wait, what could make this story a little witch-ier? Oh right,
a cat!

It was in the night and something like a cat called me out
to the meeting, and I was in Mr. Varlet's orchard with
Mrs. Judith Varlet, and she told me that she was much
troubled with the marshal, Jonathan Gilbert, and cried;
and she said if it lay in her power she would do him a
mischief, or what hurt she could.

Goody Greensmith's testimony was super helpful to the prosecution, but it did her own cause no good whatsoever. The court,
perhaps to streamline the whole paperwork thing, lumped the
cases of Mr. and Mrs. Greensmith into one, and ruled:

The indictment of Nathaniel Greensmith and of Rebecca
his wife for witchcraft: thou are here indicted . . . for not
having the fear of God before thine eyes; thy has familiarity with Satan the Grand Enemy of God and Mankind and
by his help has enacted things in a preternatural way . . .
beyond human abilities, for which, according to ye law of
God and ye established laws of this Commonwealth thou
deserveth to die.

The Greensmiths were taken to the home of the jailor, where,
for what must have been the most awkward month ever, they

awaited execution together. As they waited, their estate was charged daily for their room and board. On January 25, 1663, they, along with another accused witch, were taken to Gallows Hill in Hartford where they were hanged. Mather cheerfully concluded, "After the suspected witches were executed . . . Ann Cole was restored to health, and has continued well for many years, approving herself a serious Christian."

As a matter of fact, things went so well for Ann that less generous neighbors might have started whispering that there was something . . . *preternatural* about the whole thing. After the Greensmiths' execution, the court seized the couple's home and sold it to a local man named Andrew Benton, who moved in with his wife and children. But Benton's wife soon died, and the handsome, popular widower was quickly ready to re-marry, and get married is exactly what he did—to Ann Cole. Ann Cole finally had her groom, and she went on to raise a family of twelve children and stepchildren in the home built by the couple she claimed had bewitched her.

A Tale of Three Marys

Less is known about the other two women executed in Hartford. Mary Sanford, the mother of several children, was among those implicated by Ann Cole. There is some speculation that the Sanfords were Quakers, which definitely would have worked against Mary, Quakers at the time being considered heretics. The date of Mary Sanford's execution as well as her final resting place are unknown.

The woman executed with the Greensmiths was also a Mary. Mary Barnes was most likely in her forties and the mother of several children. She was the wife of Thomas Barnes, an immigrant from England. It's believed that she too had been implicated by Ann Cole. Mary Barnes's name makes numerous appearances in earlier court records in Connecticut, indicating that she was a bit of a problem person in Hartford. She was an illiterate servant, and her last charge before the witchcraft accusations seems to have been for adultery. Mary pleaded not guilty to the charge of witchcraft, but she was executed on Hartford's Gallows Hill and unceremoniously dumped into an unmarked grave.

After her death, Thomas Barnes was required to shell out ✷ a fee to the jailor to pay for Mary's accommodations while she awaited execution. But what Thomas Barnes did next bears mentioning: three months after his wife's execution, the suspiciously resilient Thomas Barnes remarried, first signing a marriage contract agreeing to "put out all of his children," except one. His young bride was also named Mary, and she was the daughter of the man who had arrested Mary Barnes for witchcraft.

Notes

✷ Many years later, experts examining the Elizabeth Kelly records surmised that the most likely cause of her death was bronchial pneumonia.

CHAPTER 7

An Inconvenient Witch: The Story of Eunice Cole

One Sabbath Day at night coming near the house of Eunice Cole . . . and hearing of her mutter in the house I went to the door with James Bunse and the said Eunice Cole called me Devil and said she would split out my brains and the next day I took sick.

—John Mason

G etting a stake driven through her heart was probably not the worst thing to happen to Eunice Cole.

Eunice "Goody" Cole had never had an easy time of it. Not much is known of her life before she emigrated to America. She and her husband, William, had been indentured servants in England and were in their early sixties—well past their prime by seventeenth-century standards—when they made the dangerous trans-Atlantic voyage, so it's a pretty safe bet that they were desperate for a new start. The Coles made their home in Exeter,

Massachusetts, and for a while William even held a civic office as the town's official fence viewer.* Things were looking up.

Eventually the Coles moved from Exeter to Hampton (then part of Massachusetts; it's now Hampton, New Hampshire). Hampton had been founded just a few years before the Coles arrived, but already a number of families were established and settled in as if they had been there for ages. No one really knows why the Coles moved, but it could be that disquieting rumors had already begun circulating about Goody Cole.

Hamptonites were always precariously just out of reach of the sea that had deposited them in the New World; their settlement had little but a cushion of tangled, marshy meadowland between them and the Atlantic Ocean. The almost-wilderness outskirts of town were a pastoral scene out of a dark fairytale, where deer frolicked, wolves prowled, and, according to an 1893 history by Joseph Dow, a herd of semi-wild horses so emaciated they appeared "like so many moving skeletons" pawed hopelessly at the frozen ground, snorting ghostly steam into the misty cold.

Many of the houses were clustered around the town meetinghouse; it was the kind of frontier village where any citizen who killed a wolf could earn a nice sum by cutting off the beast's head and nailing it to the tree outside the meetinghouse door. In 1640, William Cole received a land grant in Hampton, which would have been a pretty good deal even with the wolves and whatnot, except for one thing: everyone in Hampton pretty much hated the Coles. Becoming Hampton's power pariah couple was probably not what they had in mind when they moved there, but Eunice and William were barely in town before they achieved social outcast status. How bad was it for the Coles?

When a new town meetinghouse was built and congregants' permanent seats were assigned, William was given a *pretty bad* seat in the back, but Eunice's assigned spot was even worse: a bench that was in a part of the meeting house so far back it hadn't even been built yet.

Why were Eunice Cole and her husband so darn unpopular in Hampton? Well, judging by the town's court records, Eunice didn't exactly try to endear herself to her neighbors. At one point, her husband was given notice to "bring his wife to the said court to answer a presentment against her for unseemly speeches in saying to Hulda Hussie** 'where is your mother . . . that whore: she is a bed with your father that whore master?'" There was also this complaint from a neighbor named John Mason: "One Sabbath Day at night coming near the house of Eunice Cole . . . and hearing of her mutter in the house I went to the door with James Bunse and the said Eunice Cole called me Devil and said she would split out my brains and the next day I took sick."

It didn't seem matter to anyone that the twenty-year-old Mason and his friend had barged onto Eunice's property to confront her; it was taken for granted that someone like Eunice should have expected that sort of thing. Mason whined in his complaint that after Eunice had threatened him, he had stayed sick for two weeks.

And then there was the infamous "pig withholding" incident. According to court records, the Coles, for what may very well have been perfectly good reasons, had "withheld" several pigs from the plaintiff. Pig withholding was apparently the kind of thing that could get you sued, because the local constable showed up to seize the pigs after the court had decided against the Coles in an actual pig-withholding lawsuit. And this is when Eunice and William, true to form, might have overreacted just a bit: "Murder, murder!" Eunice reportedly screamed when the constable showed up at their house and tried to apprehend the pigs in question, while her husband bellowed, "Thieves!" The couple was normally acrimonious, but for this occasion they were a finely tuned machine of mayhem. Together they bit the constable's hand, tag-teamed to knock him down (presumably in the pigpen), and strong-armed a squealing pig away from him.

When not involved in pig disputes, Goody Cole seemingly spent her days wandering the town of Hampton and finding ways to push everyone's buttons. Once she taunted a young carpenter working on a house so relentlessly that he finally threw an ax at her.

It certainly couldn't have helped her reputation that Eunice Cole, peevish harridan with a hair-trigger temper and serious knack for slinging insults, was also craggy and hunched over, with a hawk-like nose and scraggly gray hair—in other words, Eunice was a witch straight out of Central Casting. And this is perhaps why between the years 1656 and 1680 she was charged with being a witch at least three separate times.

She was charged with other things, too, like making slanderous speeches (see: "Your mother that whore"), but even then what the court seemed to really mean was "You look like a witch, you act like a witch, we know you're a witch, but we admit we also just really don't like you, so we don't want to overdo it with the whole charging you with witchcraft thing."

Still, all told, Eunice would spend about thirteen years of her old age in prison for various infractions, and the criminal justice system of Hampton also occasionally added injury to incarceration. The old woman was publicly whipped on several occasions, and at least once was put in the town stockades, where, presumably, she was pelted with stuff like pig dung and old shoes.

Hampton was far from unique in its penchant for cruel physical punishments. Over-the-top penal maltreatment was the norm in colonial America, and you didn't have to be a witch to qualify. In Virginia, settlers told of criminals being left chained to trees until they starved to death, being broken on the wheel, or being committed to years of hard labor (in chains, no less) for minor offenses. In Maryland in 1648, a man who was convicted of perjury—a non-violent offense—received quite the opposite in terms of punishment. He was put in the town pillory, and his ears were nailed to the wood; he also received twenty "good" lashes for good measure. In 1662, Quakers would have taken some of the heat off Eunice if she weren't already in jail; it was at that time that a cart bearing three Quaker women sentenced to whippings (for being Quaker women, by the way) was taken from town to town. As the cart passed through Hampton, the constable dutifully applied ten lashes to the bare backs of each of the women.

So, beyond her grouchiness and unfortunate witch-like appearance, were there any Goody Cole–related events that actually poked the townspeople with a broom and screamed "witch"? You bet there were! Over the course of twenty-five years, Hampton's official records filled with depositions like the following one, which came from two of the town's many professional gossips: "We [were] talking about Goodwife Cole . . . and on the sudden we heard something scrape against the boards of the window and we went out and looked about and could

see nothing and then we went in again and began to talk the
same . . . and then we heard the scraping again."

Today, hearing a strange noise while talking smack about
someone would not set off any alarm bells, but in the 1600s, it
could only indicate one thing: Eunice just had to be a witch.
Another complaint from a local busybody claimed that Eunice
inexplicably knew about some *other* gossiping that had gone on
that she couldn't possibly have known about. Again: witch. And
then there were the cat stories.

A townswoman proffered a very convoluted story involving Goody Cole and a cat (or cats—who can tell?)—cats being
generally accepted as one of the top-10 things witches like to
turn themselves into for no apparent reason. Here's part of the
cat testimony, just in case *you* can figure it out:

> This deponent went into Goodman Wedgewood's to see
> him he being sick . . . when I arose up to go away yet stand-
> ing by his bedside I saw a cat come down . . . over his
> bed . . . and she [Goody Cole] came upon his breast: and
> he cried out Lord have mercy upon me the cat hath killed
> me, and broken my heart, and his wife asked me if that
> were the cat (which she showed me), and I thought the
> cat which I saw as aforesaid was bigger than the cat she
> showed me although she was like that cat for color, and it
> was the same evening the which Goodwife Cole was there
> about noon before.

On another occasion, a cat-like creature (probably a cat) leaped
onto the face of a man named Goodman Wedgewood as he lay
in bed; this was attributed, naturally, to Goody Cole.

* Robert Smith, the town's beleaguered constable, had his own weird problem with Eunice (in addition to having to arrest her every other day). For a while, it seemed, almost all of the bread baked in the Smith family home would turn out really bad, as in "stink and prove loathsome" bad. They couldn't even get their swine to eat it, they said. Blaming Goody Cole for bad luck had become so routine that the lawman didn't think twice about blaming this run of unsuccessful baking on a foul curse by Goody Cole and her gluten-intolerant pal, Satan.

* One of the most unfortunate incidents in the career of Eunice Cole, one that was the most damning piece of evidence for those who suspected her of being a witch, conveys just how miserable her life must have been. It occurred at her first whipping. One of Eunice's tormentors giddily reported:

> Being about to strip Eunice Cole to be whipped (by judgment of the court at Salisbury) looking upon her breasts under one of her breasts (I think her left breast) I saw a blue thing like unto a teat hanging downward about three quarters of an inch long not very thick, and having a great suspicion in my mind about it (she being suspected for a witch). . . . Hereupon she pulled or scratched if off in a violent manner, and some blood with other moistness did appear clearly to my apprehension and she said it was a sore.

"Teats"—those creepy extra appendages made for suckling the devil's familiars—are one of the true hallmarks of the colonial witch, and once one was spotted on Goody Cole, it was off to the races. Several other gentlemen were only too happy to get in on the teat action: "Also Abraham Perkins and John Redman affirmed on oath that they stood by and saw the constable tear down her shift and saw the place raw and where she had tore off her teat and fresh blood come from it."

On another occasion, a male official searching Eunice's body for teats found "a strange place in her legs being a conjunction of blue veins." Today, this would be something known to us as ordinary varicose veins; then, it was well known to the people of Hampton as yet another place on Goody Cole's decrepit body "where she had been sucked by imps or the like."

Now that it had been officially confirmed that Goody Cole was practically riddled with teats, reports of suckling incidents rolled in, and continued to roll in over the years. Townswoman Elizabeth Shaw said that she was innocently trying to go about her prayers at the meetinghouse when she was disturbed by a noise that sounded like "puppies or suchlike" suckling beneath Eunice's coat. During another service someone claimed they saw a small creature—presumably an imp—that, having finished "suckling" Eunice's teats, dropped off her and creepily scurried away across the meetinghouse floor.

As all the supposedly damning evidence against Eunice rolled in, she would get arrested for witchcraft again and again, but she was always found some variation of "not legally guilty according to indictment but just ground of vehement suspicion of her having had familiarity with the devil." This basically meant that they wouldn't hang her, but they *could* send her off to do time in the jail in Boston at their discretion, which they did as often as they possibly could.

In 1662, things went from terrible to tragic for Eunice. She had been putting in some of her routine jail time, which was normally done at a safe distance of about fifty miles away in Boston; she returned home after finally being granted leave to care for the sickly eighty-eight-year-old William. Upon arriving in Hampton she discovered that not only had her husband died several months earlier, he had also changed his will right before he died. Eunice was to receive nothing more than her own clothes, while a neighbor was awarded the remainder of the estate. William wasn't being spiteful when he changed his will; he had desperately needed someone to take care of him in his wife's absence, and the neighbor agreed to take him on only in exchange for his property. The court in turn had thoughtfully altered the will so that Eunice received half of her husband's small estate, then also thoughtfully seized all but eight pounds of that as compensation for all the money they had already put into supporting Eunice. The town now had even more of a vested interest in getting rid of their increasingly expensive witch as quickly as possible.

Goody Cole's fate may have been sealed in 1671 when the town of Hampton handed down an edict that said essentially this: *Dear townspeople, you know that old lady you all can't stand who calls your mothers whores and suckles familiars during church services? Well, now you're all going to have to take turns supporting her.* Indeed, the good folk of Hampton were officially ordered to provide food and firewood for Goody Cole; they were put on a rotation schedule of one week per family for care and feeding of their nuisance witch. The town also built a tiny hut for her, and it was there she would live—when she wasn't in jail—for the rest of her unfortunate days.

In the years that followed her return to Hampton, almost every misfortune that befell any of the town's citizens was blamed on Eunice Cole. From sickly cattle to untimely deaths, it was all the work of the witch, as time and time again the townspeople tried to get Goody Cole out of their hair. Charges that didn't even begin to approach circumstantial were leveled against her and entered as evidence. In 1673, this deposition was taken from a man named Jonathan Thing; it described an alleged incident that not only sounded like someone had taken a bad mushroom trip, but had also happened more than a *decade and a half* earlier:

> About 16 or 17 years ago I going in the street at Hampton I saw one that I did judge was Eunice Cole about 20 rod behind or in a triangle sideways of me and in a short time sooner than any man could possibly go it, I saw her as I did judge was she about 20 rods or more *before* me. Upon that I went apace wondering at the thing and when I came to her . . . I talked with her and found her to be Eunice Cole. Also about that time coming out of my gate I saw nobody nor there was nobody near as I could see and presently she, the said Eunice Cole, was before me looking into the house among my cattle, I asked her what she did there. She answered what is that to you, sawsbox***? I hastened to come up to her and she seemed as it were to swim away. I could not catch her. I then being strong and in health I followed her 20 or about 30 rod.

Because of her reputation, Eunice was excluded from many of the activities of the other women of Hampton. On one occasion she stopped by a house in town to pay her respects to a woman called Mrs. Pearson, who had just delivered a baby, and found that the new mother was upstairs with the infant and several other ladies were already present and socializing downstairs. In the words of one of these women, Goody Cole "had a desire to go see the said Mrs. Pearson and her little one" upstairs. But the women weren't about to let Goody Cole join in on the happy event. As the elderly woman tried to go up the stairs, she was yanked by the arm and pulled back down. She left, as might be expected, "muttering" to herself. Not long after, Mrs. Pearson's baby died. One of the women would later file a deposition accusing Goody Cole of causing the child's death.

In 1675, new charges of witchcraft suggested yet another source of misery for Eunice Cole. The local women had long accused Eunice of coveting their children; now they claimed Goody Cole had been using her magical powers to try to "entice" a little girl named Ann Smith to come live with her.

Little Ann was found crying in an orchard and blabbering about an old woman who had promised her "a baby and some plums" if she would come away and live with her, then promptly hit her in the head with a stone, then turned into a little dog, then ran up a tree, then turned into an eagle, and then flew away— and the conveniently gullible townspeople totally believed her. Eunice Cole may have had good reason to long for a daughter of her own. Other women had daughters and daughters-in-law to help care for them in their old age, but Eunice, needier than any, had no one who cared. But even an evil witch would know better than to try to ingratiate herself with a child by bonking her on the head with a rock, and there definitely would have been some gingerbread to go with those plums.

Nonetheless, it was back to jail for Eunice. After many months she went to trial, and again there was a verdict of not *legally* guilty, right along with the usual addendum that pointed out that there was still, just for the record, "just ground of vehement suspicion of her having had familiarity with the devil."

Little was preserved of Eunice's last charge of witchcraft in 1680; perhaps by then even Hampton was getting weary of the whole deal. But Goody Cole must have gotten a bit of satisfaction out of the proceedings, because this time a different woman was being charged with witchcraft (more specifically, causing the death of a little boy through witchcraft). Still, Eunice and several other citizens were being charged as accomplices to the supernatural murder. Inevitably, ninety-year-old Eunice was once again put in prison, and this time the court slapped a heavy leg iron on her withered leg pretty much just because they could.

The final verdict on the old woman from her final witch trial was that she was "vehemently" suspected of the usual discourse with the devil; again Eunice was sent home to the shriveled bosom of the town of Hampton, where the residents resentfully resigned themselves to again carrying on with barely supporting her. But this time, a month after she was returned to her lonely little hut, the townspeople noticed that smoke had stopped coming from her chimney; there was no sign of Eunice Cole for days. Her neighbors conveniently ignored the obvious for as long as they possibly could, and then finally, on a chilly October day, bit the bullet and entered her hovel, where they found the witch dead at last. The group lazily dug a shallow grave just outside her door, and unceremoniously dumped Goody Cole into it. But before they could fill in her grave, it is said, a case of last-minute jitters struck. What if the witch could return from the dead? They'd be in *big* trouble then, wouldn't they? And so, the story goes, the townspeople drove a stake (to be extra careful, they attached a horseshoe to it, known to ward off evil spirits) through the old, battered heart of Eunice Cole.

Hampton had officially failed in its efforts to deal with perceived problem person Eunice Cole. The town's attempt to care for its needy constituency while systematically attempting to destroy it had the obvious disastrous outcome, yet it would be reenacted in America for centuries to come in its dealings even with the non-witch problematic members of society.

In the years following Eunice Cole's death, the people of Hampton discovered what it was like to have real foes to fear as attacks by Indians escalated. The townspeople who had claimed to have been so afraid of the frail, elderly woman they called a witch now had to build a fort around their meetinghouse and spend their days and nights in constant dread of an actual danger—that the Indians who were killing and kidnapping friends in nearby towns would emerge from the darkness of their own meadows.

Decades and then centuries passed, but Hampton still hadn't forgotten its alleged witch. After only about 258 years, the town decided it was time to officially exonerate its most famous citizen, Eunice Cole. They even had a ceremony to make it official. And in 2013, they did it again; this time a memorial marker with the name Eunice Cole etched into the black marble was set into the ground. Goody Cole would probably have gotten quite a bit of satisfaction out of it, especially because of its place of honor on the edge of Hampton's Meeting House Green. The place where Eunice Cole experienced many of her most painful humiliations is now a place where people come to pay their respects to her and to contemplate her horrid mistreatment by the citizens of early Hampton.

According to some, Eunice might actually be well aware of her modern-day popularity. As you have probably already guessed, folks in Hampton still report seeing the figure of an old woman wearing a long dress and buckle shoes clutching a shawl about her thin, hunched-over frame as she wanders through the town. They say this mysterious old woman has a propensity for disappearing, then seconds later reappearing much farther away than she could have possibly walked in that time; these accounts are curious considering that folks reporting this phenomenon usually don't even know about the 1673 testimony about how Goody Cole inexplicably turned up ahead of a man on a road without ever having passed him.

Whether she's still hanging around Hampton or not, the woman who was long ago shunned, whipped, ostracized, and frequently jailed at the whim of her town has got to be having a better time now than she did back in the 1600s. When it came to unfortunate jailbird-witch Eunice "Goody" Cole, the hardest time she ever did was her whole life.

Notes

*Obscure old-time local official title, meaning, basically, one who views fences (i.e., a local official who administers the "fence laws"; for example, inspecting new fences or settling disputes arising from fence-related issues). Fun fact: in some places, this position still exists; you, too, could be a fence-viewer!

**Yes, her real name.

***As can best be determined, "sawsbox" is a variation on calling someone "saucy"—a pretty tame rejoinder by Goody Cole standards.

PART III

Slouching toward Salem

CHAPTER 8

The Goodwins' Very Bad Year: The Weirdest Case of Witchcraft in American History?

This is the Story of Goodwin's Children, a Story all made up of Wonders!

—Cotton Mather

I t was a scene straight out of *The Exorcist*—times four. It was also arguably the most fantastical case of witchcraft in American history, with many credible people claiming to have witnessed seemingly impossible things.

In 1688, four of the six children of a south Boston mason named John Goodwin and his wife, Martha, were stricken with preternatural fits. As the Goodwins and their neighbors watched in horror, the small bodies of the Goodwin children would snap into impossible positions: one moment their heels would be drawn backward to their necks in an uncanny hog-tie, and the next their heads would twist almost all the way around à la Linda Blair. Sometimes they would seem to swallow their tongues only to have them suddenly jerked out of their mouths by an unseen force until they dangled upon their chins.

The bizarre situation at the Goodwin home escalated until John and Martha finally did what any God-fearing seventeenth-century couple whose children were seemingly being tortured by demonic forces would do: they called in a physician. Well, that sounds unexpectedly logical, right? Actually, the arrival of Dr. Thomas Oakes and his examination of the Goodwin children officially began the end of logic and reason in the Goodwin home. Dr. Oakes's diagnosis of what was causing the children's strange behavior? Bewitchment.

The Reverend Cotton Mather, who would soon play exorcist to the Goodwins and then write about it in a book he prefaced by gushing that it was "a story all made up of wonders!" reported that when Dr. Oakes visited the family, he "found himself so affronted by the distempers of the children, that he concluded nothing but a hellish witchcraft could be the origin of these maladies." It was officially time to call in the big guns: the Goodwins asked for the help of the local men of God, or, as they were rather ominously referred to at the time, "The Four Ministers of Boston." Things went downhill from there.

Bewitched in Boston

The most tragic thing about a person being diagnosed as "bewitched" was that there must, by definition, be a witch who committed the bewitching. In this case, the witch in question was a woman named Ann Glover, or, as she was commonly called, Goody Glover.

It had all begun when thirteen-year-old Martha Goodwin accused a neighbor who was the family's washer-woman of stealing some linens. When the indignant Martha confronted her, the washerwoman's mother, Goody Glover, took offense and stepped in. In the words of Rev. Mather, "This woman in her daughter's defense bestowed very bad language upon the girl." Unfortunately, Goody Glover's words were not preserved, but they must have been really something: Mather continued, "Immediately upon which the poor child became variously indisposed in her health, and visited with strange fits." And no sooner had Martha's fits begun than several of her siblings—John, age eleven; Mercy, age seven; and Benjamin, age five—started display-ing the exact same symptoms. Soon the four children were manifesting alarming behavior:

> They would make most piteous out-cries, that they were cut with knives, and struck with blows that they could not bear. Their necks would be broken so that their neck-bone would seem dissolved unto them that felt after it . . . and if main force at any time obstructed a dangerous motion which they seemed to be upon, they would roar exceedingly.

And the Goodwin kids were just getting warmed up.

The scenes inside the Goodwin home were truly eerie, and Mather's account of the strange goings-on reads like someone gushing about a great horror movie they've just seen. Mather especially seemed to appreciate the special effects. He wrote:

> They would have their mouths opened unto such a wideness, that their jaws went out of joint; and anon they would clap together again with a force like that of a strong spring-lock. The same would happen to their shoulder blades, and their elbows, and hand-wrists. . . . They would at times lie in a benumbed condition and be drawn together as those that are tied neck and heels; and presently be stretched out, yea, drawn backwards, to such a degree that it was feared the very skin of their bellies would have cracked.

He also noted with great credulity that when he tried to pray with one of the children, "The child utterly lost her hearing till our prayer was over."

The Goodwins versus Evil

By all accounts, the Goodwins were a family with a particularly good reputation. Governor Hutchinson, when he wrote his *History of the Province of Massachusetts Bay*, described them in glowing terms, saying John was "a grave man and good liver." And before their bewitchment, the Goodwin kids weren't just any kids. These were straight-up godly kids, upstanding in every way. Mather said, "They had an observable Affection unto Divine and Sacred things." Rev. Mather also had it on totally good authority that the Goodwin children were not only kept constantly busy with religious education, doing chores, and generally being perfect little Puritans, but also "they took a delight in it." In other words, they were the perfect targets for a bitter witch.

Rev. Mather also had it on good authority (i.e., some juicy neighborhood gossip) that Goody Glover had a reputation as "an ignorant and scandalous old woman in the neighborhood, whose miserable husband before he died had sometimes complained of her that she was undoubtedly a witch."

Between the local scuttlebutt, which he referred to as "undoubted information," and what Mather called "my own ocular observation," he was certain the Goodwins' situation was an honest-to-God case of "stupendous witchcraft." The scene was now set for a showdown between "Good"—the Goodwins, God, and Rev. Mather—and "Evil"—the devil's local rep, wicked witch Goody Glover. *Somebody* was outnumbered.

A complaint was filed against Goody Glover with the local magistrate, and in short order she was arrested and put in jail. Then, in Mather's words, "the Witch thus in the trap, she was brought upon her trial." Meanwhile, a search was made of Goody Glover's home, which yielded some damning evidence: "several small images, or puppets, or babies, made of rags, and stuff't with goat's hair, and other such ingredients." These strange objects, often called "poppets," looked like arts and crafts projects made by the insane and were used like the archetypical voodoo doll. They were also hallmarks of a witch, and as such were presented as evidence during the trial. Rev. Mather wrote that during the courtroom proceedings, also attended by the Goodwin children, "when these (poppets) were produced the vile woman acknowledged that her way to torment the objects of her malice was by wetting of her finger with her spittle and streaking of those little images." Goody Glover licked her finger and demonstrated her technique, and, as if on cue, the Goodwin children quickly fell into fits. Not satisfied to see this just once, the judge asked Glover to repeat her actions, which she did, with the same entertaining results.

Another neighborhood woman got into the act and testified that she had a really good "Goody Glover is a witch" story, and nobody even cared that it had happened six years before. The woman testified that *another* neighbor, while on her death-bed as the result of a bad bewitchment, had told her that the witch Goody Glover was to blame for her sad situation. Glover, the dying woman said, would come down her chimney at night; in this pre-Santa era, coming down a chimney was known generally as *the* go-to creepy way for witches to enter your house. But the neighbor woman should have known better than to testify against a known witch. Immediately her son started having the same problems as the Goodwin children, but with some very special touches: "One night particularly, the boy said he saw a Black Thing with a blue cap in the room, tormenting of him; and he complained most bitterly of a hand put into the bed, to pull out his bowels." No one could argue that this was a legit thing to complain "most bitterly about," and Glover, supposedly, confessed to it: "I tried to pull out the boys bowels but I could not." The next day, apparently in a much better mood, Goody Glover saw the boy in court and "expressed her good wishes for him." The boy's torments ended.

In the end, Goody Glover was found guilty of being a witch and sentenced to death. On November 16, 1688, the old woman was loaded into a cart and pulled through rutted streets to the Boston Common as onlookers jeered. According to some accounts, the hangman dragged the witch to the gallows, a heavy chain on her leg painfully holding the old woman back even as the hangman pulled her harder and harder. Waiting ringside was Cotton Mather and the Goodwin children. As they watched the sad procession, Mather, in his dark robes, leaned over and hissed in a stage whisper to the wide-eyed children, "She is being pulled to the fires of hell!"

It was said that one of Goody Glover's cats, a "fearsome creature," also came to observe her execution.

Goody Glover had proclaimed that putting her to death would not help the Goodwin children, and she was right. Their terrifying fits did not end after her death. As a matter of fact, they got even worse.

The Furnace Grows Hotter

The youngest of the Goodwin children had proven the least bewitched, and Mather claimed that the prayers of the Four Ministers of Boston had cured him. But after the death of condemned witch Goody Glover, Martha, John, and Mercy Goodwin all continued—as the witch had predicted—to be bewitched. But even the witch didn't realize how freaky the situation would become. Cotton Mather was excited to write about it:

It came to pass accordingly that the three children continued in their furnace as before, and it grew rather seven times hotter than it was. . . . They would bark at one another like dogs, and again purr like so many cats. They would sometimes complain that they were in a red-hot oven, sweating and panting. . . . They would cry out of dismal blows with great cudgels laid upon them; and tho' we saw no cudgels nor blows, yet we could see the marks left by them in red streaks upon their bodies afterward.

The children's behavior became lavishly, spookily theatrical:

> And one of them would be roasted on an invisible spit, run into his mouth and out of his foot, he lying, and rolling, and groaning. . . . Sometimes also he would have his head so forcibly, tho not visibly, nailed unto the floor, that it was as much as a strong man could do to pull it up. . . . Yea, they would fly like geese, and be carried with an incredible swiftness thro the air, having but just their toes now and then upon the ground, and their arms waved like the wings of a bird. One of them, in the house of a kind neighbor . . . flew the length of the room, about 20 foot, and flew just into an infant's high armed chair; (as tis affirmed) none seeing her feet all the way touch the floor.

Finding it inconvenient to have to be at the Goodwins' house all the time in order to monitor the bewitchment situation, Mather decided to take Martha, still the star attraction, home to live with him and his absurdly patient wife. The reverend was not disappointed; the girl's symptoms worsened:

> Variety of tortures now seized upon the girl. . . . She often would cough up a ball as big as a small egg, into the side of her wind-pipe, that would near choke her, till by stroking and by drinking it was carried down again. . . . She kept

oddly looking up the chimney. . . . When I bade her cry to the Lord Jesus for help, her teeth were instantly set; upon which I added, "Yet, child, look unto Him," and then her eyes were presently pulled into her head, so far, that one might have feared she should never have used them more.

Worst of all, Goody Glover continued to torment her sassy-mouthed nemesis Martha Goodwin. "She likewise complained that Goody Glover's chain was upon her leg," Mather wrote. It was a creepy sight indeed: when the girl tried to walk, she struggled in the same fashion that the witch had done, pulling the heavy chain behind her as she trudged to the gallows.

Martha had other phantom-chain problems as well. As the girl sat by the hearth before a snapping fire, for instance, an invisible chain was suddenly clasped around her and, as the minister frantically struggled to unshackle her, an unseen force on the other end kept pulling her closer and closer toward the fire, the girl shrieking with terror all the while; just as it seemed she would be plunged into the flames, the minister managed a mighty tug and plucked her from the devil's grasp.

When Martha wasn't busy coughing things up or trying to keep out of the fire, she was being experimented on by Mather, who was thrilled at having a live subject for his witchcraft obsession. The reverend tried various "trials," as he called them, to see what effect they might have on the bewitched child. He stomped on Martha's invisible chain (it "hurt her back") and had visitors pitch in to determine if the voices of other people reading the Bible put her into fits or if it was just his voice (she was "cast into terrible agonies" no matter who read it to her). "A few further trials, I confess, I did make," Mather wrote, but in an admission that only enhances the creepiness of the whole situation, he added that he would not relate them out of fear of offending his reader. Indeed, some of Mather's recounting of his work with the Goodwin children reads like the transcript from a child molestation trial: "It gave me much trouble to get her into my arms, and much more to drag her up the stairs"; "She was pulled out of my hands, and when I recovered my hold, she was thrust so hard upon me . . . her own breast was sore afterwards"; "With incredible forcing (though she kept screaming 'They say I must not go in . . . ')"; and "This was found when the children were to be undressed. The devils would . . . wonderfully twist the part that was to be undressed so that there was no coming at it."

Martha's stay with the Mathers grew even stranger when the girl acquired an invisible horse, which she would mount and charge furiously through the house upon. Sometimes, she would take her phantom horse ride while seated in a chair, girl and horse/chair shaking as if in a mad gallop, often without her feet even touching the floor. The hijinks were endless. Once Martha had a falling out with the horse, and after arguing with it, threatened to cut off its head with a knife. An obliging Mather handed her his sheath, which she instantly slashed across her own throat, then complained when it didn't cut. The invisible horse became an almost constant preoccupation; the girl also had invisible demonic companions that she would chat with or sometimes argue with as she rode along.

The horse—perhaps remembering the knife incident— would occasionally throw Martha violently to the floor, but the brave girl would always climb back on. Visitors gathered regularly at Mather's home to watch what their host called "her Fantastic Journeys," which, he said, "were mostly performed in her chair . . . but sometimes would she ride from her chair and be carried oddly on the floor, from one part of the room to another, in the postures of a riding woman."

One spectator asked if Martha could ride her horse up the stairs to the second floor. Of course she could! Mather wrote, "To our admiration she rose (that is, was tossed as one that rode) up the stairs."

But eventually Martha got fed up with her long-suffering phantom horse, and grouchy with her demonic acquaintances, complaining, "You have brought me such an ugly horse, I am angry at you!" She huffily called the demons "filthy witches" and informed them they would be hanged, something she knew a thing or two about by now.

Martha's bewitchment woes continued, however. She managed to fight off an unseen force that tried to drag her into a burning oven, but Mather said that another incident, involving an invisible hangman's noose, left her "black in the face." He reported that she developed a fondness for picking on her host, treating him "with a sauciness I had not been used to be treated with." She amused herself by knocking at his study door to tell him he had visitors when there were none—a prank Mather hilariously fell for again and again—and she grew fond of throwing things at him. His further experiments at praying in her presence caused her to whistle, sing, roar, throw herself on the floor and kick, or cry out for someone to strike him. "He has wounded me in the head!" she screamed. Eventually the devils and Mather wore her out entirely, and she took to playing possum: "She would be laid for dead, wholly senseless and (unless to a severe trial) breathless; with her belly swelled like a drum, and sometimes with croaking noises in it, thus would she lie, most exactly with the stiffness and posture of one that had been two days laid out for dead."

Finally, in the throes of an especially terrible fit, Martha dramatically announced that she was definitely dying, and then, oddly, uttered something about "the state of the country." But she didn't die, and it was the last fit she had at the home of Cotton Mather. The bewitchment had finally run its course.

Aftermath of the Story All Made Up of Wonders

And what of the woman who had been executed because of ☞ the claims of the Goodwins and Cotton Mather? Witch or not, Ann Glover had good reason to be a really, really grouchy old woman. Historians have only been able put together a blurred sketch, but what *is* known of her life is a sad tale indeed. Glover was born in Ireland, but during Cromwell's occupation she, along with thousands of others, was sold to plantation owners and deported to Barbados. (The English captured and sold hundreds of thousands of Irish people, proving that evil, if not witches, was alive and well in the seventeenth century.) In other words, Ann Glover had been sold into slavery. It's believed that Ann's husband was executed in Barbados for refusing to renounce his religion (Catholicism), so the husband the neighbors mentioned who had supposedly complained of Goody Glover being a witch remains a bit of a mystery.

It's not known how Goody Glover and her daughter ended up in Boston, but as an Irish, or as Mather said, "wild Irish," person in Puritan New England, her status would have been the same or lower than that of a Native American or an African. To the Puritans, the Irish were an unruly, uncivilized lot. But Ann Glover had one more black mark on her Puritan report card: she was Catholic. To the Puritans, Catholicism, much like Quakerism, was essentially the same thing as witchcraft. The icons! The saints! And don't even get them started on the Pope. In 1702, in his typical, understated way, Cotton Mather referred to Catholicism as "the Kingdom of Antichrist." To the Puritans, the Pope was the devil and the Catholics his witches. More likely than not, from the time she appeared in Boston, the Irish-speaking Catholic Ann Glover was suspected to be nothing more or less than a witch.

⁋ Looking at the situation from Goody Glover's point of view is an exercise in misery: deported from her homeland, sold into slavery, husband executed, making it to Boston only to find herself despised and called a witch. It's enough to make a lady want to cast a spell on somebody. Oh, and P.S.: no one is even completely sure what Goody Glover's first name really was; many accounts say it was Ann, but some say Mary. Sadly, at the time, nobody really cared enough to learn it or record it. Rev. Mather once referred to her merely as the "hag."

It is also very likely that *speaking* Irish was a big factor in Goody Glover being convicted and executed as a witch. In his account, Mather alternated between claiming the woman spoke nothing but Irish, which he did not speak, and claiming to have had conversations with her. The language issue definitely brings her supposed confession into question: if no one understood her well, did she really confess? Did she really understand what was happening to her? And for that matter, how did Martha

Goodwin understand the "very bad language" spat at her by the Irish-speaking witch?

Goody Glover, though never officially bestowed with the title, is often called a Catholic martyr, and a plaque in her honor in Boston calls her "the first Catholic Martyr in Massachusetts." And in 1988, the Boston City Council officially declared November 16 Goody Glover Day, an honor intended to have a lot more to do with portraying the evils of bigotry than recalling the days of witchcraft trials.

And what of the Goodwin children and the truly creepy ⟡ and disturbing things so many people claimed to have witnessed inside the Goodwin and Mather homes? And what about Mather's breathless credulity at these otherworldly antics? There were some aspects of the children's bewitchment that seem a bit *too* convenient: it never kept them up at night, and it never interfered with their dinners. And the Goodwin children were more than familiar with the expected behaviors of the bewitched: if there had been a *New England Times* bestseller list, numerous books about witches would have been on it. And one of those books was written by Cotton Mather's own father. *Remarkable Providences*, by Increase Mather, had been published in 1684 and featured sensational tales of bewitchment. But that doesn't explain the super-spooky supernatural things witnesses claimed to have seen firsthand at the Goodwin and Mather homes, like the children flying around and their bodies contorting into impossible positions.

Many who lived in Boston during this episode never doubted the story, and in his book Governor Hutchinson reminisced about how the Goodwin family had joined Rev. Mather's church after the bewitchment. He related how the children ultimately returned to their ordinary ultra-religious behavior, then grew to adulthood and became even more ultra-religious. He wrote, "One of them I knew many years after. She had the character of a very sober, virtuous woman and never made any acknowledgement of fraud in the transaction." Well then. And Nathaniel Goodwin, the fortunate son who'd had only a "touch" of bewitchment, was named an executor of Mather's estate.

The bewitchment of the Goodwin children, which lasted less than a year, turned out to be the beginning of another, more vastly terrifying story. In 1692, no small thanks to Mather's publication of *Memorable Providences, Relating to Witchcrafts and Possessions,* which documented the Goodwin case in giddy, gory detail, the bizarre bewitchment of the Goodwin children would be mirrored by several children in the town of Salem. Before that year was over, 150 people would be arrested as witches, and twenty-five would be dead. The story "all made up of wonders" would become a nightmare.

CHAPTER 9

What's the Mather with Witches?

*Alas! We are not aware of the Devil if we do not think
that he aims at inflaming us one against another; and
shall we suffer ourselves to be Devil-ridden?*

—Cotton Mather

The Reverend Cotton Mather was a man of God and a calm,
understated sort of fellow. In 1692, he wrote:

We have been advised by some Credible Christians yet
alive, that a Malefactor, accused of Witchcraft as well as
Murder, and Executed in this place more than Forty Years
ago, did then give Notice of, a Horrible PLOT against
the Country by WITCHCRAFT, and a Foundation of
WITCHCRAFT then laid, which if it were not season-
ably discovered would probably Blow up, and pull down
all the Churches in the Country. And we have now with

Horror seen the Discovery of such a Witchcraft! An Army
of Devils is horrible broke in upon the place . . . and the
Houses of the Good People there are filled with the doleful
Shrieks of their Children.

Hmm . . . "Army of Devils," you say? "Shrieks of their Children,"
you say? Well, perhaps we'd better take a closer look at Rev.
Cotton Mather.

We have seen the interest Mather took in the bewitched
Goodwin children and his punitiveness toward the alleged
witch in that case. But our friend Cotton is also the guy who
has borne the brunt of the responsibility for the persecution of
witches at Salem—pretty damning, since those persecutions led
to twenty deaths. Cotton Mather encouraged the Salem prosecutors in their "dark methods," wrote a contemporary, Robert
Calef, who painted a chilling portrait of Mather as a dark figure
on horseback egging on executions. Nineteenth-century historian Charles Wentworth Upham wrote, "No historical fact has
ever been so steadily recognized as the action and to a great
degree controlling agency of Cotton Mather in supporting and
promoting the witchcraft proceedings of 1692." Luckily for us,
history left behind accounts of Cotton's very personal involvement in some of these cases—involvement that seemed to range
from "foaming at the mouth" vengefulness to very un-Puritan-
ical lasciviousness.

Cotton Mather and his father, Increase Mather, were
VIPs: Very Important Puritans. Their pedigree was about as
good as it got in early colonial America. Cotton's maternal
grandfather was John Cotton, author of *God's Promise to His
Plantation* and America's first superstar minister. Increase,

Cotton's father, was the son of Richard Mather, who had immigrated to America for religious freedom and become minister of the First Parish Church at Dorchester in the Massachusetts Bay Colony. Increase had entered Harvard College at the age of twelve and graduated at seventeen. The fact that he married his stepsister Maria Cotton (he was "brought into acquaintance with her by means of my father having married her mother," he unnecessarily explained) just reinforced the family aristocracy in close-knit early New England. In 1664, Increase became minister of Boston's North Church, positioning himself as one of the most influential men in New England. His son, Cotton, would take over the ministry of the North Church at a young age; Increase would go on to be named president of his alma mater, Harvard.

But things weren't quite as rosy for the ambitious Mathers as they seemed. Increase was given to frequent premonitions that he was about to die, and he would sometimes startle his congregation by announcing that he was not only pretty sure he was about to die, he *wanted* to die. The sooner he saw God the better. When his beloved son, Cotton, who was preordained to follow in his footsteps, was small, Increase was frequently certain *he* was about to die as well. The elder Mather's diary notations about little Cotton, who as a precocious toddler was already referring to himself in the third person with the abbreviated "Ton," portray a father and son who shared a tendency to expect the worst. These were typical entries: "Fears of Cotton's death because so ill"; "This day Cotton taken very ill of vomiting and purging. I troubled because I loved him so strongly." And then there was his report of the feverish two-and-a-half-year-old

Cotton announcing, "Father, Ton would go see God." Like father, like son.

As he grew, Ton developed other issues besides being overly dramatic. He was plagued by severe toothaches that made it difficult to eat. He had a delicate constitution and was prone to frequent attacks of "the vapors"—the seventeenth century's handy name for panic attacks. Perhaps Cotton's anxieties were stoked by the types of things his father preached would happen to naughty children: "It is to be feared that such children will come to the Gallows, and be hanged in Gibbets for the ravens and eagles to feed upon them," he warned.

If little Cotton had been vying for the Most Unpopular Puritan Kid award, he couldn't have done a better job. He described one of his favorite childhood pastimes like this: "I composed forms of prayer for my schoolmates and obliged them to pray. . . . I rebuked my playmates for their wicked words and ways." As a result, he admitted, he "suffered from them the persecution of scoffs not only, but blows, also." After each church service, Cotton would rush home and try to rewrite the sermon from memory, fearful that he might forget something of vital importance to his soul. To play it extra safe, he tacked on days of self-imposed fasting and prayer. Not a fun childhood, even by seventeenth-century standards.

The worst news though: Cotton developed a bad stutter, a troubling condition for a boy who was expected to become a preacher. But no need to be self-conscious about that stutter, Ton! Increase noted in his diary: "I fasted and prayed before the Lord because of my son Cotton's Impediment in his speech. . . . I called him and his mother into my study. We prayed together and with many tears bewailed our sinfulness and begged of God mercy in this particular." Meanwhile, Increase added mania, chronic kidney stones, terrible nightmares, and creepy premonitions to his own curriculum vitae.

While Cotton continued to cultivate his neuroses, his stubborn determination did bring some successes: he entered Harvard at twelve. (He was sent back home after a few weeks in a state of nervous exhaustion—naturally—but he eventually returned.) He also worked hard on curing his stutter, with some success, and he was preaching in earnest by his teens.

As Cotton reached young adulthood, some found his sermons a bit *too* earnest. Future witch trial judge Samuel Sewall mentioned Cotton's sermons in his diary. In a critique of one especially memorable sermon, Sewall remarked that he was "disgusted" by some of the young Rev. Mather's more quirky prose, such as "sweet scented hands of Christ" and "Lord High Treasurer of Ethiopia," but allowed that he was "sorry for" it because the homily was "otherwise well-handled."

In 1686, Cotton obtained a "young gentlewoman" for a wife, and for a few moments there, it almost seemed as if things were looking up. But there was to be no peace for Cotton Mather. Politically, it was a time of turmoil in the Massachusetts Bay Colony. Increase left Boston to spend an indefinite amount of time in England to work toward obtaining a restoration of the Charter for the Colonies of New England. He probably wasn't surprised when he got this note from his newlywed son:

> I am sorry for myself, who am left alone in the midst of cares, fears, anxieties, more than, I believe, any one person in these territories, and who have just now been within a

few minutes of death by a very dangerous fever, the relics whereof are yet upon me. . . . I write with a most ill-boding jealousy that I shall never see you again in this evil world . . . and it overwhelms me into tears which cannot be dried.

Cotton added that if his father didn't see fit to return soon, he was definitely going to die, but, you know, no biggie. Cotton may have been a bit self-absorbed in whining for his father to return given that Increase was currently in meetings with the king of England about the future of the American colonies, but he did get Dad's attention. Increase wrote to a friend in Boston expressing concern for his high-strung son: "Do not let him kill himself. He will do it if you do not hinder him."

Indeed, things at home had taken a turn for the even-worse for Cotton. His favorite sibling, Nathanael, died at age nineteen. His wife had given birth to a baby that he, with typical understatement, described as "one of the comeliest infants that have been seen in the world." But the baby died of convulsions at five months old. "The dying of a child is like the tearing of a limb from us," he preached a few hours later, determined not to let a little thing like grief cause him to miss giving a sermon. After all, life in colonial America was nothing if not one long, sad parade of baby coffins. And Cotton now had a more pressing problem on his hands: witches.

The Witch Factor

Cotton Mather inherited something else from his father besides hypochondria and a morbid preoccupation with death. Father and son were both totally sold on witches.

In 1684, Increase had published *Remarkable Providences,* a minister's attempt to reconcile religion and science (such as it was). The book consisted of a whole lot of strange, anecdotal stories about bad weather, shipwrecks, terrible accidents, possessed people, and a lot of other weird, random stuff. While Increase took a great interest in science, he was a Puritan, so he also believed that nature was controlled by God—and that meant pretty much anything was possible—and what seemed to be supernatural could be all too real. A lot of the tales Increase related were pretty screwy (like the story of a man who would fall into "convulsive Sardonian laughter" at the sight of pork, or the woman who would fall into delirium if she saw cheese).

The book also had a lot to say about witches—mostly that there were a lot of them around and they were often doing seemingly awesome things like causing knives to be thrown at unwelcome visitors and enabling people to speak in languages they didn't know. But even though Increase firmly believed in witches, he cautioned readers to remember who actually called the shots when it came to evil: Satan. In an ironic foreshadowing of Salem, Increase related the story of a young woman named Elizabeth Knapp, who in 1671 had shown all the classic signs of bewitchment: thrashing around, speaking in the voice of a demon (this was done ventriloquist-style, with Elizabeth's lips clamped tight while a guttural and presumably nasty voice croaked from deep within her throat), and having her tongue pulled out of her mouth "to an extraordinary length"—you know, the usual.

But, as Increase warned his readers, the devil had also pulled an especially dangerous trick: he made Elizabeth Knapp implicate an innocent woman as having bewitched her. Finally

Elizabeth came to her senses: "She confessed that Satan had deluded her, making her believe evil of her good Neighbour without any cause"—thankfully before anyone could get up any hanging parties. In 1692, Salem would remember the stories of witchcraft and possession, but conveniently forget the caveat that witchcraft accusations should be taken with a big ol' grain of salt.

As a wee Puritan, Cotton had learned about witches directly from his father, as well as from some of the awesomely lurid books in his father's library, such as the English classic, Glanvill's *Relations of Witchcraft* (unofficial subtitle: *All the Crazy S**t Witches Do That They Should Probably Be Executed For*), and, of course, the Bible ("Thou shalt not suffer a witch to live," etc.). The mid-1680s found the young minister increasingly obsessed with the threat witchcraft posed to the New World. Between all the witch lit and the relentless misfortunes he and New England seemed to be experiencing, Cotton came to the reasonable conclusion that the devil totally had it in for the tender new country; it was all quite simple:

> The New Englanders are a People of God settled in those which were once the Devil's Territories; and it may easily be supposed that the Devil was exceedingly disturbed when he perceived such a People here accomplishing the Promise of old, made unto our Blessed Jesus, That He should have the Utmost parts of the Earth for his Possession . . . I believe that never were more Satanical Devices used for the Unsettling of any People under the Sun than what have been employed for the extirpation of the Vine which God has here planted.

"Devil's Territories," by the way, was Cotton's way of describ- ⸙
ing America as populated by Indians. And that "Vine" that
God planted had the roots of what would come to be known as
"American exceptionalism."

In 1688, Cotton witnessed firsthand what a witch was capa- ⸙
ble of when he inserted himself in the Goodwin case, where four
Boston children became dramatically possessed after one of them
pissed off a witch. The case resulted in the execution of an elderly
Irish woman as a witch, and in Cotton writing a popular book,
Memorable Providences, Relating to Witchcrafts and Possessions.

For the Mathers and most of their contemporaries, witches
were very real—and very formulaic. It was all pretty simple:
start with the devil, add witches and/or demons (i.e., minions),
send minions to zero in on a nice Christian, smite said Christian
with hideous torments, let the now-bewitched person know that
he only need sign a certain book (while not drawing attention
to the really, really small print saying, "You are now obligated
to serve Satan for all eternity, and P.S., you're going to hell"),
and—voilà—the torments cease. Those who refused to sign The
Book could expect *a thousand preternatural Torments*. It was the
minister's job to act as middleman for the Lord by discouraging
Satan's minions, which he could do by helping the bewitched
person resist the impulse to sign The Book. This convoluted
self-imposed duty held great meaning to Cotton Mather, who
was eager to distinguish himself amongst his formidable family.

The Mathers versus the Devil

If you are living in the 1600s and are somehow, through some ⸙
weird glitch of the time-space continuum or the like, reading
this, then please don't panic, but . . .

The Devil is now making one attempt more upon us; an attempt more difficult, more surprising, more snarled with unintelligible circumstances than any that we have hitherto encountered, an attempt so critical that if we get well through, we shall soon enjoy Halcyon Days* with all the Vultures of hell trodden under our feet.

See—there's always something to look forward to in colonial New England! This attempt by the devil to take over, as described in *The Wonders of the Invisible World* written in 1692, was Mather's explanation for what was going on in Salem. And what was going on in Salem was sheer madness—a hysteria that would sear a black mark onto the reputations of the Mathers that remains to this day. William Phips, who had recently been sent to America from England to serve as governor of the Province of Massachusetts, described the "What did I get myself into?" situation:

When I first arrived I found this province miserably harassed with a most horrible witchcraft or possession of Devils . . . some score of poor people were taken with preternatural torments, some scalded with brimstone, some had pins stuck in their flesh, others hurried in the fire and water, and some dragged out of their houses and carried over the tops of trees and hills for many miles . . . there were many committed to prison upon suspicion of Witchcraft.

Phips wasn't kidding. It had begun in the winter of 1692 when bizarre accusations made by several young girls who claimed to be bewitched snowballed beyond imagination and the dark jail cells of Salem Village filled with witches.

Parris Shakes Up Salem

He was a sometimes merchant and Harvard dropout who ˙
desperately needed a career change. Samuel Parris may have
been born with a silver spoon in his mouth, but that didn't
mean he knew what to do with it; he just couldn't stick with
anything long enough to make it a success. He even inherited a large plantation in Barbados, but he wasn't interested
enough to rebuild after a hurricane went through and damaged his property. Instead, the fickle young man headed
back to colder climates—good old New England. He brought
a few valued souvenirs with him from Barbados, though:
two slaves.

Parris married in Boston and soon after, restless with business dealings, began moonlighting as a minister in a nearby
town known for its pious, if quarrelsome, inhabitants. For once
he settled in and stuck with it; 1691 found him the minister
of Salem Village, settled cozily in the parsonage with his wife,
three children, twelve-year-old niece, and, of course, his slaves.
True to form, his disagreeable parish had begun bickering over
their new minister, whom, as they had with those who came
before him, many had taken an unchristian dislike to. In a
fine display of passive aggression, the parish stopped paying
Parris his wages. Parris, in turn, spitefully continued preaching, unsettling the parish with warnings that Satan was setting
his sights on Salem. It was very similar to the ominous stuff
that a nice young minister at the Old North Church, Cotton
Mather, had been spouting. Adding to the disquiet was the fact
that Indian attacks had been hitting towns closer and closer to
Salem. Political instability was the order of the day. And don't

even get anyone started on that other scourge from Hell: smallpox. Uncertainty reigned in Salem Village in February 1692.

With grown-ups causing so much stress and anxiety, you could hardly blame a couple of little girls for trying to distract themselves. Little Betty Parris, nine, and her live-in cousin, Abigail, eleven, may or may not have been hanging around the kitchen and pestering household servant/slave Tituba, the woman brought by Parris to New England—chances are, they were. Tituba may or may not have been tantalizing the girls during those cold, dreary days of February with tales and even demonstrations of magic and sorcery from her days in Barbados—possibly she was. Spells and magic were far from the sole domain of slaves, however; the settlers of New England had brought their own folk magic with them from the Old World, and even Puritan girls would sometimes hear of these intriguing practices. Abigail and Betty, it seems, had been dabbling in their very own white girl magic, using fortune-telling tricks in attempts to find out which of the goofy village boys they were destined to marry. But indulgence in the dark arts could not long coexist with the frightening and punitive Puritan doctrine the girls were exposed to every day in the home of Rev. Parris and at church; something had to give.

Abigail was discovered scurrying around the house on all fours; one moment she was barking like a dog, another she was braying like a mule. She wasn't playing. Meanwhile, Betty also began making strange noises. She threw her Bible and announced she had been damned. Things went downhill fast. The girls complained of being pinched and bitten by unseen fiends and displayed the bite marks to prove it. Rev. Parris suspected witchcraft from the get-go, and confronted his obvious suspect, the ultimate outsider, Tituba. And sure enough, she confessed to witchcraft—after the good reverend had beaten her, promising her more if she didn't own up. When pressed to name other witches, she again did as she was told. But no one in Salem, despite their seemingly awesome imaginations, could have imagined what would happen next.

As talk of witchcraft crept and lurched throughout Salem Village, more and more people began to have strange, supernatural visions of their neighbors doing bad things. Local women appeared in spectral form, crouching on top of men in bedrooms across town in the middle of the night. People saw witches flying through the sky on poles, on their way to covert witch get-togethers. Everywhere witches were said to be seeking recruits, pressuring folks to sign The Book and join them in the fulfilling job of serving the world's most provocative boss, that CEO of Hell, Satan.

Those initially accused of witchcraft had been some of the vicinity's more marginalized citizens, like the slave Tituba and the bad-tempered beggar Sarah Good. Soon, long-festering animosities between neighbors became accusations of witchcraft. When someone was "named" as a witch, they were expected to name others, and they often did. Sometimes someone would even accuse a person whose name they had heard, but whom they had never even met. Soon almost everyone in Salem knew a witch, was bewitched by a witch, or was accused of being a witch.

Courts were convened; accused witches were tried. Women, men, even children sat in filthy, dank cells, stunned and at the mercy of a justice system where logic needed not apply. And then the hangings started. Cotton Mather once began a letter to a relative with this happy greeting: "Our Good God is working miracles. Five witches were lately executed."

The Mathers versus the King of Hell

Early in the witch frenzy a rumor began to circulate about a male witch who was said to be the very king of Hell himself. The most shocking thing of all? No, not that the king of Hell was on the loose in, of all places, the rural town of Salem. What appalled the villagers in the late winter of 1692 was that the king of Hell was, it turned out, a *minister*.

The first inkling as to the identity of the double-agent minister came when a little Salem girl said she had seen witches gathering in a local pasture to celebrate their Sabbath. The girl's family had heard her cry out, "Oh dreadful, dreadful! Here is a minister come! What are ministers witches, too?" After a great deal of prodding by the adults, the girl fingered the Chief Witch: former Salem minister George Burroughs. What may have been even more significant, however, was the name of the little girl. She was Ann Putnam, daughter of the wealthy and powerful Thomas Putnam. While Ann had never met the non-spectral version of George Burroughs in person, she had heard his name often enough. Her father had entertained a well-known feud with the little man some years back and had never gotten over it. Thomas Putnam, Ann well knew, hated George Burroughs.

George Burroughs, like the Mathers, was a Harvard graduate and a minister. In 1680, the short, swarthy Burroughs, lately of Maine, had been offered the job of minister of Salem Village. He accepted the position but, like William Phips, quickly discovered the meaning of the phrase "ye bad career move." Community discord and feuding parishioners—including a faction that opposed his appointment—grew ever more belligerent. Many members of the parish, as they would later with Rev. Parris, spitefully refused to tithe (face it, the Salem Villagers were just really pretty cheap), and the new minister soon found himself without an income. As his resulting debts accrued, sentiment against him grew. On top of this, some even suspected him of *being a Baptist*—almost as bad as being a Quaker or even a witch to the Puritan purists. This accusation had put the reverend from Maine on Cotton Mather's "people who might be a witch" radar. Despite being a minister, Burroughs had never had his children baptized, an oversight that seemed deliberate and about which Burroughs would always change the subject whenever it was brought up. Burroughs also admitted that he had not taken communion in a very long time; in short, as far as Cotton Mather was concerned, Burroughs was a blasphemer of a Baptist.

One of the most vehement of Burroughs's detractors was John Putnam, who, in what was surely just a coincidence, was also his biggest creditor. Putnam went so far as to have the minister arrested for his debts and helped spread the rumor that an abusive Burroughs had been responsible for his wife's recent death. George Burroughs took the first opportunity to get out of dysfunctional, spiteful Salem, leaving his nemesis Putnam quivering with anger and resentment. Meanwhile the minister high-tailed it back to Maine, where he lived a rough but satisfying life with his third wife, her daughter, and his seven kids. They were living on a frontier fraught with attacks by Indians and their French cohorts, and, we can safely assume, the occasional wolf. But it was all just fine with Burroughs, who was apparently something of a badass. Though he was small, he was cartoonishly muscular; at Harvard he had been a legendary athlete.

But it was the other man who harbored a simmering hatred for George Burroughs who would prove the most deadly of all his detractors: Cotton Mather. When Burroughs started appearing around Salem in spectral form as the "King of Hell," the self-righteous Cotton was beside himself. It seemed the worst type of blasphemy when someone who was supposedly a man of God and had the title of reverend—the same title Cotton had—was discovered to be working for the other side.

While rumors of the ongoing witch hunt in Salem may have trickled out to the frontier, no one could have imagined that its craggy, grasping fingers would reach all the way to Maine, but the Burroughs family was about to learn that there were some things even scarier than Indians and wolves. In early May 1692, George was eating dinner with his family when the door burst open and a group of men dispatched from Salem burst in, arrested him for witchcraft, and hustled him out the door. It was said that it all happened so suddenly that his family was left sitting at the dinner table in shock, their food still warm. Not long after this, Mrs. Burroughs, terrified of the possibility that her husband really *was* a witch, and also that the court of Salem would send for her next—and, well, quite possibly having second thoughts about this whole "life on the frontier with the widower with seven kids" thing—packed up her daughter and everything of value she could carry, and left George's children to fend for themselves. George Burroughs would never

return to his home. Cotton Mather summed up what awaited
Burroughs in Salem:

> This G.B. was indicted for Witchcraft, and in the prose-
> cution of the charge against him, he was accused by five
> or six of the bewitched as the author of their miseries; he
> was accused by eight of the confessing witches as being an
> head actor at some of their hellish rendezvouses, and one
> who had the promise of being a King in Satan's Kingdom.

It was probably not a coincidence that during this very same
month, Cotton Mather, taking advantage of his respected family name and his status as a man of God, sent a carefully composed letter to the judges of the Salem Court. In it he cautioned
the court to exercise caution in executing the trials, but concluded with a strongly worded edict recommending "the speedy
and vigorous prosecution of such as have rendered themselves
obnoxious, according to the direction given in the Laws of God
and the wholesome statutes of the English nation for the detection of witchcraft."

The Rather Bizarre Trial of Reverend Burroughs

The bizarre trial of the Rev. George Burroughs began in August
1692. Increase Mather traveled from Boston for the spectacle;
like Cotton, he had felt Burroughs was a dangerous religious dis-
sident and was gratified when witchcraft charges were brought
against him. Burroughs's would be the only witch trial either
of the Mathers would attend. This one was serious business, all
right, as Burroughs had not only been living as a minister while

actually serving the devil, but also he was believed to be *the* ringleader, or as those court-admissible rumors went, "King of Hell." One after another, folks took the stand and testified against him; it seemed that almost everyone had a "George Burroughs is a witch" story. Cotton Mather, who probably got a firsthand account from his father, related a typical one: "And now upon the trial of one of the bewitched persons, testified that in her agonies, a little black haired man came to her saying his name was B. and bidding her set her hand to a book which he showed to her."

There was more bad news for Burroughs. He had a couple of skeletons in his closet in the form of two deceased wives— wives he was rumored to have abused during his marriages. (In this case, unfortunately, the rumors were quite credible.) And now these two dead wives, wrapped in white sheets, kept appearing and complaining to whoever would listen that George had murdered them. And while they had everyone's attention, they also wanted everyone to know that George was responsible for several other unsolved murders. Finally, the murdered wives took it upon themselves to make an appearance at the trial, standing before Burroughs in the courtroom, shrieking, "Vengeance!" Or at least that was what a number of his accusers who were there said; the bewildered Burroughs said he did not see anything.

Somehow moving on from these ghostly shenanigans, the court heard some other strange testimony: it was also being alleged that Burroughs's former home had been badly haunted *and* infested with toads. These were generally agreed upon as indicators of demonic activity on the part of a home's owner. Under oath, Burroughs indignantly denied his house was haunted but, according to records, "owned there were toads." Many witnesses also testified that George had preternatural strength courtesy of his witch powers, having witnessed such feats as the compact little man lifting a full barrel of molasses over his head. Perhaps most damning of all: eight confessed witches testified that the Rev. George Burroughs had been the one to make them sign the dreaded Book o' Satan. And, of course, several plaintiffs managed to throw in not-so-subtle mentions of the money they said he still owed them. The court found George Burroughs guilty, an outcome to which Increase Mather gave a thumbs-up. He wrote, "Had I been one of the judges I could not have acquitted him." The execution of George Burroughs was the instance that, above all others, would inexorably brand Increase's son Cotton Mather as Salem's Witchfinder General.

Gallows Hill

August 19, 1692, was an especially strange and tragic day in the history of Salem witchcraft. Five convicted witches were taken from the Salem jail to make the short, torturous ride to Gallows Hill. Four of the condemned were men, and one of these men was king of Hell, George Burroughs. The convicted witches were ceremoniously pulled through the town in a cart, followed by a swelling crowd eager to savor the sight of a real live, and real righteous, witch execution. Joining the horde was an unexpected figure on horseback: the Rev. Cotton Mather had, for the first time, come to Salem to attend an execution of witches. Also said to be present were several of those who claimed Rev. Burroughs had bewitched them. Although names were not given, some accounts referred to these particular attendees as "the afflicted girls."

As the condemned witches mounted the gallows, they were allowed to speak; all proclaimed their innocence, and all of them prayed. When it was George Burroughs's turn to say his final words, he was, by accounts, the most self-*possessed* of all the witches. It was a precarious moment, with Burroughs on the gallows, poised to be executed, facing the crowd to speak as the noose swung above his head like a pendulum ticking off the remaining seconds of his life. The power of Burroughs's conviction and his strong personality—he was a preacher, after all— had the potential to turn the tide of the witch hunts, or at least stay his execution. A man named Robert Calef described the dramatic moment when Burroughs addressed the onlookers:

> When he was upon the ladder, he made a speech for the clearing of his innocence with such solemn and serious expressions, as were to the admiration of all present: his prayer (which he concluded by repeating the Lord's prayer) was so well worded, and uttered with such composedness, and such (at least seeming) fervency of spirit, as was very affecting, and drew tears from many, so that it seemed to some that the spectators would hinder the execution. The accusers said the black man stood and dictated to him.

The crowd was stirred, and folks muttered to one another as they wiped away tears. Moments before they had been foaming at the mouth to see Burroughs executed; now it seemed they were having second thoughts. Meanwhile, several of those who had made accusations against Burroughs said the devil was on

the gallows with him, and had whispered the words of the Lord's ⸶
Prayer into his ear that he might say it correctly. The hangman
grew anxious, uncertain as to how to proceed with this unexpected turn of events, when the imposing, dark figure on horseback spoke up, his voice authoritative as he looked down on the
agitated crowd. Calef described what happened next:

> Mr. Cotton Mather, being mounted upon a horse,
> addressed himself to the people, partly to declare that he
> (Burroughs) was no ordained minister, and partly to pos-
> sess the people of his guilt, saying that the devil has often
> been transformed into an angel of light; and this some-
> what appeased the people, and the executions went on.

George Burroughs, who mere weeks before had been enjoying life with his young wife and family, was hanged, along with
Martha Carrier, George Jacobs, Sr., John Proctor, and John
Willard, all of whom insisted until the end that they were innocent of witchcraft. Calef felt that Burroughs, in particular, was
singularly mistreated in death as in life:

> When he was cut down, he was dragged by the halter to a
> hole, or grave, between the rocks, about two feet deep, his
> shirt and breeches being pulled off, and an old pair of trou-
> sers of one executed put on his lower parts; he was so put
> in, together with Willard and Carrier, that one of his hands
> and his chin, and a foot of one of them, were left uncovered.

Cotton Mather remained especially vehement about George
Burroughs, refusing to refer to him by name (he called him

"G.B."). Although he clung to the belief that Burroughs was a witch, Cotton's writing on the subject indicated he may have felt at least some discomfort with the subject; he wrote, "Glad should I have been, if I had never known the name of this man." But Cotton soon found a distraction: "About this Time, I had many wonderful Entertainments, from the Invisible World, in the Circumstances of a Young Woman horribly possessed with Devils."

Saving Mercy Short

In the summer of 1692, another haunted girl emerged from Cotton Mather's overwrought neighborhood. Early in the witch craze, seventeen-year-old Mercy Short seemed to be coming down with a *touch* of bewitchment, but as that strangest of years skulked on, Mercy's symptoms heated up. But being bewitched probably seemed like a picnic to Mercy compared to an earlier life experience. As described by Cotton:

Mercy Short had been taken captive by our cruel and bloody Indians in the East, who at the same time horribly butchered her father, her mother, her brother, her sister, and others of her kindred and then carried [her] and three surviving brothers with two sisters . . . unto Canada, after which our fleet returning from Quebec to Boston, brought them with other prisoners that were then redeemed. But although she had then already born the yoke in her youth, yet God Almighty saw it good for her to bear more of that yoke, before seventeen years of her life had rolled away.

Even Cotton Mather wondered sometimes at the trials God placed on his constituency. Mercy Short had watched as her family was massacred by Abenaki Indians at their Salmon Falls, New Hampshire, homestead, and she had experienced the unspeakable during her captivity.

The "yoke" Mercy would next bear would be a more fanciful one. According to Mather, the poor girl was now in the throes of a sound bewitchment at the hands of Sarah Good, one of the accused witches languishing in the Boston jail. Her fits continued even after Good's execution in July 1692.

The teenage Mercy Short had arrived in Boston as an orphan and was placed with a family as a servant. During the witch trial crisis, her mistress had dispatched her on what was most likely a mission of mercy: taking alms to the jail. But Mercy wasn't feeling so merciful that day. When accused witch Sarah Good had the nerve to ask the girl for some tobacco, Mercy picked up a handful of shavings from the dirty floor and threw them at the woman, snarling, "That's tobacco good enough for you!" Predictably, the woman "cursed her" for her nastiness.

Flash forward to the next church service, and we find Mercy throwing a noisy fit; spectators said it was as bad as or worse than any from the recent witchcraft cases. As Mercy's bewitchment gathered steam, her attacks became more frequent and seemed to be provoked by prayer; at one point, while being preached at by Cotton Mather, she lunged at him and tore a page from his Bible. Finally, during a church service, she threw a fit so terrible that she had to be carried out by "many strong men." She ended up at the home of a concerned neighbor, which is where she rode out the following weeks in the clutches of a very theatrical bewitchment.

Cotton Mather inserted himself right into the thick of things, paying frequent visits to the girl. He described some of the visions Mercy was tormented with:

> A Devil having the figure of a short and a black man . . . of the same stature, feature, and complexion with what the histories of the Witchcrafts beyond-sea ascribe to him; he was a wretch no taller than an ordinary walking-staff; he was not of a Negro, but of a tawny, or an Indian color; he wore an high-crowned hat, with straight hair; and had one cloven-foot.

Mather completely ignored the possibility of lingering trauma stemming from the orphan's Indian captivity experience. He was blithely gratified to have another devil to take down. And Mercy's devil meant business.

The strange scenes were witnessed by the dozens if not hundreds of people who would come and go from what Mather called "the Haunted Chamber" (i.e., Mercy's bedroom) to watch the young woman "in her Ecstatic Circumstances." (Fifty was given as the approximate record number of people who filled the Haunted Chamber at one time.) Many of the onlookers were young people—the teenage members of the Salem population. A group of teens who held regular prayer meetings took to meeting up in Mercy's bedroom, which was undoubtedly the most fun any of them had in Salem for a long time. Cotton, of course, seized the opportunity to recruit new church members. Seeing Mercy's torments, he said, had "awakened" them to the danger Satan posed to those who neglected God. Day after day, Cotton held vigil, leading visitors in prayer and hymns and imposing days of prayer and fasting on the beleaguered community on the bewitched girl's behalf. But week after week, the demons held tight.

Before gaping onlookers, the girl experienced an onslaught of intense phantom attacks. At the hands of invisible fiends, a hot iron was shoved down her throat as she thrashed and gagged. She was forced to swallow pins, and she was stuck with pins that left bloody marks on her body. Her jaw was pried open, as unseen demons forced her to swallow poison; afterward, she was unable to eat for days. The demons seemed particularly fond of tormenting Mercy with fire; according to Mather, he and other witnesses could smell brimstone in the girl's room as she was tortured with flames that left actual blisters on her skin. Finally, the girl lost her vision and hearing. Cotton wrote,

> Reader, if thou hadst a desire to have seen a picture of hell, it was visible in the doleful circumstances of Mercy Short! Here was one lying in outer darkness, haunted with the devil and his angels, deprived of all common comforts, tortured with most excruciating fires, wounded with a thousand pains all over, and cured immediately, that the pains of those wounds might be repeated.

Cotton monitored Mercy carefully, spending every moment he could in her chamber. He observed that the easily bored devils would change tactics on occasion: "Her tortures were turned into frolicks, and she became as extravagant as a wild-cat." But Cotton wasn't content with being an onlooker to the spectacle; he was a man of science, after all: it was time to do some experiments!

As he had with the Goodwin children, Cotton seized the opportunity to see how Mercy's demons would react to some cause-and-effect experimentation. When Mercy claimed to be mesmerized by visions of "hellish harpies" fluttering around her bed, Mather wanted to see if he could distract her fixed gaze: "Although we (Cotton was probably using the royal "we," but may have been referring to himself and his father) made as if we would strike at her eyes, it would not make her wink." Mercy was so engrossed in her invisible assailants, he noted, that even when he "hallooed extremely loud in her ears," she did not react. A sword waved at her invisible assailants, however, caused her to shut her eyes and cringe. Cotton recorded every word the demons uttered and everything they or Mercy did; there was definitely a book in this.

In this manner, with gawkers coming and going and Cotton hovering at her bedside, weeks passed, but Mercy's demons stayed put. When December 25 came around, Mercy said her demons were eager to get in on the merriments of Christmas, a holiday that horrified the Puritans for its supposed hedonism. Mather wrote,

> On the twenty-fifth of December it was that Mercy said they were going to have a Dance; and immediately those that were attending her most plainly heard and felt a dance, as of barefooted people, upon the floor.

Soon there were disturbing developments that seemed to indicate the devils were tiring of Cotton's interference. They began playing tricks on the minister, keeping Mercy up to date on their hijinks. She informed the minister that some local witches had used a book from his very own library—a Catholic devotional he kept for study—for their depredations. On retrieving the book from its shelf he found—gasp—a page folded over. Then Mercy told him that the witches were planning something especially bad for Cotton and his wife, who was, as usual, pregnant. Sure enough, things took an especially ugly turn:

> On March 28. Tuesday, between 4 and 5 A.M. God gave to ⤴
> my Wife, a safe Deliverance of a Son. It was a child of a most
> comely and hearty Look, and all my Friends entertained
> his Birth, with very singular Expressions of Satisfaction.
> But the Child was attended with a very strange Disaster;
> for it had such an obstruction in the Bowels, as utterly hin-
> dered the Passage of its Ordure from it. We used all the
> Methods that could be devised for its Ease; but nothing we
> did, could save the Child from Death. It languished, in its
> Agonies, til Saturday, April 1, about 10 P.M. and so died,
> unbaptized.

"It languished in its agonies." If the devil himself had planned a punishment for Cotton Mather, it would have been this. So perhaps that's why Cotton decided that this tragedy had been engineered from the very depths of Hell. Especially after—well, we'll let him tell you:

> When the Body of the Child was opened, we found, that
> the lower End of the Rectum Intestinum, instead of being
> Musculous, as it should have been, was Membranous,

and altogether closed up. I had great Reason to suspect a Witchcraft . . . because my Wife, a few weeks before her Deliverance, was affrighted with an horrible Specter, in our Porch, which Fright caused her Bowels to turn within her; and the Specters which both before and after, tormented a young Woman in our Neighborhood, bragged of their giving my Wife that Fright, in hopes, they said, of doing Mischief unto her Infant.

Well, that was unexpected. The Mathers' baby had been cut open and examined. The first official autopsy performed in America, on little Elizabeth Kelly in 1662, was most likely Mather's inspiration for the autopsy, such as it was, on his infant. Kelly's autopsy had revealed no discernible cause of death, which proved, according to the physician who carried it out, that witchcraft was the cause of death. Mather's infant's autopsy had revealed the opposite—gross deformity of the internal organs—and somehow this *too* meant witchcraft. But probably the most interesting aspect of this particular autopsy was the conveniently unnamed person who performed it. Many historians believe it was most likely done by a man who had studied physiology at Harvard, practiced medicine as a sort of amateur hobby, and wrote pamphlets and books on the subject of health: none other than the grieving father, Cotton Mather, himself.

At any rate, having finally outdone themselves with this especially macabre trick, the demons finally began to tire of the whole affair. One night Mather listened as the girl held a lively exchange with her unseen tormentors, who huffily told her, "Go and be damned, we can do no more!" Mercy, channeling some of the saintliness she was picking up from

Rev. Mather, no doubt, retorted, "O ye cursed wretches; is that ⸙
your blessing? Well after all the wrong that you have done to
me, I do not wish that any one of you may be damned; I wish
you may all be saved, if that be possible. However, in the name
of the blessed Lord Jesus Christ, be gone, let me be no more
troubled with you." Mather wrote, "Upon that, they flew away
immediately." Whew.

In his diary, Mather modestly noted what had caused
the demons to skidaddle. The tenacious demons had outlasted everyone, he wrote; the townspeople were "now either
too weary or too busy" to keep up the onslaught of prayer on
Mercy's behalf. Only one man remained to take on the fiends
of the Haunted Chamber: the hero of the story, Cotton Mather.
"I did alone in my study fast and pray for her deliverance. And
unto my amazement . . . she was finally and forever delivered
from the hands of evil angels." He would not have long to savor
his triumph, however, before the witches would strike again.

A Hard Master

When the witch craze had wound down and something resem-⸙
bling reason descended on Salem, folks naturally started looking for someone to blame. Most fingers pointed right at Samuel
Parris. "He started it," inhabitants of the embarrassed town
seemed to agree of the reverend from whose home the witchcraft accusations had first emerged.

Meanwhile, as everyone was "looking over there," Cotton
Mather got into some more witchcraft action. In the autumn
of 1693, another teenage girl from Cotton's congregation came
down with a bad case of possession. Cotton and Increase

persisted in believing in witchcraft and that it needed to be dealt with severely, but, they diplomatically added, dealt with *cautiously*. The newly possessed girl, Margaret Rule, was promptly put to bed, which had become the unofficially agreed-upon best place for such girls. There she received frequent visits from both of the Mathers, associates of the Mathers, and assorted rubber-neckers—and no wonder. There was quite a show going on in the bedroom of Miss Margaret Rule. Cotton wrote, "There were wonderful noises every now and then made about the room, which our people could ascribe to no other authors but the specters; yea, the watchers affirm, that they heard those fiends clapping their hands together."

But no one was prepared for what the demons pulled off next: "Her tormentors pulled her up to the ceiling of the chamber, and held her there, before a very numerous company of spectators, who found it as much as they could all do to pull her down again."

Margaret Rule's levitation was not just anecdotally witnessed by numerous spectators; many of the men who were present wrote and signed sworn affidavits, like this one from a man named Samuel Aves:

> I do testify that I have seen Margaret Rule in her afflictions from the invisible world lifted up from her bed wholly by an invisible force a great way toward the top of the room where she lay when . . . a strong person hath thrown his whole weight across her to pull her down.

Folks were stopping by at all hours by now to take in the activities of New England's newest star. Margaret Rule's possession was quickly becoming a sideshow, and, according to at least one account, an NC-17 kind of sideshow.

Robert Calef, who had witnessed the execution of *
George Burroughs, was a Boston merchant who took an interest in the Mathers' interest in witches, and especially in their interest in young girls who were supposedly possessed by witches. He paid several visits to the Rule home—more specifically, Margaret's bedroom—documenting and then, to the Mathers' horror, eventually publishing the details of her possession and the Mathers' activities in her Haunted Chamber. What follows is Calef's shocking account of what he witnessed, with Cotton thinly disguised as "Mr. M" and Increase called "the Father." It's super creepy, in more ways than one. We give you here an evening with the Mathers as they treat a bewitched teenaged girl in her bedroom, as transcribed by observer Robert Calef:

> September the 13th, 1693. In the evening when the sun was withdrawn, giving place to darkness to succeed, I with some others were drawn by curiosity to see Margaret Rule, and so much the rather because it was reported Mr. M would be there that night. Being come to her father's house into the chamber wherein she was in bed, found her of a healthy countenance of about seventeen years old, lying very still, and speaking very little, what she did say seemed as if she were light-headed. Then Mr. M, Father and Son, came up and others with them, in the whole were about 30 or 40 persons, they being sat, the Father on a stool, and the Son upon the bedside by her, the Son began to question her:

Question: Margaret Rule; how do you do?

(Then a pause without any answer.)

Question: Do a great many Witches sit upon you?

Answer: Yes.

Q: Do you not know that there is a hard Master?

(Then she was in a fit; he laid his hand upon her face and nose, but, as he said, without perceiving breath; then he brushed her on the face with his glove, and rubbed her stomach her breast not covered with the bed-clothes and bid others do so too, and said it eased her, then she revived.)

Q: Don't you know there is a hard Master?

A: Yes.

Reply: Don't serve that hard Master, you know who. Do you believe?

(Then again she was in a fit, and he again rubbed her breast, &c. about this time Margaret Perd an attendant assisted him in rubbing of her. The Afflicted spoke angrily to her saying don't you meddle with me, and hastily put away her hand. He wrought his fingers before her eyes and asked her if she saw the Witches?)

A: No.

Q: Do you believe?

A: Yes.

Q: Do you believe in you know who?

A: Yes.

Q: Who is it that afflicts you?

A: I know not there is a great many of them.

(About this time the Father questioned if she knew the Specters? An attendant said if she did she would not tell; the Son proceeded.)

Q: You have seen the Black-man haven't you?

A: No.

Reply: I hope you never shall. You have had a Book offered you, haven't you?

A: No.

Q: The brushing of you gives you ease, don't it?

A: Yes.

(She turned herself and a little groaned.)

Q: Now the Witches scratch you and pinch you, and bite you, don't they?

A: Yes.

(Then he put his hand upon her breast and belly, viz. on the clothes over her, and felt a Living thing, as he said, which moved the Father also to feel, and some others.)

Q: Don't you feel the Live thing in the bed?

A: No.

Q: The great company of people increase your torment, don't they?

A: Yes.

(The people were desired to withdraw. One woman said, I am sure I am no Witch, I will not go: so others, so none withdrew.)

Q: Shall we got to prayers?

(Then she lay in a fit as before. But this time to revive her, they waved a hat and brushed her head and pillow therewith.)

Q: Shall we go to P-R-A-Y (spelling the word)?

A: Yes.

(The Father went to prayer for perhaps half an hour, chiefly against the power of the Devil and Witchcraft, and that

Yep—she's a witch, all right! This seventeenth-century engraving shows what happens when a witch is bound and thrown into water: she floats. In the forefront, a non-witch goes slowly under.

A medieval illuminated manuscript showing witches perpetuating a favorite stereotype. From *Champion des Dames*.

Ships are known to be favorite targets of witches, as shown in this woodcut of a witch "pouring out the contents of a cauldron to sink ships." The image appears in Olaus Magnus's fantastic sixteenth-century book, *History of the Northern Peoples*, which contains lots of important witch-related information.

Examination of a Witch; painting by Tompkins H. Matteson.

THE WITCH No.3.

"In like distemper she died," wrote witness Rev. John Hale of Margaret Jones, who probably looked something like this as she gave her accusers a piece of her mind, not long before they hanged her for witchcraft.

"Just come with us, nice little old lady—we want to show you something . . ." A suspiciously witch-like old lady gets picked up on the street and taken downtown in this Howard Pyle illustration.

The Mohawk have had just about enough of Jesuit priest Isaac Jogues and his brethren.

An old woodcut depicts a rare non-teat feeding of her familiars by a witch.

Witches and swine just go together. The colonial American witch's go-to sidekick was also a favorite with English witches, as shown on the cover of this seventeenth-century book.

THE
WITCHES
OF
NORTHAMPTON-
SHIRE.

Agnes Browne. } Arthur Bill.
Ioane Vaughan. } Hellen Ienkenson } Witches.
Mary Barber. }

Who were all executed at *Northampton* the 22. of
Iuly last. 1612.

LONDON,
Printed by *Tho: Purfoot*, for *Arthur
Iohnson.* 1612.

Witches frolic with feline familiars in an image from an old children's book, *The History of Springfield in Massachusetts.*

1938 image of Goody Cole created for Hampton's Tercentenary Celebration. (Courtesy of the Hampton Historical Society.)

The travails of being an old lady who looks like a witch are depicted in this old image.

OPENING OF THE WITCH-HUNTING SEASON.

Cotton Mather, enemy of witches, making a fearless fashion statement wearing the subject of at least one of his sermons, a periwig.

A nineteenth-century depiction of George Burroughs in chains.

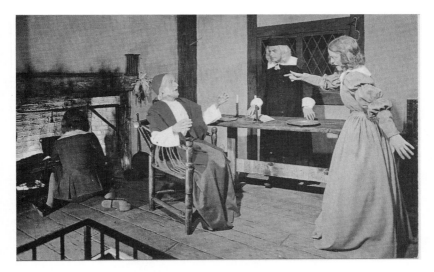

This isn't going to end well. The accusations are flying in this dramatic scene depicted on a vintage Salem postcard.

"SOUL-KILLING WITCHES THAT DEFORM THE BODY."

An image from an 1828 edition of Cotton Mather's least-favorite book, *More Wonders of the Invisible World.*

Houdini's personal bookplate graces a copy of *The Witches of New York*, covering over an advertisement for another Philander Q. Doesticks book. (Courtesy of the Douglas Bast Collection.)

The only illustration inside *The Witches of New York* is rather inexplicable, but still fun. (Courtesy of the Douglas Bast Collection.)

Investigating the witches of New York may have been the last fun Mortimer Thomson ever had. He's shown here sporting his trademark mustache and a hard-earned sad look.

The Christian Science Church in Boston, Mass. Quite an accomplishment for Mary Baker Eddy, one-time impoverished social pariah.

Mary Baker Eddy during her heyday.

"Hex" Slaying Stirs York County

Peru Sho
Presider
Held Ai

he con-
ght was
ysicians
his tem-
last 24
activity

e fight
against
ficial re-
has been
leep and
therwise
evening
ned." On
ture has
bulletin
scence of

lent hat
anxiety
as again
the fact
by four

hich they
row fur-
y's heart,
hysicians
that his
which
om their
give the
pe in the
sovereign.
Mary to-
ry after-
vere com-
he crown
um con-
he Duke
r Stanley
ocuments
e the ill-
ys ago,

hich are
in Buck-
ut in full
ent the
m enter-
eorge and

LIMA, F
linking of tl
and South a
system of a
night by H
dinner giver
dent Leguia
The pre:
would not
devise a Pa
tem were th
of the gove:
council table
would realiz
another 12 1
Hoover e
aviation. "I
munication
would be "
destroys th•
ples and c
them."
Proud To A
"Every e:
of intelligen
of our peo:
"adds to tha
derstanding :
makes for n
will. I shou
might contr
of so great
"I have +
than recreat
satisfaction
have had th
that I coul
further rei:
peace and
ideas which
since the b
have though
pare myself
knowledge o
of our siste:
"A centur
history. We
can do but
minute part
forgotten. B
to diminish
can strength
and spiritua
build the in
which assu:

The witch murder house, above, near York, Pa., where Nelson D. Rehmeyer, recluse farmer, was beaten and strangled to death. Police have arrested three accused of slaying Rehmeyer in an effort to obtain a lock of his
hair to break a spell supposedly cast by a "hex" or witch. Below, Mrs. Milton
Hess, mother of Wilbert Hess, one of the accused trio, and two of her other
sons, Leonard and Woodrow.

The mother of one of the York Hex Murderers is shown in front of what the
newspaper called "the witch murder house."

FACE WITCHCRAFT MURDER CHARGE

John Blymer (left), professed witch doctor, and two youths,
Wilber Hess, 18, and John Curry, 14 (right), are charged with the
murder of Nelson D. Rehmeyer, aged recluse farmer near York, Pa.
Rehmeyer was killed, according to statements by the defendants,
during a struggle when they attempted to cut a lock of hair from his
head to break a spell alleged to have been cast over Hess.

Newspaper photo of the young men known as the Hex Murderers (with one of the
many alternative spellings of John Blymyer's name).

The York Hex Murder brought to light a deep-seated belief in folk magic in America in the early twentieth century. Shown here are unidentified members of the Zittle clan, a Pennsylvania Dutch family who relocated to South Mountain, Maryland, where they were associated with folk magic. Note the open scissor next to the door; this was a charm to protect the home from evil. Michael Zittle, known as "Wizard Zittle," worked wonders using a copy of the same spell book that got Nelson Rehmeyer killed. (Courtesy of the Douglas Bast Collection.)

Shenanigans abound in the courtroom as bewitched girls point out phantom birds flying around the head of an accused witch in this Howard Pyle illustration.

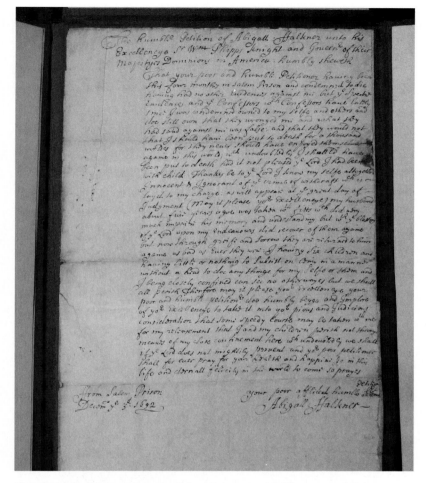

Original document written in Salem Prison in 1692 by accused Salem witch Abigail Falkner and sent to Gov. William Phips. The return address is "Salem Prison." In it, the pregnant Falkner, mother of six, begs the governor for mercy for herself and her family. It reads in part: "Having been this four months in Salem Prison and condemned to die having had no other evidences against me but ye spectre evidences . . . I . . . do humbly beg and implore of your Excellency to take it unto your pious and judicious consideration that some speedy course may be taken with me for my releasement that I and my children perish not through means of my close confinement here which undoubtedly we shall if ye lord does not mightily prevent and your poor petitioner shall forever pray for your health and happiness in this life and eternal felicity in the world to come." (Courtesy of the Douglas Bast Collection.)

Mayhem was often the order of the day during the Salem witch trials.

Burkittsville, Maryland: no witches here.

❖ God would bring out the Afflicters: during prayer-time, the Son stood by, and when they thought she was in a fit, rubbed her and brushed her as before, and beckoned to others to do the like. After prayer he proceeded)

Q: You did not hear when we were at prayer, did you?

A: Yes.

Q: You don't hear sometimes passed a word or two, do you?

A: No.

(Then turning him about said this is just another Mercy Short: Margaret Perd replied she was not like her in her fits.)

Q: What does she eat or drink?

A: Not eat at all; but drink rum.

(Then he admonished the young people to take warning, saying it as a sad thing to be so tormented by the devil and his instruments. A young-man present in the habit of a seaman, replied this is the devil all over, than the Ministers withdrew. Soon after they were gone the Afflicted desired the women to be gone, saying, that the company of the Men was not offensive to her, and having hold of the hand of a Young-man, said to have been her Sweet-heart formerly, who was withdrawing; she pulled him again into his seat, saying he should not go tonight.)

⚑ Ahem . . . is it getting hot in here, or is it the "30 or 40 persons" crowded into the little bedroom in the late-summer heat? Yeah, it's both. It's definitely both. At any rate, six days later the bewitched girl was again holding court in her bedroom. Calef paid another visit to the best show in town, this time missing

Cotton Mather, who had already come and gone that evening. But several handlers were standing by, ready to employ the Mather Method of Bewitchment Management on their star:

> September the 19th, 1693. This night I renewed my visit, and found her rather of a fresher countenance than before, about eight persons present with her, she was in a fit screaming and making a noise. Three or four persons rubbed and brushed her with their hands, they said that the brushing did put them (the fits) away, if they brushed or rubbed in the right place; therefore they brushed and rubbed in several places, and they said that when they did it in the right place she could fetch her breath, and by that they knew. She being come to herself was soon in a merry talking fit.

The Mather Method having worked its magic, Margaret is ready to turn on the charm for a male visitor:

> A young-man came in and asked her how she did? She answered very bad, but at present a little better; he soon told her he must be gone and bid her good night, at which she seemed troubled, saying that she liked his company and said she would not have him go till she was well, adding, for I shall die when you are gone.

She was feeling better, but she wasn't particularly pleased with her stylists in the Haunted Chamber: "Then she complained they did not put her on a clean cap, but let her lie so like a beast, saying she should lose her fellows."

She also tried to get a feel as to what sort of press she was getting around the village:

> She said she wondered if any people should be so wicked as to think she was not afflicted, out to think she dissembled (faked), a young-woman answered yes, if they were to see you in this merry fit, they would say you dissembled indeed.

And she name-dropped:

> She replied Mr. M said this was her laughing time, she must laugh now. She said Mr. M had been there this evening. . . . She said, he stayed alone with her in the room half an hour.

As might well be expected, Calef's titillating account of the suggestive goings-on in Margaret's bedroom created quite a scandal—and that was the point. As the Mathers were interested in witches, so was Calef interested in exposing the dark side of religion.

Robert Calef versus the Mathers

Robert Calef was a progressive man for his time. Born in England, one of the reasons he left that country was because of its persecution of Quakers; he had no tolerance for such intolerance. It was surely a bitter revelation when he found America not only into persecuting Quakers, but also in the process of revving up witch hunting. In 1693, it seemed the

deadly witch craze had come to an end and New Englanders
were finally coming to their senses. So when he heard that the
Mathers had now diagnosed a new case of bewitchment, he
feared the worst: the Mathers were going to start the whole
thing all over again. This time, Robert Calef was going to do
something about it. After witnessing the bizarre and provocative scene in the bedroom, he returned when Cotton was
there and confronted him about the situation. Mather became
enraged and stormed out.

The confrontation in the Haunted Chamber set off a bitter
exchange between Cotton and Calef via letters, pamphlets, and
books—the seventeenth-century version of a Twitter war. "You
cannot know how much this representation hath contributed to
make people believe a Smutty thing of me," Cotton complained
indignantly.

At one point Calef managed to persuade Cotton to lend
him the handwritten treatise on witchcraft the latter was
working on. When Cotton got his manuscript back, Calef had
scrawled sarcastic comments all over it. In 1700, Robert Calef,
without first lending the manuscript to Mather, published *More
Wonders of the Invisible World*, which was basically an expose of
the witchcraft craze featuring the lurid Margaret Rule story and
the Mathers' role in it. It also included his unflattering account
of Mather's actions at the execution of George Burroughs.

Cotton Mather Defeats the Devil

But in 1693, Mather continued to pray for Margaret Rule's deliv-
ery from the devil, finally making the case with the Evil One,

during one of his conversations with him through Margaret, that the girl, as a member of his congregation, was *his* rightful property. The next time he visited Margaret Rule, she addressed him for the first time as "Father." A white spirit had come to her, she explained, and told her that God had "given her" to Rev. Mather. Here, Cotton humbly admits that he had, once again, done the whole three-day prayer/fast thing, and that it was this that had loosened the devil's grip. Voice of reason that he was, he added this gem: "I must earnestly entreat all my readers to beware of any superstitious conceits upon the number Three." Either way, it was a done deal: Cotton Mather had beaten the devil. Again.

With the devil and his witchy minions finally giving up on the young ladies of Boston, the Mathers were free to go back to writing long-winded sermons and composing exciting books about witches, which they did. But their bedside vigils had yielded some valuable information. Mercy Short and Margaret Rule, like the other possessed girls, had named names: the names of those who had attended the witch-gatherings, and the names of those who had tempted them with the dreaded book. Cotton and his father had tactfully withheld those names, but apparently the pair *did* find another good use for this information, as evidenced by this note from Secretary of the Colony of Connecticut, John Allen, who was definitely going to owe the guys a really big favor:

As to what you mention, concerning the poor creature in your town that is afflicted, and mentioned my name to yourself and son, I return you hearty thanks for your intimation about it, and for your charity therein mentioned, and have great cause to bless God, who of his mercy hitherto, hath not let me fall into such an horrid evil.

And it may be that the nights of bedside vigils had ended *because* of the possessed girls' name-dropping. For, during their possessions, both girls had uttered another name, the name of one who the devils said was a witch. It was a name that hit very close to home: *Cotton Mather.*

Periwigs, Pigs, and Pox

Life went on for the Mathers. Babies were born, babies died. At *the age of fifty-one, Cotton set down a sad tally in his diary: of fifteen children, nine were now dead, six were living. Cotton's wives sickened and died, too. Cotton would have three wives during his lifetime; Increase would have two.

There were a few things unexpected, even progressive, about Cotton Mather, though, and not just the fashionable periwig he took to wearing. (His defense of the scandalous trend caused Samuel Sewall to remark: "I expected not to hear a vindication of periwigs in Boston Pulpit by Mr. Mather," after Mather managed to bring up the subject in a sermon. God wanted him to have a warm head—geez, it got cold in the meetinghouse in the winter, and a fella couldn't very well wear a hat in church, could he?)

Though he never wrote a book about the wonders of periwigs, Cotton did enjoy writing about other amazing things besides witchcraft. Behold his comments about the wondrous creature known as the pig:

> How surprisingly is the Head and the Neck of the Swine adapted for his rooting in the Earth! The strong snout of the Swine such that he may sufficiently thrust it into the Ground, where his Living lies, without hurting his eyes . . . and even his wallowing in the mire is a wise contrivance for the suffocation of troublesome insects!

Later in life, Cotton undertook a witch hunt against another unseen evil: the smallpox virus. His interest in science led Cotton to be an early and unlikely champion of the smallpox vaccine. Having lost so many loved ones to the disease and being understandably panicked each time he was exposed to a contagious disease when making godly visits to the chambers of the sick, Cotton turned into one of the most controversially forward-thinking men of his day. His late-life calling was introducing the use of the vaccine to the American colonies, an undertaking which got him a bomb thrown into his house.

It's a popular belief that witches were burned at the stake in Salem. This is a falsehood; no witches were burned in Salem: they were hanged. But in 1700, Increase Mather, then president of Harvard College, had a large bonfire set in Harvard Yard and ordered something even more repellent to him than witches to be burned: a copy of the book that had caused him and his son so much embarrassment, Robert Calef's *More Wonders of the Invisible World.*

Notes

* "Halcyon Days," Mathers-style, would presumably mean the awe-some time when the godly would spread out their picnic blankets, unwrap their sandwiches, and smugly savor the sight of the ungodly swinging from nooses while having their eyeballs plucked out by righteous American eagles.

CHAPTER 10

Salem by the Numbers

And now Nineteen persons having been hang'd, and one prest to death, and Eight more condemned, in all Twenty and Eight, of which above a third part were Members of some of the Churches of New England, and more than half of them of a good conversation in general, and not one clear'd; about Fifty having confest themselves to be Witches, of which not one Executed; above an Hundred and Fifty in Prison, and Two Hundred more accused.

—Robert Calef, doing some Salem math in 1700

Number of People Executed at Salem for Witchcraft

Twenty. This number includes Giles Cory, who was crushed to death for "standing mute" (i.e., refusing to stand trial).

Ages of Those Executed for Witchcraft at Salem (Also Known As That Time Salem Found a Really Terrible Way to Get Rid of a Lot of Its Old People)

Bridget Bishop was fifty-something; Rev. George Burroughs, forty-two; Martha Carrier, fifty; Giles Cory, eighty; Martha Cory, seventy-two; Mary Esty, fifty-eight; Sarah Good, thirty-something; Elizabeth How, fifty-something; George Jacobs, Sr., eighty; Susannah Martin, seventy-something; Rebecca Nurse, seventy-one; Alice Parker, unknown; Mary Parker, fifty-five, John Proctor, Sr., sixty; Ann Pudeator, seventy-something; Wilmott Redd, fifty-something; Margaret Scott, seventy-something; Samuel Wardwell, forty-nine; Sarah Wildes, sixty-five; John Willard, twenty-something.

Number of Accused Witches Who Died in Jail

Five: Lydia Dustin, Ann Foster, Sarah Osborne, Roger Toothaker, and infant daughter of accused witch Sarah Good. Although the infant was technically not accused of witchcraft, she was born and did pass away in Salem Prison. The infant's sister, however, *was* accused of witchcraft. (See: Age of Youngest Person Jailed for Witchcraft.)

Age of Youngest Person Jailed for Witchcraft

Four. Imagine that you're lying in bed, surrounded by the portentous quiet of a New England night, when the apparition of a four-year-old witch—a girl-child fiend—creeps out of the shadows, and, as you lie frozen in fear, climbs onto your chest, bites at you with sharp little teeth, pinches you, and then finally wraps her supernaturally strong hands around your neck and begins to squeeze. Well, that was exactly what Ann Putnam said happened to her in 1692. Her testimony got four-year-old Dorothy Good, whose pregnant mother, Sarah Good, was already imprisoned for witchcraft, seized and thrown into jail.

It was one of the most appalling moments in the saga of the Salem witch craze. Dorothy (also called Dorcas) Good was not only imprisoned for nine months without actually being charged with anything, she was also, once arrested, separated from her mother until she did what the magistrates wanted by testifying that her mother was a witch. Her reward: being cast into the same prison cell as her mother. A heavy chain was clamped around Dorothy's ankle; it scraped her skin and hurt her constantly. The tiny jail cell was cramped and insufferably hot that summer; the little girl could barely recall what it was like to be able to run about free in the meadows outside Salem with the other children. But at least little Dorothy had her mother there to comfort her—at least until July 19, when Sarah Good was wrenched from her daughter's side, driven to Gallows Hill in a rickety cart, and hanged.

But the Salem court wasn't done with little Dorothy Good; she was held in prison for five more long months. By the time her father, William Good, was able to raise the bond money to free her, Dorothy Good was a lost cause. Years later, when William petitioned for restitution for what he called the "destruction of my poor family," he complained to the court that his daughter "being chained in the dungeon was so harshly used and terrified that she hath ever since been very chargeable having little or no reason (with which) to govern herself."

There was one small but telling sidelight to this terrible story; it can be found scribbled on a series of frayed, time-worn court documents. It seemed the marshal charged with apprehending the little girl couldn't bring himself to perform this particular duty. He deputized another man, Samuel Braybrook, to take over the distasteful job; Braybrook did as he was ordered and took the girl into custody. But instead of taking her to jail, he went against orders and took her to the local inn, where prisoners were sometimes temporarily remanded. The court was relentless though, and yet another man was dispatched to bring four-year-old Dorothy to Salem Prison. Bring her he did, but it is believed that this man carried Dorothy in his arms the distance from the Ingersoll Inn to the jail, it being too far for the little girl to possibly have walked. It has to be noted that at least one of the men who apparently found the job of arresting Salem's tiniest witch distasteful also testified against other accused witches in the courtroom. But at least in the unwillingness, however tentative, of several men to arrest four-year-old Dorothy Good, we could see that there was at least a morsel of humanity still lurking beneath the mania of the Salem witch craze.

Number of Witches in America in 1692 (according to Courtroom Testimony of Those Who Had Attended the Big Witch Get-Together in Salem)

305, according to one accused witch; 307 according to another; we can safely assume that the Witch Census of America in 1692 would have recorded a number somewhere in the low 300s.

Number of Dogs Executed for Witchcraft

꜡ Two. Witch dog #1 was the familiar of accused witch John Bradstreet, who, it was said, had been "riding" it, although accounts are unclear as to whether this dog belonged to Bradstreet or not. In October 1692, Bradstreet fled Salem—without benefit of riding on the dog—and escaped prosecution for witchcraft. The dog, however, was not so fortunate; since it was considered a witch's familiar, it was killed.

Witch dog #2, identified as a male dog, was shot to death after being accused of causing the bewitchment of one of the girls of Salem. After the dog's execution, Rev. Increase Mather helpfully announced that "this dog was no Devil; for then they could not have killed him"—an exoneration that came a bit late to be of any benefit whatsoever to the dog.

Largest Number of Ghosts to Attend a Witch Trial

꜡ Eight. That's a lot of ghosts to have show up at your witch trial—almost enough for a whole jury of spirits. It became commonplace for ghosts to appear and accuse the Salem witches of having killed them. These ghosts were mostly random people from the area who had died in previous years, usually in non-mysterious ways. Even by Salem standards, however, eight ghosts was a lot. But according to the court records, on June 7, 1692, as a certain Job Tookey was questioned by judges, including John Hathorne, a small army of ghosts showed up: two children, three men, and three women. The spirits had gone old-school for the occasion, dressed for effect in shrouds that wound round them like sheets; they were there to testify against Tookey via very over-the-top glares and cries for vengeance. All had been victims of Tookey's bewitchment, they said—mostly through the "pin stuck in a poppet" method, which could be, it seems, quite deadly. Despite the best efforts of the eight ghosts, Tookey was released from Salem Prison in January 1693.

Number of "Deadly" Wounds Sarah Bishop Was Accused of Inflicting on a Victim via Witchcraft

Three. Goody Trask could be sort of a fun-spoiler. According to testimony, she became royally indignant about the behavior of neighbor Sarah Bishop because "the said Bishop did entertain people in her house at unseasonable hours in the night to keep drinking and playing at shovel-board.*" One night, Goody Trask had paid a visit to Sarah Bishop. Trask had "gone into the house and finding some at shovel-board had taken the pieces they played with and thrown them into the fire."

Besides being a lady who really, really hated shovel-board, Goody Trask could also be a little bit confrontational. She "had reproved the said Bishop for promoting such disorders but had received no satisfaction from her about it."

This incident was recounted during the Salem witch trials several years after it happened. It came to light as prosecutors tried to gather information against accused witch Sarah Bishop because it seemed something very bad had happened to Goody Trask after her confrontation with Bishop. At first Trask had become "very distracted" (i.e., began having mental issues); supposedly she had told folks she thought Goody Bishop had bewitched her. Not long after, Trask's body was found in a very gruesome state. According to a witness, "As to the wounds she died of I observed 3 deadly ones. A piece of her windpipe cut out and another wound above that through the windpipe & gullet & vein they call jugular." The witness, who was not a physician, felt confident in asserting that it was "impossible for her with so short a pair of scissors to mangle herself so without some extraordinary work of the devil or witchcraft."

So it seemed that witch Sarah Bishop had taken control of Goody Trask and caused her to hack herself to death with scissors. Okay, now that that was settled (and no one was suggesting any alternative theories, like that perhaps the small scissors were the very reason it had taken such butchery for Trask to take her life), the court could move on to other somehow relevant evidence against Bishop, like how several people had once heard her have an argument with her husband.

Fun-spoiler Goody Trask may have had good reason for her bad moods. At twenty-nine, she was the mother of five—no wonder she complained about neighbors being rowdy at night. And she had just given birth a few months before she took her life. A woman who became "distracted" a few months after childbirth today would be evaluated for post-partum depression. In the end, Goody Trask's death was ruled a suicide—a sin against God according to the court—and so instead of a headstone in the town graveyard, Goody Trask received an unmarked resting place in a ditch and a load of rocks dumped on top of her mangled body.

Sarah Bishop made out better than many others accused of witchcraft at Salem; she and her husband, who was also arrested for witchcraft, escaped from jail and survived the witchcraft craze.

Total Amount of Restitution Ordered by Governor Dudley in 1710 (to Be Distributed among Victims of the Salem Witchcraft Trial Victims)

578 pounds and twelve shillings. The amount was paltry, and for most, too little, too late. Giles Corey and his wife, for instance, got twenty-one pounds in the settlement, which probably wasn't especially appreciated since they were both dead. An aside: sixty pounds was the amount of money that the son of Martha Cory petitioned the court for because that was the amount of money that had been taken from her when she was arrested. Amount he was awarded: fifty pounds.

Number of Foster Family Generations Arrested for Witchcraft

Three. Widow Ann Foster was seventy-two when she was arrested for witchcraft. Her daughter, Mary Foster Lacey, Sr., was forty, and her daughter's daughter, Mary Foster Lacey, Jr., was eighteen when they were also arrested and charged with "detestable witchcraft." All three women confessed to witchcraft. Mary Sr. stated in court that she had traveled to the big witch get-together in Salem on a pole with her mother, Ann Foster, and another woman, and that (unsurprisingly) the pole had broken.

What Cost Two Pounds and Ten Shillings in Salem in 1692?

Two pounds and ten shillings was the price Abraham Foster had to pay to the jailor in order to obtain the body of his mother,

Ann Foster, after she had died in prison while awaiting execution for witchcraft.

Notes

* Shovel-board was an English game, sort of a combination between shuffleboard and air hockey.

PART IV

After Salem

Lifestyles of the Witch and Infamous: The Black Arts and Bad Neighborhoods of the Witches of New York

The Witches of New York exert an influence too powerful and too wide-spread to be treated with such light regard.

—Mortimer Thomson

After the embarrassment of Salem, witchcraft charges began to wane in America. A few cases were brought before courts in Virginia and Maryland only to result in acquittals and then countersuits for slander. Witch hunting just wasn't as satisfying as it had once been. The *Acte Against Conjuration and Witchcraft* was repealed in 1735, and the separation of church and witch hunting meant no more fun witch executions to attend. But although witch trials died out, belief in witch- ⸙ craft was alive and well in America in the 1700s and 1800s. In lonely mountain huts, small rural villages, and even cities teeming with immigrants and industry, people still held tight to old beliefs that magical spells could be used to effect cures, get revenge, foretell the future—all the things that made American life fun and satisfying. *That* meant there was money to be made in witchcraft. And that's exactly what brought wry journalist Mortimer Thomson—a.k.a. Q.K. Philander Doesticks—to New York City's most dangerous neighborhoods. In his efforts to expose the witches of New York, he left a one-of-a-kind snapshot of that city's gritty underside.

Doesticks Does New York

It was the late 1850s, and America was on the hell train to ⸙ civil war. In Kansas, John Brown executed the "Pottawatomie Massacre," a bloody raid on pro-slavers, then began stockpiling weapons for a much bigger raid. In Washington, the Supreme Court informed an enslaved man named Dred Scott that he was *property*, not a *citizen*, thank you very much. And in Illinois, the man who would change everything—then Senate-hopeful Abraham Lincoln—made a speech that warned "a house divided against itself cannot stand."

Meanwhile, in New York City, a reporter named Mortimer Thomson wriggled into a corset, donned a bonnet, and went looking for witches.

Thomson was on a mission to expose the city's fortune-tellers, or, as he called them, "The Witches of New York." For variety, he also called them "dangerous criminals."

Thomson's purported purpose was twofold: to protect the citizens of Gotham from the devious deceptions of the witches, and to divert vulnerable young women from resorting to the soothsaying profession. (He said it led to prostitution, although the connection was a bit vague.) But what the reporter actually exposed was much more interesting. Mortimer Thomson's visits to the witches—all of whom operated out of their homes— was a socio-economic excursion into conditions in the city's tenements. And some of the conditions the reporter smarmily described were factors that, in a few years' time, would have a significant impact on the Union's ability to win the Civil War. Oh, and those fortune-tellers? Thomson may not have known it at the time, but there was an eerie thread of accuracy woven through their predictions.

Mortimer Thomson had a skeleton or two in his own closet. He was expelled from the University of Michigan for what his *New York Times* obituary called "too much enterprise in securing subjects for the dissection room." After a stint as an actor with an itinerant theater company, the paunchy young man with the droopy mustache settled in New York City. He now had at least one definite ambition: "As soon as I had become comfortably established as a citizen of New York . . . I made up my mind to devote the next six months of my life to seeing the sights, and becoming acquainted with the celebrities of the town." As usual, Mortimer's career ambitions were on the understated side. He was toiling as a store clerk when he accidentally found his calling: Mortimer Thomson had landed in the newspapers, and this time not for stealing bodies. He had become a writer.

Hiding behind the mouthful of a pseudonym, Q.K. Philander Doesticks, Thomson inflicted a satiric, elaborately ornamental

style on an apparently easily entertained public in 1854 with ⋆
"Doesticks on a Bender." This tongue-in-cheek first-person
account of a trip to Niagara Falls is believed to have first been published in the school newspaper during Mortimer's University of
Michigan days, and then slowly, without its author knowing, was
picked up by other papers; soon it was getting national attention.
It read like a frat boy's drunken stream-of-consciousness word
salad of a travelogue destined to be rejected by *Vice*, but readers
ate it up. Thomson—er, Doesticks—became an accidental sensation. It was a welcome surprise for the new New Yorker, and so
was the offer to work for the *New York Tribune* penning humor-
ous columns, funny letters, and parodies of poems. A few years
and many laugh-riot bylines later, Thomson got a bee in his bonnet about the city's many professional fortune-tellers, and all bets
(and at one point his pantaloons) were off.

It was true that what could get you a good hanging in the
1600s could fetch you a tidy sum in the 1800s. Spiritualism,
usually involving communicating with the dead through mediums, was thriving. Some estimates say that during this era there
were close to 30,000 mediums active in America, busily con-
ducting séances, tipping tables, and receiving messages from
the beyond in the form of knocks and disembodied trumpet
solos. The wily witches of New York were ready to take advantage of the trend. They had a business plan: they cut out the
otherworldly middlemen and, they claimed, received their intel
directly from the other side. New York newspapers regularly
ran advertisements for their services, like this one:

Astonishing To All. Madame Bruce, the Mysterious Veiled
Lady, can be consulted on all events of life, at No. 513

Broome St. She is a second-sight seer and was born with a natural gift.

"Witchcraft" as practiced by the witches of nineteenth-century New York consisted mostly of predictions regarding love, money, and health, and their ads threw around a lot of supernatural yet vague buzzwords like "oracles," "horoscopes," "zodiacs," and "magnetism."

These ads (many sold, it's worth noting, by Thomson's own employer, the *Tribune*) were apparently quite effective. Thomson wrote in his exposé, "It may open the eyes of . . . innocent querists to the popularity of modern witchcraft to learn that the nineteen she-prophets who advertise in the daily journals of this city are visited every week by an average of sixteen hundred people." Thomson—concerned citizen, conscientious journalist, and questionable mathematician (eighty-four clients a week per witch seems pretty high)—worried that the witches could, theoretically, have *way* too much influence on the powerful men of the city. Among the witches' clientele were, he claimed, "Not a few men engaged in respectable and influential professions, and many merchants of good credit and repute, who periodically consult these women, and are actually governed by their advice in business affairs of great moment."

By now, some of us may be thinking, "But wait—wouldn't the public good have been better served by the reporter investigating those 'influential' bigshots who were allegedly basing decisions of great social import on fortunes told by witches?" Fair enough—but that wouldn't have been nearly as fun for Mortimer Thomson.

Besides, it was the ladies Thomson was *really* concerned about. Yes, those helpless, silly New York gals needed saving,

and he was just the man to do it. Women with disposable income
to fritter away on fortune-telling needed to be saved from their
own gullibility, and the less-fortunate girls—the young, pretty
ones, anyway—needed to be rescued from the inevitable short
walk from dubious profession #1—witchcraft—to dubious profession #2—prostitution. Thomson wrote,

> The most terrible truth connected with this whole subject
> is the fact that the greater number of these female for-
> tune-tellers are but doing their allotted part in a scheme
> by which, in this city, the wholesale seduction of ignorant,
> simple-hearted girls, in the lower walks of life, has been
> thoroughly systematized.

Spoiler alert: Thomson is not exactly successful in demonstrating this connection, unless his premise is supposed to be that
shady shenanigans of one sort are proof of shady shenanigans
of another sort. Whether he was sincere in his concern or not
is hard to say, but the humor and the chance to peek inside the
operations of New York's witches would have been enough to
justify his undertaking.

So, like a nineteenth-century Geraldo Rivera, the intrepid
mustachioed reporter went undercover to infiltrate the shady
world of the urban witch. Thomsen's M.O. was this:

1. Visit witch as paying customer;
2. Have fortune told;
3. Write snarky article for *Tribune*;
4. Repeat until there are enough articles for book;
5. Call book *The Witches of New York*.

"But wait a minute!" we stubbornly protest. "Witchcraft and fortune-telling are two different things, right?"

"Well," Thomson might fire back, "try telling that to those girls in Salem whose experimentation with divination allegedly conjured up the deadly Salem witch trials." Good point, Mortimer.

The journalist, who was at least as interested in himself as in witches, prefaced *The Witches of New York* with a description of himself as "a cash customer, who paid liberally for all he required, and who, by reason of the dollars he disbursed, was entitled to the very best witchcraft in the market. And he got it."

Similarly, later in the book Thomson, a "referring to one-self in third person" enthusiast, achieved unimagined heights of literary self-description by describing himself as "a man with Hope in heart and money in his pantaloons."

To get an idea of what the witch world was like in the 1850s, we're going to accompany Thomson, the judgmental cash customer, and experience some of the highlights of his encounters. Keep in mind that in doing his witchcraft exposé, our reporter inadvertently gifted us with an important glimpse into life in New York City's pre-Civil War tenements. And now, it's time to visit the witches of New York. Hold onto your pantaloons . . .

Mortimer Thomson's Guide to the Witches of New York, or Witchcraft Can Be a Drag

In order to get to know our reporter a little better, we'll first take a look at the extent he was willing to go in order to secure an audience with one particular witch, and how a chapter in *The Witches of New York* ended up with the awesome title

"How the Cash Customer visited the 'Astonisher'—How he was
Astonished—and How he saw his Future Husband."

This witch was known as Madame Morrow the Astonisher,
and she didn't "do" men. That is, Madame Morrow was a witch
with a caveat: she only accepted female customers. Thomson
attributed this restriction to her shrewdly taking advantage
of her own sex's credulity, but it seems much more likely that
the wise Madame Morrow had one scary experience too many
with male customers and decided that working with them just
wasn't worth the risk. And as if to confirm that Witch Morrow
has good reason to be *so over* men, Thomson breezily suggests
that she was, in her pre-witch days, a prostitute.

Madame Morrow's soothsaying specialty was predicting
"matrimonial bliss" prospects for her lady customers, and, as a
grand finale, giving them a sneak preview of their future hus-
bands in something called a "magic mirror." This was a proposition that Mortimer Thomson simply could not resist. Call
it dedication. Call it a taste for the theatrical. Call it a lifelong
desire to put on a dress. Whatever it was, Thomson quickly
formed a plan to gain an audience with the ladies-only witch
and gain "a look at his future husband": "Yes, he would petticoat
himself up to the required dimensions, if it took a week to tie
on the machinery. Off with the pantaloons; on with the skirts."
Again with the pantaloons?

Thomson did indeed secure the required garments, and
with the help of "two discreet married men, who knew the
ropes," he was transformed by ribbons, lace, corset, skirts, and
a bonnet into *Miss* Thomson. Somehow it wasn't until he was
otherwise dolled up that the guys realized there was still one
grave impediment standing between Thomson and full-blown

femininity: his billowing black mustache. Already gowned up, he was in too deep to turn back now. The fellows considered the predicament: what would Thomson do with his trademark mustache? The solution resulted in this memorable sentence: "At last he knelt down, which was the nearest approach he could make to a sitting position, and Jenkins, mounted on the bed, shaved him as well as he could at arm's length."

Thus de-pantalooned and gussied up, the nineteenth century's (presumably) homeliest woman sallied forth, sashaying toward what he hoped would be a glimpse of his future husband. Madame Morrow may or may not have seen worse, but somehow Thomson passed muster and was admitted. At last he was face to face with the exclusive witch, but, ironically, his description of Madame Morrow makes her sound like the opposite of the type of party girl he alleged she had been: "She is a tall, sallow-looking woman, with a complexion the color of old parchment . . . attired in a handsome delaine dress of half-mourning."

It's worth pausing here for a moment to imagine the strong possibility that the severely dressed Witch Morrow probably took one look at "Miss" Thomson and determined that *she*, in her over-the-top get-up, was probably a streetwalker of questionable marketability.

Witch Morrow, gazing into her customer's marital prospects and probably suppressing a snigger, proceeded to inform Thomson that there were not one but *two* gentlemen who wanted to marry "her," and that there was a wedding in her near future. Meanwhile, her client fidgeted in her petticoats, pining for the long-awaited gander of the image of her future husband, until at long last the witch produced a small pine box: the magic mirror!

At one end of the box was an eyehole covered by a small black curtain; the witch positioned Miss Thomson before it, then— drumroll!—the witch dramatically pulled back the tiny curtain. And at that moment, the face of the future husband of Mortimer Thomson was revealed in the hazy image inside the box. It was "a bloated face with a mustache, with black eyes and black hair; it was a hang-dog, thief-like face, and one that he would not have passed in the street without involuntarily putting his hands on his pockets to assure himself that all was right."

It was a face not unlike his own—before the makeover. And so Thomson (quite disappointed in the appearance of his future husband, we assume) went home, took off his gown, pried off his corset, wrote unpleasantly about his visit to Witch Morrow, sulked for a while, and began the slow process of re-growing his own black hang-dog mustache.

Witch Zero

Thomson's inaugural encounter with a New York City witch had been a bit less theatrical but just as entertaining. The witch in question was one of the city's most notorious: the renowned Madame Prewster. To Thomson, she was witch zero. He wrote, "She has been engaged in the Witch business in this city for more years than has any other one whose name is now advertised to the public." Then, since it was the good old days and reporters were little inconvenienced by things like lawsuits, he threw around a lot of adjectives like "illicit," "criminal," and "evil." And that was just in the first paragraph.

Thomson set off to see Madame Prewster, declaring dramatically that he was "fully prepared to encounter whatever of the diabolical machinery of the black art might be put in operation to appall his unaccustomed soul." Madame Prewster worked her wonders out of 373 Bowery, and Thomson, strolling squeamishly into the witch's neighborhood, described it as being full of cats, clotheslines, stables, and really bad smells.

Like most of the witches of New York, Madame Prewster employed a receptionist, a sort of "the witch will see you now" person who answered the door and collected the fee. When this young woman greeted Thomson at Madame Prewster's door, he didn't ask her relation to the witch or her name, being quite satisfied with calling her "a greasy girl." She was not particularly charmed by him either:

> The juvenile female who had admitted him thus far, evidently took him for a disreputable character, and stood prepared to prevent depredations. She planted herself firmly before him in the narrow hall in an attitude of self-defense, and squaring off scientifically, demanded his business. Astrology was mentioned, whereupon the threatening fists were lowered, the saucy under-jaw was retracted, and the general air of pugnacity was subdued into a very suspicious demeanor.

For a guy who claimed to be all about protecting women, Mortimer Thomson was conveniently oblivious to the very real dangers faced by the witches, whose profession often involved allowing strange men into their homes. The New York City of the 1850s was a hotbed of crime, as the glittering, growing wealth of some segments of the population awkwardly banged elbows with the hopeless poverty of others. Savvy citizens navigated the streets armed with small arms, knives, and black-jacks, and violent gangs did the same. Cases of what we would now call home invasions and gang rapes were common. But in 1858, Thomson got a guffaw out of the fact that Prewster's "belligerent girl" seemed poised for a fight, observing mirthfully that "one fist she still kept loaded" as she led him from a dilapidated and sparsely furnished front room to his consultation with the witch.

The witch, as it turned out, was in the basement. The basement, as it turned out, was also being used as a kitchen, and the suspicious hostess unceremoniously returned to some dishes she had been washing. Also present was a "feeble child" playing on the floor with some pots and pans; whether boy or girl we don't know, as the reporter referred to the toddler as "it." And in the midst of this gloomy domestic scene sat the great witch herself, shrouded in a shawl and lounging in a rocking chair of "extra size" to accommodate her ample girth. Thomson wrote,

> Grim, grizzled, and stony-eyed, is this juicy old Sibyl; and she glared fearfully on the hero with her fishy optics. . . . She was evidently just out of bed, although it was long past noon, and when she yawned, which she did seven times a minute on a low average, the effect was gloomy and cavernous, and the timid delegate in search of the mysterious trembled in his boots.

Witch Prewster then produced a worn deck of cards from her voluminous folds. Unfortunately, Thomson, a man of great snarkiness but little curiosity, doesn't describe the cards, but they were very likely Lenormand cards. Lenormand decks were fortune-telling cards widely published in Europe, and subsequently in the German and French immigrant communities in America. While they were named for the famous French fortune-teller Mlle. Lenormand, the origin of the cards themselves has been attributed to everything from an old German board game to images inspired by reading coffee grounds. Witch Prewster had her cash customer shuffle these cards, then proceeded to read them in a casual, Magic 8 Ball sort of way. She vaguely predicted a generic-type future for Thomson, full of the usual ups and downs in matters of love, marriage, and money. She concluded by attempting to name the reporter's future wife, a detail he almost certainly received with an eye-roll.

As the reader ponders the alleged evil threat imposed by an obese woman holding a deck of cards in a rocking chair, the intrepid reporter exits the basement lair, but not before making a really scary face at the child, which, he proudly noted, "Caused that weird brat to fling itself flat on its back and scream in agony of fear." Lack of empathy? Check. Sense of irony? Not so much.

Then, as the young hostess led Thomson to the door, he noted that, hidden beneath her worn apron, she was clutching a heavy wooden rolling pin. Apparently the "greasy girl" wasn't taking any chances with Mortimer Thomson.

Broome Street and Other Witch 'Hoods

Something most of Thomson's witches had in common was that they lived in very bad neighborhoods. Sounds about right for witches, no? And so to visit these witches, the fussy Thomson had to deign to venture into some very interesting communities, places that probably would have made him want to bathe in hand sanitizer, had it been invented, when he got home. For Thomson, these sketchy surroundings spoke to the character of the said witches, and so he seemed to relish describing them. While his commentary was often very mean-spirited, it was also very telling, for many of the witches of New York lived in the slums with many of the other struggling immigrants of that city.

Awesomely, many of the witches Thomson investigated just happened to live on *Broome Street*. Just as the street's name was eerily appropriate, it was also a bit ironic considering it was pretty much covered in, well, *manure*. And that, Thomson says, explains some of the other things one might see on Broome Street:

> This prolific and valuable deposit that covers Broome Street bears perennial crops: in the spring and summer, dirty-faced children and mean-looking dogs seem to spring from it spontaneously; they are succeeded during the colder weather by a crop of tumble-down barrels, and cast-away broken carts; while the humbler and more insignificant things . . . such as potato parings, and fish heads, and shreds of ragged dish-cloths, and bits of broken crockery, and old bones, are in season all the year round.

But that's not all. There are pawnbrokers' establishments! Rum shops! Stagnant gutters! Mounds of decomposing trash! And for our skeevy scratch-and-sniff entertainment, Thomson adds that there was "a stench so thick and heavy that it be-slimes everything it touches, and makes a man feel as if he were far past the saving powers of soap and soft water, and was fast dissolving into rancid lard oil."

Broome Street was also the very epicenter of criminality, according to the reporter, who claimed parents there schooled their children in thievery from infancy. And don't even think about setting foot on Broome Street after dark unless you want to be the subject of a newspaper story of a garroting* or other really bad things.

On a side note, these days the neighborhood has spiffed itself up a wee bit. You can actually still buy yourself a nice little place on Broome Street—that is, if you have a few million bucks to spend. But even in its modern, upscale version the area retains an uneasy aura: it was inside a multimillion dollar penthouse on Broome Street that actor Heath Ledger was found dead of a drug overdose in 2008.

Another witch neighborhood, Mulberry Street, may sound more innocuous but was just as crappy and just as full of abandoned broken-down carts and stray broken-down dogs. Yes, it seemed any time the beleaguered cash customer wanted to find a witch, he had to navigate a veritable gauntlet of smelly stables, rock-throwing boys, and always, always those ever-present mounds of putrescent refuse.

🕯 The actual living quarters of the witches of New York were not exactly *Godey's Lady's Book*–ready either, but they *were* a sort of nineteenth-century urban equivalent of the classic cobwebs-and-cauldrons look. Like many folks in the poorer sections of town, many of the witches lived in tenement houses. The tenements, well worn by scores of immigrants and other struggling New Yorkers, were overpopulated and under-maintained, so it was little wonder they were shabbier than Thomson was used to. Factor in the fragrances of cabbage-heavy dinners simmering in dozens of poorly ventilated apartments and, well,

you get the idea. The witches' housekeeping left something to be ꜜ
desired as well. After a visit to one tenement house, Thomson
reported, "The walls were stained, discolored, and bedaubed,
and the floor had a sufficient thickness of soil for a vegetable
garden; at one end of the hall, indeed, an Irish woman was on
her knees, making experimental excavations, possibly with a
view to planting early lettuce and peppergrass." Then Thomson,
in one of his trademark pantaloons-related non-sequiturs,
remarked that the cash customer had been going to kneel but
was afraid that it "would result in the ineffaceable soiling of his
best pantaloons; so he stood sturdily erect."

Despite the heaps of unwashed dishes and, especially offensive to his sensibilities, cheap furniture, Thomson does occasionally give the witches a little credit; in one landmark comment he
even concedes that one witch's rooms are "small but neatly furnished." In another witch house, he expands his horizons and turns
art critic when he spies paintings of "St. Somebody taking his ease
on an X-shaped cross, St. Somebody Else comfortably cooking
on a gridiron, and St. Somebody, different from either of these,
impaled on a spear like a bug in an Entomological Museum."

A trademark of New York's witches seemed to be the
assortment of colorful, and, according to Thomson, unwashed
young women who answered their doors. (Since access to clean
water wasn't a standard amenity in the tenements, this was very
likely an accurate observation.) These gals, most of them identified by Thomson as Irish, were no-nonsense types; there was
nary a how-do-you-do, let alone a curtsey. The witches' host-
esses were essentially the bouncers of the fortune-telling world,
letting any questionable visitors know that they and the witches
were not to be trifled with.

Thomson also encountered and described other residents of the tenement houses, like this young man who seemed to be a sort of middle-management person between the hostess—a French woman who basically just didn't want to climb the stairs—and the second-floor fortune-teller: "The cash customer was next handed off to a shock-headed boy sporting a double-barreled black eye." The bruises on this little character seemed to personify the violence the slums were famous for.

Fighting was notoriously one of the most popular pastimes in the rough neighborhoods, and boys weren't the only ones getting in on the action. Thomson was shown into one witch domicile by a young woman who could barely pull herself away from a physical altercation with another girl, and he watched with unabashed glee as the pair went after each other with large straight pins. The fight ended, he says, with one of the girls cowering under a table while being kicked by the other, who reluctantly pulled herself away from her victory to escort the visitor to see the witch.

Then, in another witch home, yet another brawl: Thomson observed two small children fight a large yellow dog for their dinner; this altercation was eventually broken up by the obligatory Irish girl, who administered a sound whack to each of the children. The dog, apparently, made out much better.

Men were notably absent when Thomson visited the tenements, and it wasn't because they were scared of witches and tough Irish girls. Most men from the witches' 'hoods spent their days toiling as poorly paid day laborers, helping to build the ever-expanding city. When the Civil War came a few years later, enlisting was a lucrative proposition for many immigrants, who were offered bonuses and subsidies for their families. Ultimately the Union Army would be as diverse as the tenements themselves, since these immigrants made up a significant portion of that army.

Something else that would ultimately benefit the Union was exposed when Thomson encountered another scary resident of the tenements: smallpox. In the midst of his witch investigations, the reporter ran into an unexpected problem. It seems Mortimer Thomson contracted smallpox, which he blamed, of course, on his visits to the witches and their unsanitary neighborhoods. If Thomson did contract smallpox from venturing into the crowded tenements, it was a pretty good foreshadowing of what would happen to many troops. The Confederate Army would be hit hard right out of the gate by infectious diseases, foes their men were helpless to resist. Many of the South's volunteers were country boys who'd had little opportunity to be exposed to the infectious diseases to the extent the Northern boys had—until they found themselves crowded into dirty camps. The diseases spread quickly and cost both sides, but especially the Confederates, precious manpower.

Witchy Demographics

So just who *were* these witches, and where did they come from? The witch demographic seemed to be pretty much in line with the non-witch population. New York was a city of immigrants, and immigrants were well represented in the fortune-telling business, with witches of all ages hailing from France, Germany, Ireland, England, and even Brazil.

Most of the witches kept it simple; few shared Thomson's affinity for theatrics. He did report that one of them made an effort to adapt a mysterious look by wearing a long black veil over her face, but otherwise, according to the reporter, it was a lot of this: "A dirty slatternly young woman of about twenty-three years, with filthy hands and uncombed hair whose clothes looked as if they had been tossed on with a pitchfork." So just why would someone want to visit a witch in an unsavory hovel and fork over a whole dollar for the pleasure? (The fact that $1 then was the equivalent of about $22 in today's money suggests the witches of New York didn't do as much business as Thomson purported, or they would have been living quite a bit better.)

In the 1800s, a woman might have had good reason to consult witches. The desire to know one's future—to have reassurances in matters of love, family, and good fortune—is certainly not news to anyone. The witches of New York were also frequently consulted in another matter: "absent friends." In the 1800s, it was easy to lose track of people and common to go long periods without hearing from loved ones far away. And if someone wanted to get lost and stay lost, the people they left behind couldn't exactly track their cell phone calls or check their Facebook. But a trusted fortune-teller could be counted on to deliver peace of mind with psychic updates on their well-being. And then there was the matter of fortune-telling as entertainment—a concept apparently lost on Mortimer Thomson altogether.

The Witches' Whatchamacallits, and What They Foretold for Thomson

There was nary a crystal ball deployed by the witches of New York, but one witch, Madame Widger, or as Thomson affectionately called her, "The Widger," used her own sort of budget version: a bunch of ordinary-looking rocks that she held up to her eye one by one while saying things like: "I see by looking into this stone that you was born under two planets . . . "

Cards were the number-one apparatus used by the witches. Some of these were run-of-the-mill playing cards, but by and large most of them were some variation of the Lenormand deck, which looked like tarot cards but were bedecked with things like ships (for the inevitable upcoming "voyage"), rings (for the inevitable upcoming wedding), and dogs (one witch told Thomson he might "die by a dog," although this was probably just wishful thinking on her part). And not to worry: predictions of bad times ahead were always tempered with an opportunity to purchase a good luck charm on the spot.

There was also, of course, Witch Morrow's magic-mirror doo-hickey, the wooden box with a likeness of a random and not exactly attractive man inside. Other witches consulted astrology books, while another jabbed at Thomson's open palm with a long, witchy finger.

They may have used a variety of techniques, but there was a definite theme to the witches' predictions for Thomson's future. Many of the witches of New York informed the reporter that he would be married twice, and that his first wife would die not long after marriage. Thomson didn't seem to be fazed by this cheery news, and when one of the witches, Mrs. Pugh, told him he would be married twice and also predicted the deaths of numerous children, he seemed to be quite the good sport about it all: "The inquirer was charmed with the lively prospect of so many funerals, and mentally resolved to buy a couple of acres in Greenwood (cemetery) for the accommodation of his future family."

The Witches' Wake

❧ So what happened *after* Thomson visited the witches of New York? Did the journalist's exposé have any effect on New York's witches? The answer is a bit murky; it's true some of the witches were no angels, and a number of them were rounded up on various other charges (fortune-telling itself was not illegal); but they were quickly released and returned to their prognostication businesses. Life in the slums continued to be bleak and generally crummy, and its residents continued to find creative ways to try to get by. Mortimer Thomson's attempt to control the witches, women, and girls of New York was ultimately unsuccessful, and fortune-telling and the efforts of women to make a living continued. Sorry, Mortimer.

And what about the author himself? As it turned out, the cash customer didn't have to marry a man with a hangdog look and droopy mustache after all. Thomson had had a potential wife waiting on the sidelines all along in the form of a petite, very pretty, dark-haired sixteen-year-old named Anna. This, by the way, would be a good time to note that *Anna* was the name Madame Prewster had predicted for Thomson's first wife. (Okay, it was her second choice, after Emma, but *still.*) Anna Van Cleve was the daughter of family friends and, according to family interviews done by Fletcher Daniel Slater, a student who researched Thomson in 1931, was "promised" to Thomson by her parents. The Thomsons and the Van Cleves had an *understanding,* which Mortimer apparently understood to mean he could send for his intended bride any time he was ready to give up bachelorhood, which he was soon after finishing his witch exposé.

But the witches of New York may have had the last, bitter ◈ laugh over the journalist—and no, it wasn't just the smallpox they gave him. Mortimer Thomson had wed the lovely Anna in October 1857, and in December 1858, four days after the publication of *The Witches of New York,* Anna died after giving birth to their son. Only twenty-seven years old, Thomson was a widower—just as the witches had predicted.

In 1861, Thomson acquired wife number two—again, as the witches had predicted. In 1862, however, in a sad déjà vu, this wife also died after giving birth to a daughter.

Mortimer Thomson died in 1875. His obituary told the sad tale of the once jolly writer's life after his second wife's death: "His unfortunate habits, including a use of opium, clouded his later years."

Decades after his death there would be yet another strange twist to the story of Mortimer Thomson and the witches of New York. The carnage of World War I was providing spiritualists a well-paid resurgence as the bereaved sought contact with their dead. This time, it was the most famous magician in the world who was out on a mission to expose the crafty tricks of mediums. Harry Houdini, mourning the loss of his beloved mother, was really, really offended (or perhaps disappointed) by those who claimed they could talk to the dead. He attended hundreds of séances in disguise and was able to reverse-engineer the ectoplasmic ejaculations and tipping tables he witnessed. Soon he incorporated this exposé into his magic act; he would perform his own dramatic séance, followed by a finger-wagging debunking. He even wrote a book about the subject: *Miracle Mongers and Their Methods.* In 1926, he was on tour performing and lecturing on the topic of spiritualist fakery when he received the blow that was said to have expedited his death on Halloween that same year.

❧ We know Houdini had a strong distaste for spiritualists because of his mother's death, but what had given him the idea of doing an undercover exposé? The answer could lie in the archives of a private museum in the small town of Boonsboro, Maryland. There, amid a collection of rare old books, is a very battered first edition of *The Witches of New York* by Q.K. Philander Doesticks. If you open the book, the first thing you'll see inside the dusty cover is a personalized bookplate glued there by the book's long-ago owner, who is depicted in profile. The top of the bookplate reads, "Ex Libris"—"from the library of"—and below, there is a single name: Houdini.

Notes

* Garroting: old-timey way of murdering someone by strangling them with something handy and also old-timey, like piano wire.

CHAPTER 12

Christian Science and the Last Witch Trial in American History (So Far)

And all this deviltry as revealed by God! All this medieval witchcraft in the name of Christ! Out upon it, I say! Let it no longer be tolerated amongst us.

—Frederick W. Peabody, writing about
Christian Science in 1910

T he small girl lay stiff as a board on her bed in the old New
Hampshire farmhouse, her hands clenching the sides of the
mattress for dear life. She had heard the voices before, and it
seemed as if there had always been the fits—the strange episodes that left her thrashing on the floor or sometimes even frozen like a statue—but never this, this *pulling* from above. Now,
suddenly, there came over her a peculiar sensation of lightness
and then she was actually *rising above her bed*. She didn't panic,

but she didn't let go of the mattress, either. Three times the voice called her name; three times she answered. Each time, she rose off the bed to a height of about a foot, and each time her little body seemed to float back down onto the bed, gently, like a small feather released from a great height.

A Founding Fall

During the winter of 1866, a middle-aged Massachusetts woman slipped on an icy sidewalk and founded a major religion—a religion that sounded an awful lot like witchcraft. And its controversial female founder would instigate a court case based on allegations of behavior so much like witchcraft that the press called it "Second Salem."

The woman who took this fortuitous fall was once the little girl who had endured the Salem-like fits and bedroom levitation. She would soon become known to the world as Mary Baker Eddy, a name that would become synonymous with the religious movement she founded: Christian Science. According to Mary, she didn't so much found the religion as *discover* it. Mary's company, the Christian Science Publishing Company of Boston, published an account of this pivotal failure to stay upright, and as you will see, it was quite some fall:

> In company with her husband, she was returning from an errand of mercy, when she fell upon the icy curbstone, and was carried helpless to her home. The skilled physicians declared that there was absolutely no hope for her, and pronounced the verdict that she had but three days to live. On the third day, calling for her Bible, opened to the

healing of the palsied man, Matthew 9:2. The truth which set him free she saw. The power which gave him strength she felt. The life divine which healed the sick of the palsy restored her, and she rose from the bed of pain healed and free.

Mary revealed what it was that she had discovered that enabled her to cure herself:

> I discovered the Christ Science or divine laws of Life, Truth, Love, and named my discovery Christian Science.

But wait—just what, exactly, was this discovery? And what effect did it have on Mary?

> My discovery, that erring, mortal, misnamed mind produces all the organism and action of the mortal body, set my thoughts to work in new channels, and led up to my demonstration of the proposition that Mind is All and matter is naught as the leading factor in Mind-science.

In case you're having difficulty following Ms. Eddy's thought process there, she has a handy mathematical formula that should clear that right up for you:

> My conclusions were reached by demonstrable evidence, allowing the evidence of this revelation to multiply with mathematical certainty and the lesser demonstration to prove the great, as the product of three multiplied by three, equaling nine, proves conclusively that three times

three duodecillions must be nine duodecillions, not a fraction more, not a unit less.

• Got it now? There's the lesser demonstration and the demonstrable evidence and the duode . . . Okay, never mind. We can't all be math prodigies. But we can take a look at the genuinely odd story of Mary's life, with its recurring themes of witchcraft and dark powers, as well as the bizarre accusations that colored it—which led to the equally bizarre court case that would go down in history as Second Salem.

From Pet to Pariah

§ Mary Ann Morse Baker (later Glover, then Peterson, and finally Eddy) was born in New Hampshire in 1821 to a Bible-wielding farmer and his wife. The youngest of six, Mary, with her small stature and dark ringlets, quickly became the family pet. And by many reports, the family pet was spoiled, sickly, and prone to strange fits and convulsions reminiscent of those afflicting the girls who started the Salem witch craze. At home, when Mary would fall to the floor and commence dramatically thrashing around and screaming, her family would send for the village doctor, sometimes with the exclamation, "Mary's dying!" When the fits occurred in public places, however, observers were more likely to say Mary was having herself a tantrum. But sometimes the fits left her in what looked like a weird state of suspended animation, and it was easy to imagine that the attacks were of supernatural origin. Finally, perhaps because of the acrobatic contortions her small body would undertake during her fits, Mary was plagued by chronic spinal pain.

When she wasn't writhing on the floor or frozen in place like
a statue, Mary liked writing flowery poetry and considered herself
quite a scholar, although reports indicate she was not a particularly gifted student. Although her formal schooling was minimal,
Mary was fond of using big, impressive-sounding words, and
didn't care whether they were real words or not; she would also
perplex listeners with her distinctive, affected pronunciation.

The family pet had other issues as well. She was prone to
stomach problems and claimed that *not eating* was the only
thing that helped. It was perhaps her first stab at "healing," but
it wasn't fun. She wrote that most of her childhood was spent in
"hunger, pain, weakness, and starvation." This self-prescribed
starvation treatment could possibly have been the cause of
one of her other strange symptoms: hearing voices. Over the
course of one year, little Mary Baker was plagued by a loud
voice, unheard by anyone but her, which would always repeat
her name three times. It was this voice that seemed to have trig-
gered the childhood levitation in her bed.

Despite the host of strange afflictions and self-imposed
starvation, Mary was growing up, and the teenaged Mary was,
according to accounts, pretty hot. After years of the local fellas salivating over her, Mary married a smalltime businessman
named George Glover. Six months later, courtesy of yellow
fever, she went from new bride to widow overnight. And just a
few months after that, Mary gave birth to a baby boy she named
George. In under a year's time, the pampered family pet and village beauty had become an impoverished widow with an infant
and no home of her own. Though George had left her enough
money to get by on for a bit, no one expected the high-strung
young woman to be up for taking care of a baby. Sure enough, a

despondent Mary returned home and took to her old bed in her parents' home for several months, while her mother, with help from a maid, cared for little George.

For several years Mary floundered and struggled. She tried to earn a living as a writer, but even in Victorian times poetess was not the most practical career choice. She spent very little time with baby George; perhaps her family had assumed so much of his care so quickly that she failed to bond with him. Then in 1849, the death of her mother cinched the deal: the family pet would soon become the family pariah. Mary's father had quickly remarried and the new wife, playing evil stepmother to the high-maintenance spinster-widow, cleaned house—at least according to Mary's version of events. Little George was taken in by the family maid and her husband, who soon left town and took the boy with them. This, Mary would later assert, was the beginning of a "plot" to keep her and her child apart.

Mary had moved in with her sister and her family and was living as an invalid, both physically and emotionally, when a new interest caught her imagination: the occult. Spiritualism, a movement devoted to the belief that it is possible to communicate with the dead, was then revving up toward its heyday. People all over the country were sitting in dark rooms, holding hands, and talking to the dead—and sometimes the dead talked back. Spirits sent regards from the other side via knocks on walls, and bolder ghosts made their presence known by tipping tables in séances. It all seemed a perfect fit for the still-young woman prone to strange trances. Mary started practicing automatic writing, going into a trancelike state and writing out messages she said were coming from the dearly departed. Once, when a friend stayed over, Mary kept her awake all night, claiming to see spirits hanging around the bedroom; the friend ↖ also reported hearing strange rapping on Mary's walls through-out the night.

In her new séance circle of Spiritualist friends, it seemed that at last Mary had found a group where she fit in; she would remain part of the occult community for nearly a decade. Eventually, thanks to the untreated anxiety and physical pain that just would not go away, Mary began a new relationship, one that purportedly lasted the rest of her life. Mary's new best friend? Morphine.

And maybe Mary's infatuation with morphine also had ↗ something to do with the next love of her life: Daniel Patterson, fun-loving itinerant dentist. The good-looking Dr. Patterson enjoyed catering to his sickly bride, and neighbors said that while Mary was able to get around just fine in his absence, she would suddenly lose the ability to walk when he was home, requiring him to carry her from room to room.

The neighbors also complained that the new Mrs. Patterson was prone to hysterics, and, according to one fre-quently repeated story, they were particularly annoyed about the time Mary had summoned neighbors while her husband was away treating a patient in another town. They found Mary in bed, moaning that she was barely clinging to life; she asked one of the men to go find Dr. Patterson and bring him back to her. She just wanted to see her husband one last time before she died, she said pathetically. The neighbor dashed through the winter night on barely passable, snow-covered roads, at one point even stopping to trade off his horses for fresh ones, in a panic lest Mary should die before he could return with Dr. Patterson. When the neighbor finally returned, exhausted and half frozen, with Dr. Patterson in tow, Mary was sitting up in a chair and smiling; she seemed to have completely forgotten about her close call with death.

ℰ   The fun and games at the Pattersons' ended, as they did for much of America, during the Civil War. The dentist was captured behind enemy lines in Virginia while trying to smuggle supplies to Union troops. He was held in a Confederate prison, where he would languish for close to a year. When she heard her husband had been arrested, Mary wasted no time in writing to relatives asking for money. She had a new interest, and it was going to cost somebody a bit of cash.

A Method for Her Madness

If ever there was a fantastic name for a faith healer, it was Phineas Parkhurst Quimby; and if ever there was an ideal customer for a faith healer, it was Mary. Rumors of Quimby's healing powers were spreading like smallpox through certain New England circles, and Mary quickly became obsessed with the controversial healer from Maine. As always completely dependent on the grudging kindness of relatives, she relentlessly badgered her sister—who had married much better than she had—to finance a trip to Portland, Maine, where she could visit the healer for a dose of what was called "the Quimby Method."

Mary's sister refused to pay for the trip to Maine, but as a consolation prize sent her to Dr. Vail's Hydropathic Institute, which was closer, for a "water cure." Also called "hydrotherapy," water cures could involve the startling process of immersing the patient in tubs of very hot then very cold water, or sleeping in wet clothing, or sometimes simply taking a bath and then taking a walk. Water cures were a very big deal, but they were also a pretty lightweight solution for problems the size of Mary's. But conveniently for Mary's sister, not only was Dr. Vail's establishment the cheapest place of its kind, the water cure was also guaranteed to take a good couple of months. So Mary was packed off to Dr. Vail's in New Hampshire. In no time Mary was hitting her sister up for what she said was "spending money." It was a small price for Mary's sister to pay to keep the problem patient out of her hair, and so she began sending her cash on a regular basis. But Mary had a plan; as she endured the stay at Dr. Vail's—the Motel 6 of invalid treatment centers—she faithfully squirreled away the money sent by her sister.

By October 1862, Mary finally had enough money to make the pilgrimage to see Dr. Quimby. Unsurprisingly, the water cure hadn't helped her one bit, but her stay at Dr. Vail's had inadvertently put her on the bizarre trail that would change her life.

Mesmerizing Science

Gnomish, twitchy former clockmaker Phineas Parkhurst ♦ Quimby went by the honorific title of "Doctor," but this title was a whimsical one since he had actually only gone to school for a few years early in childhood. But what he lacked in formal training, Quimby made up for in not caring what people thought of him.

Mesmerism, pioneered by the German physician Franz Mesmer, was a process whereby the mesmerist was able to impose his own will on his subject through the power of his mind. It was a theatrical undertaking, in which the mesmerist would position himself close to his subject and, through a series of hand gestures, touches, and spoken instructions, appear to put the person into a state sort of like unconsciousness but not really. Once the mesmerist had his subject in this strange condition, he could then take his choice of getting the person to do whatever he told them (preferably something embarrassing) or heal them of some nagging impairment. Mesmerism seemed to work best when performed in front of a large, paying crowd.

⚓ Inspired by a demonstration given by a popular mesmerist, Quimby, then a self-described "skeptic," decided to try his luck at the intriguing new fad. He pursued his new interest with a clockmaker's precision; soon he developed his own demonstration and took it on the road. In his show, he routinely hypnotized a teenage boy, and yes, as evidenced by an essay Quimby published in 1863, this was actually every bit as weird and awkward as it sounds:

> I will now introduce myself as a mesmerizer, with all the superstitions of a powerful operator. The first trial was with another gentleman, or young man. We all sat down and took hold of each other's hands. Then the gentleman and myself placed our minds on the subject, willing him to sleep. So we sat, puffing and willing him and forcing the electricity out of us into the subject, until we had filled him full. . . . Sometimes he would be so full that we would have to make passes to throw it off. At last he came into the right state. Then, as we had him between us, I wanted to know which had the most power over him. So we sat him in the chair and the gentleman stood in front of him and

I behind him . . . he tried to draw him out of the chair but
he could not start him. We reversed positions, and I went
in front, and I drew him out of the chair. This went to show
that I had the most power (or will).

Soon Quimby began to tweak his act. He dropped the term "mesmerism" and focused on healing. "Whatever you believe is what
you create," Quimby would tell patients. (It was an early sort
of law-of-attraction/vision-board type thing.) "Quimbyism"
would be a prototype for the next century's New Age movement. It was at this point in his career that Quimby awarded
himself an honorary doctorate, just to make everything official.

Quimby's degree may have been fake, but he impressed
many with his apparent sincerity, his gentle manner, and his
devotion to healing the sick. The Quimby Method was based
on a theorem that went something like this: bodily illness is
caused by the mind, or, more specifically, the *beliefs* of the
patient's mind; ergo, the patient's mind can also *remove* the illness. Sickness was merely a mistaken belief, an "error." "Science"
could correct the error (science in this case being the will or
thoughts of the person or healer). It was "science" because it
was the new way; using medicine was the old way. It sounded
like hogwash to many, but there were some credible folks who
were totally sold on the Quimby Method, such as a once-blind
ex-mayor who said the little man's technique had restored his
eyesight.

There were also a lot of folks who regarded what Dr.
Quimby was practicing—using an unseen force to affect the
well-being of other people—as nothing more or less than good
old all-American witchcraft. But Quimby didn't seem to mind

the witchcraft comparisons; as a matter of fact, he was fond of the subject himself, and found the metaphor useful when discussing traditional medicine: "The means used to destroy the evil creates it, as it was in the days of the Salem witchcraft. The course taken to put down the evil was the very way to make it. . . . Now the witches are in the people in the form of disease." Dr. Quimby goes on to tell, in witch terms, the story of a theoretical (or real, who can tell?) patient, a sick young woman who is brought to a physician by her parents because they are certain she has consumption:

> Here she stands before her tormentors like the innocent girl of Salem, accused of being bewitched. She stands pale with quivering lips and glassy eyes . . . nervously suppressing the little nervous cough for fear she would expose herself to the worst of all devils (or barbarians), who stand ready to tear (or choke) her to death . . . or to bind her and cast her into prison for the safety of society.

Anyway, Quimby's story went that the girl did *not* have consumption and that there was no such thing as consumption unless you believed there was; the girl merely had a "nervous cough," yada yada yada. But if the girl's doctor and her parents told her that she had consumption and she *believed* it, the girl would surely languish and die from the disease.

Mary Meets Her Mesmerist

She was a quirky, emaciated, middle-aged woman who had to be half-carried up the stairs to meet Quimby in his office for

the first time on that autumn day. Mary made such an impres- ↲
sion on the others present in Quimby's office that morning that
the meeting was still fresh in their minds many years later: the
thin, shabby woman and her dark, rather dirty hair curled into
long ringlets greasily brushing the shoulders of her severe black
dress. Everything about her screamed poor and needy, and
she seemed a peculiar combination of feeble and agitated. The
first thing Mary did, they recalled, was to inform the great Dr.
Quimby that she was very poor; could he possibly help her get a
cheap place to stay? It wasn't the most auspicious kickoff, but by
the time Mary left the office, she wanted to tell the whole world
the news: she had been cured by Dr. Phineas P. Quimby.

Quimby was Mary's newest and soon-to-be-greatest
obsession. She hunkered down in Portland to devote herself to
learning the Quimby Method; she believed she could do what
he did. By the time Mary's hapless husband finally escaped from
the Confederate prison and headed north, Mary was so devoted
to Quimby-ism that she barely acknowledged his return. Daniel
Patterson ended up having to travel to Maine to see her; they
would eventually divorce.

Mary finally had to leave Portland when the cash ran out,
but she kept up a steady stream of plaintive letters to her idol
Quimby. Her neediness knew no bounds; if it wasn't "Why hast
thou forsaken me," it was "I wish you would come to my aid,
help me sleep, and relieve the confined state of my bowels." She
reported to the healer that his apparition had paid her a visit
one night; it had shown up in the parlor at exactly midnight,
formally attired in hat and dress coat.

Not satisfied with the ghostly Quimby doppelganger,
she soon made the trek to back to Maine, living in a cheap

boardinghouse. She pored over Quimby's manuscripts—he had put together ten volumes expounding his ideas and methods—sat in on lectures and healing sessions, and, one assumes, annoyed Mrs. Quimby quite a bit. She also made friends with other Quimby devotees and pretty much lived a full-immersion Quimby Method lifestyle. Soon Mary began lecturing on the Quimby Method and found she enjoyed speaking before crowds. Then, when she started to perform cures on her own, she knew she had finally found her vocation.

During this time Mary also began experimenting with Spiritualism again and amazed her friend Mrs. Crosby with communications to her from Mary's dead brother, Albert, at least according to what was called a "sworn affidavit" by Mrs. Crosby years later. Albert, whom Mary had adored, was for some reason really interested in chatting up Mrs. Crosby. Mary would fall into a deep trance and then Albert would speak through her in a deep, manly voice. Albert told Mrs. Crosby that he was her "guardian spirit" and that Mary was his "only earthly medium." Once, Albert informed the women that if they looked under a certain sofa cushion, they would find a letter from him, and sure enough, they lifted the cushion and—voilà—there was the letter!

But there was another very strange aspect to Albert's communications to Mrs. Crosby—strange even for a paranormal occurrence. Through Mary's lips, Albert, who had never met Mrs. Crosby in life, warned her to beware of his sister. Mary, the spirit brother said, just might use Mrs. Crosby to further her own ambitions. Albert helpfully added that Mary had had a most difficult life and that she loved Mrs. Crosby very much, so, you know, she shouldn't be too hard on her friend. It was the strangest message Mrs. Crosby had ever received.

From Morphine to Moral Science: Mary Takes Over

Mary's new Quimby-centered lifestyle was destined to end eventually, and within a few years of the commencement of her infatuation it did—Phineas Quimby was dead. Two weeks after the death of her mentor, Mary took the slip on the ice that would change everything.

And about that fall—Dr. Alvin M. Cushing, a non-Quimby Method physician who treated Mary after her slip on the ice, left an account of that pivotal event that differed in some key aspects from Mary's infamous version. He wrote,

> I was called . . . to attend a Mrs. Patterson, wife of Daniel Patterson who had fallen upon the icy sidewalk in front of Mr. Bubier's factory and had injured her head by the fall. Mrs. Patterson has since become Mrs. Baker Glover Eddy. I found her very nervous, partially unconscious, semi-hysterical, complaining by word and action of severe pain in the back of her head and neck.

Okay, so far not so different. Dr. Cushing attended Mary at the home of Samuel Bubier, in front of whose factory she had fallen. He stopped in again the next morning to check on her and found her still crying in pain and insisting on being taken home. Cushing remembered that Mary had proclaimed that "she was going to her home whether we consented or not." No worries: Dr. Cushing had just the thing to deal with hysterical women: "On account of the severe pain and her nervousness, I gave her one-eighth of a grain of morphine, not as a curative remedy, but as an expedient to lessen the pain on removing."

Dr. Cushing, a full-service physician if ever there was one, then went off to secure a sleigh and a pile of blankets so his patient could be transported to her home. When he had the sleigh ready to go and went to get the ailing Mary, he was surprised to find her sleeping like a baby. Dr. Cushing had his new patient carried to the sleigh, and even rode along to her home—and that was where the scenario really turned bizarre. Once they carried her into the house, even several men working together couldn't manage to carry the lightweight patient up the stairs to her bedroom, because, related Cushing, "she was so sound asleep and limp she doubled up like a jack-knife."

Again, Cushing went the extra yard: "So I placed myself on the stairs on my hands and feet, and they laid her on my back, and in that way we carried her upstairs and placed her in bed, and she slept . . . so long I began to fear there had been some mistake in the dose." He then rather unnecessarily added that Eddy "proved to be a very interesting patient." Cushing continued to visit Mary and dose her with morphine. She seemed to have reconsidered the usefulness of traditional medicine; Dr. Cushing said his patient told him she could "feel each dose to the tips of her fingers and toes, and gave me much credit for my ability to select a remedy."

Whether it was Dr. Cushing and his soothing morphine or the wonders of what would come to be called Christian Science that ultimately healed Mary after her terrible accident, it was a new woman who arose from the sickbed. With Quimby gone and a (according to her) miraculous cure under her belt, Mary reinvented herself. She was, she wanted everyone to know, Quimby's prodigy—and she was ready to take over. Her lectures became more and more crowded, as folks looking for solutions to their problems flocked to listen to the strange, compelling woman who was preaching about the powers of what she was now calling "Moral Science." The mind was the cause of all illness, she proclaimed, and she could teach anyone (with enough cash to pay the fee for the course) how to tap the power of the mind to heal themselves and others.

Strange Science

By 1875, Mary was officially calling her movement "Christian Science," and she even bought a building to use as its headquarters. Hanging out the sign that read *Mary Glover's Christian Scientist Home* made it official: Mary was the head of her own religion. Bam.

Also in 1875, a book Mary had long labored over was finally published. It was a tome of a whopping 456 pages, and she titled it *Science and Health*. (For your information, Quimby had called *his* system the Science *of* Health, so, obviously, nobody was *copying* anybody or anything.) While she would soon be accused of stealing Quimby's work, Mary's book did have original, very Mary-esque ideas as well. Mary would continue to update the work and publish revised editions for the rest of her life; today there are over 400 editions of *Science and Health*. Here are a few examples of the important things Mary had to say about health and science and corpses and worms and whatnot:

> Not to admit disease is to conquer it; All disease is the result of education, and disease can carry its ill-effects no farther than mortal mind maps out the way; When there

are fewer prescriptions, and less thought is given to sanitary subjects, there will be better constitutions and less disease—In old times who ever heard of dyspepsia, cerebro-spinal meningitis, hay-fever, and rose-cold? A child may have worms, if you say so, or any other malady, timorously held in the beliefs concerning his body; It is profane to fancy that the perfume of clover and the breath of new-mown hay can cause glandular inflammation, sneezing, and nasal pangs; Man is the same after as before a bone is broken, or a head chopped off; Contemplating a corpse we behold the going out of a belief.

You had to give Mary credit: few other religions going had the panache to use imagery such as corpses and decapitations; it was all really quite attention-grabbing, and quite a few people whose attention it got considered the new Christian Science nothing less than the same old work of the devil.

Mary was now the iteration of herself that would stick: Mary Baker Eddy. Christian Science was entering its heyday, and Mary, perhaps the John Lennon of her time, considered herself somewhere between a doctor and Jesus Christ. While her formal education was sketchy and she was unimpressed with actual medical science—she said a knowledge of medicine was a hindrance to healing—Mary was quite comfortable with practicing medicine herself, right down to prescribing medications. Her style was a bit more like experimentation than doctoring. In *Science and Health* she reported on one of her own case studies on a woman with "dropsy" (edema, or an abnormal accumulation of fluids somewhere in the body); needless to say the *Journal of the American Medical*

Association did not pick it up, but let's give it a run-through anyway:

> A case of dropsy, given up by the faculty, fell into my hands. It was a terrible case. Tapping had been employed, and yet, as she lay in her bed, the patient looked like a barrel.

Diagnosis: terrible case of dropsy with barrel characteristics. Barrel tapped unsuccessfully.

> I prescribed the fourth attenuation of Argentum nitratum with occasional doses of a high attenuation of Sulphuris. She improved perceptibly.

Treatment: a bunch of dangerous-sounding chemical compounds. But it seems to be working!

> Believing then somewhat in the ordinary theories of medical practice and learning that her former physician had prescribed these remedies, I began to fear an aggregation of symptoms from their prolonged use, and told the patient so, but she was unwilling to give up the medicine while she was recovering. It then occurred to me to give her un-medicated pellets and watch the results.

Uh oh. Treatment seems to be working, but . . . it's probably the same treatment an actual physician would prescribe. Treatment stopped. Successful treatment promptly replaced with obviously superior "un-medicated pellets."

I did so, and she continued to gain. Finally she said that she would give up her medicine for one day and risk the effects. After trying this she informed me that she could get along for two days without globules; but on the third day she again suffered, and was relieved by taking them. She went on in this way, taking the un-medicated pellets, and receiving occasional visits from me, but employing no other means, and she was cured.

And so . . . because of or in spite of Mary's capricious doctoring, the patient gradually got better, at least as far as Mary could tell from her "occasional visits." Next patient!

The New Witchcraft Heads to Court in Salem

From the get-go, however, Mary ran into problems with disgruntled students. One young man, Wallace Wright, dutifully paid $300 for the full Mary course. To give a general idea of the value of $300 during this era—in the year 1870, a carpenter in Boston could expect to earn a whopping $2.13 a day. Having shelled out big bucks, Wright was a devoted practitioner of Moral Science for a while before deciding that what Mary had taught him was nothing more or less than good old-fashioned mesmerism, simply hypnotizing people into *thinking* they were well. He also took issue with some of Mary's more over-the-top claims, particularly her assertions that she could walk on water, and *especially* the one that she could raise the dead. He demanded his money back and proceeded to have a knock-down drag out with Mary in the pages of the local newspaper. Then another ex-student sued Mary to get her money back for what she, too, had now determined had been just a whole lot of mumbo jumbo, and the student won.

Mary ran into another big obstacle in her pursuit of fame ⚹ as a healer besides unappreciative students. She continued to have health problems of her own, and she wasn't always able to hide her weakness and pain from her audiences. It was a bit awkward to be proselytizing about the power of the mind over the body and then faint dead away in the midst of a sentence. But it didn't take long for Mary to come up with an explanation that made her health science movement that much more interesting: it was the malignant thoughts of others that caused her illness, she announced. More specifically, one of her followers who had learned the method had then fallen out with her and was now using her own method *against* her. She even had a name for this: malicious animal magnetism, or M.A.M. It was something Quimby had warned could happen.

According to Mary, malicious animal magnetism consisted of transmitting malign thoughts in order to cause harm to another person. M.A.M., she explained, accounted for all of her personal health problems: those frequent fainting spells, and the strange "fits" that continued to afflict her and that were so reminiscent of those that had plagued the bewitched girls of Salem in 1692. If bad thoughts could indeed cause physical harm to someone else, Mary was in big trouble; the roster of her disgruntled students was continuing to grow.

Richard Kennedy was a handsome young man Mary had briefly taken on as a partner; for a while the pair was close. But the magnetic mesmerism of money came between them. In the faith-healing pyramid scheme, Mary believed she was entitled to a cut of any money anyone she had "taught" ever

⁋ earned. In 1872, when Mary demanded that Kennedy turn over a large part of his income to her, he left the organization in a huff. Now, Mary said, Kennedy was out to kill her. She needed the help of her faithful followers for her life to be saved, so she did the obvious thing: she asked her followers to use her method and aim the powers of their minds against Kennedy on her behalf. Whether she specifically thought Kennedy could be killed this way is uncertain, and there was no evidence that they were even close to successful in the dubious endeavor.

⁋ But there was love in the air for Mary as well. On New Year's Day 1877, Mary, who had long claimed she had no use for marriage, surprised her followers by announcing she had married one of her students. Gilbert Eddy was short, quirky, and quiet. He was given to wearing a knitted cardigan jacket— an unusual look for the day, especially for a sewing machine salesman, which was what he was. But Gilbert's most striking feature was the several inches of upward-combed hair that stood at perky attention above his forehead.

But there was still more turmoil on the horizon for the new bride; in 1878, Mary found herself with another problematic ex-student: Civil War veteran Harrison Spofford. The situation with Spofford would go much farther than it had with Kennedy, and before long the case wound up in court in just the town you'd expect a trial about something called "witchcraft" to be held: Salem, Massachusetts.

Mary, being Mary, had brought the case on through expertly played passive aggressiveness. At first, in April of that year, she took Spofford to court to try to recover royalties she believed she was owed; Spofford had been making money practicing her Christian Science on his own, and, as usual, she wanted a cut. This case was quickly dismissed.

Mary decided to crank it up several notches, while still keeping within her passive-aggressive comfort zone. She charged that Spofford had inflicted harm upon the person of one of her female students, Lucretia Brown, of Ipswich, Massachusetts. The case brought Christian Science to public attention as never before, and it wasn't exactly good PR. As local newspapers bemoaned the reemergence of what some were calling the "witchcraft delusion," and others tittered, the judge heard these charges:

> That the said Daniel H. Spofford of Newburyport is a mesmerist, and practices the art of mesmerism, and that by his power and influence he is capable of injuring the persons and property and social relations of others, and does by said means so injure them. That the said Daniel H. Spofford has at divers times and places since the year 1875 wrongfully, maliciously and with the intent to injure the plaintiff, caused the plaintiff by means of his said power and art great suffering of body, severe spinal pains and neuralgia, and temporary suspension of mind.

It was of course what Mary called malicious animal magnetism, but for an added flourish of evil, Mary also called Spofford a "demonologist." All the M.A.M. shenanigans were quickly labeled "the New Witchcraft," and the ensuing court cases became known as the Ipswich Witch Trials, or, inevitably, Second Salem.

In the end, the unorthodox case had the judge scratching his head, if not rolling his eyes. Even if there were such a thing as "M.A.M."—and you could be pretty sure the judge didn't think so—if Spofford were jailed for using it, there would be no way to prevent him from continuing to deploy his malicious mind powers from prison, would there? Under that premise the judge dismissed the case, basically saying, "Now, for the love of God, get out of here with this nonsense." Meanwhile, newspapers accused Mary of setting the country back 200 years, to the time when people dangerously blamed their misfortunes on the evil powers of others. This time, however, there were no courtroom hysterics (it didn't get far enough for that), no chains or dark dungeons, and no swinging nooses high on Gallows Hill; nonetheless, Second Salem is often referred to as the last witchcraft trial in America. And, in support of the "there's no such thing as bad publicity" premise, after Second Salem more people than ever knew the name Mary Baker Eddy, and Christian Science continued to grow.

Like most witchcraft, M.A.M. was only evil when somebody *else* was doing it, and so Mary again resorted to attempting to give her persecutor a taste of his own medicine. She took out a psychic hit on Spofford, recruiting a team of her followers to take turns concentrating their thoughts against him. Apparently this was unsuccessful, because soon Mary allegedly did the unthinkable: she took out an *actual* hit on Spofford.

Gilbert Eddy and Edward Arens, another of Mary's students, were arrested on charges of conspiracy to commit murder, namely the murder of Daniel Spofford. This time, however, nobody was accusing anyone of using their minds; Mary's henchmen had attempted to contract out. They had hired a hitman—one who, unfortunately for Christian Science, double-crossed them.

The charges against Eddy and Arens were eventually dis- ✦ missed. The sensational court case brought Christian Science and Mary Baker Eddy to more national attention than ever, but somehow the publicity seemed to bring in even more followers. In 1881, Mary founded her own college, Massachusetts Metaphysical College, in Boston. As per usual, Mary's life was about to take another unfortunate turn. And, according to Mary, it was all because of an especially devious spell cast on her and her husband by Edward Arens.

Arens had been on Mary's you-know-what list since the hitman debacle, and when Gilbert became ill in early 1882, it could only mean one thing, according to Mary, who just kind of *knew* these things: "arsenical poison, mentally administered." This was, as far as is known, not only the first ever diagnosis of mentally administered arsenical poisoning, but the first *two* diagnoses; Mary was certain that Arens was also poisoning *her*. She experimented by taking what she called "large doses of morphine" to see what effect they might have on the psychic attacks, but ultimately she said it was the power of her mind, not the drug, that fought off the attack. Gilbert, however, continued to get worse until the founder of Christian Science finally called in a regular physician, who said Gilbert had heart disease, not mental arsenical poisoning. Neither Mary nor Gilbert believed him, and Gilbert Eddy died shortly thereafter. And that was when Mary did what others in centuries before her had done to try to confirm a case of death by bewitchment: she asked for an autopsy. According to the story, the physician, knowing Mary's disbelief in physical maladies, actually brought Gilbert's heart directly to her on a tray and pointed out to the new widow the obvious effects of heart disease. Mary took a look at her husband's damaged heart on the tray and then announced to the world that her husband had been assassinated by mental poisoning.

Mary never filed charges against Arens for the murder of her husband, but she did take him to court for stealing parts of *Science and Health* and using them in his own book. Arens's defense was that the work was actually Quimby's, not Mary's, and Quimby had failed to copyright it. Despite Arens's frank and convincing testimony, Mary finally won a case in court; it may have been the highlight of her career. As she saw it, the tenets of Christian Science were officially hers, not Quimby's—and certainly not Arens's. And then, as a nice Salem witch-era flourish, the judge ordered all copies of Arens's book destroyed; Mary wrote, with great satisfaction, that the books were "chopped into pieces by the officers of the law."

In 1908, Mary founded the *Christian Science Monitor*, mostly as an outlet to respond to criticism in other media. A highlight of the publication was Mary's annual listing of all the Christmas presents her followers had sent her, along with the name of each giver—a practice that almost certainly guaranteed her even more gifts the next year. When her publisher gently suggested it might be a good idea to discontinue the practice, Mary informed him that, duh,

> Students are constantly telling me how they felt the mental impression this year to make me no present, and when they overcame it were strengthened and blessed. For

this reason—viz, to discourage mental malpractice and encourage those who beat it—I want that notice published.

The *Monitor*, to the surprise of many, evolved; eventually it earned a reputation as a reliable news source, and long outlasted Mary herself.

Early in the twentieth century, Christian Science membership continued to grow, and so did the large Christian Scientist church complex in Boston—and so did Mary's income. The modest founder began to appear in public resplendent in diamonds and velvet.

Haunted, Hounded

She may have looked like a woman who had it all, but Mary didn't have everything. She had never managed to resume a relationship with her son George, even though at times she lived quite close to him. As an adult George wrote to his now-wealthy mother and asked to come visit; Mary's response was to inform him he was forbidden to visit her. But in 1888, when she was well into her sixties, Mary's maternal instincts found their way to the forefront and she adopted a son. Her new son was named Ebeneezer Foster, and he was forty-one years old. After legally adopting the man, she began calling him Foster Eddy. Another small, quiet, affable guy, Foster obeyed his mother's every wish and was rewarded with the chance to do his mother's errands while wearing a fur-lined coat and diamond pinkie ring. The whole motherhood thing worked so well for Mary that she began instructing her followers to refer to her as "Mother." But after a pretty good decade as mom and son,

⚥ the charm of motherhood began to wear off. Amid rumors of Foster's dalliances with married ladies and the annoyance of his careless bookkeeping, Mary shipped Foster off—literally, on a ship—and ceased calling herself his mother. Before long, Mary was also accusing Foster Eddy of using malignant mesmerism against her.

Instead of enjoying the successes of her endeavors, Mary spent her later years obsessing over the activities of those she considered her enemies. Mrs. Woodbury was to become Mary's greatest female nemesis. A one-time close associate of Mary's turned rival in the science of mental healing and generally being a weird lady, Mrs. Woodbury outdid Mary's adoption of an adult son by giving birth to her own late-life baby—a baby that, she maintained, had been conceived through immaculate conception. Just to make sure folks remembered her son's lineage, Mrs. Woodbury gave him a name from his father's side of the family: the Prince of Peace.

Mary seethed for half a decade before excommunicating Woodbury and presumably the Prince of Peace, too. Woodbury then wasted no time in telling everyone everything she could think of that might embarrass Mary. Mary Baker Eddy, she said, was consumed by fear of witchcraft. She was also fond of reminding folks that Mary had at one time been a Spiritualist medium. Mary inevitably accused Woodbury of using malicious magnetism against her. And so Mary found herself back in the courtroom in her old age, defending herself against charges of libel placed by Mrs. Woodbury. This time, Mary won. Still, she poetically wrote in a letter, "Why O why are the declining years of a life like mine so haunted hounded soulless unpitied?"

While Mary tortured herself throughout her golden years with the belief that her enemies were using mesmerism against her, she was at least able to do it in luxurious surroundings. During the final years of her life she mostly holed up in her mansion in Brookline, Massachusetts, taking morphine. Meanwhile, the elaborate complex of buildings that would become known as the Christian Science Center continued to expand. Mary's estate, which was worth millions, would ensure that the cause of Christian Science would continue to thrive should that dreadful witchcraft she called malignant animal magnetism catch up with her and cause her death.

Mary died on December 3, 1910, of pneumonia. No physician was in attendance. Mary had long viewed death as a sort of reversible condition, and perhaps this is why, after her death, rumors arose and persisted that she had been entombed with a telephone in her vault. Should she find herself healed, the story went, she could pick up the phone, call her house, and let everyone know that Mother had at last reversed the malicious animal magnetism—the dreadful witchcraft—that had almost done her in for good. That is, if anyone answered the phone.

Mary Baker Eddy and Second Salem helped redefine witchcraft for a new century; while the stereotype of Satan's hags riding on poles across moonlit skies was passé, Second Salem did confirm that once endowed with witch-like powers, people were unable to refrain from trying to use them to harm their enemies. It was the dawn of the Progressive Era in America, but it seemed that the primeval pulse of witchcraft was still beating beneath the shiny veneer of the new century.

CHAPTER 13

Bad Times in Booger Hole

The end.

Okay, there is more—but doesn't it seem like just the name "Booger Hole" is enough? Well, it could be, but this is also where we tell you that people from Booger Hole were sometimes called "Boogers." And, on top of that, the fabulously named town of Booger Hole, West Virginia, has its very own witch story. And we're going to begin it like this:

There were unsavory things happening in Booger Hole. Of course there were. In the early 1900s, the unincorporated town in the backwoods hinterland of Clay County had become an epicenter for unsolved murders and strange disappearances. The story usually goes that there were "about a dozen," though nobody seems to really know for sure, and these murders were really only related in the fact that all of the folks in Booger Hole either knew each other or were actually related to one another. But the most infamous of the murders was that of a very formidable little old lady who was allegedly a *witch*.

Booger Hole, it is often said, is named after the Booger Man, a.k.a. Boogie Man, a.k.a. the person or entity Booger Holers sometimes conveniently blamed for all those murders. But since many say the area had been known as Booger Hole even before that series of unfortunate events, there may be a different but certainly just as interesting origin for the name, especially since the scrappy little log cabin village was also sometimes referred to as "Bugger Hole."

It did seem folks had a way of disappearing in Booger Hole, leaving behind nothing but whispered rumors and occasionally an abruptly ending trail of blood. The list of folks involved in the mysterious and violent Booger Hole saga reads like the cast of characters in a pitch for a quirky, soon-to-be-cult-favorite HBO series:

Lacy Ann Boggs. Said to be a "peculiar old woman"; new in town, she lived alone and weren't a-feared of no man. Also, she was a witch.

The Cottrells. Father and son farmers; believed they were bewitched by Lacy Boggs.

Joe Clark. Fixed clocks. Time ran out for him when he came to Booger Hole.

John Henry, a.k.a. "The Peddler." Booger Hole wasn't buying what he was selling.

Caroline Moore. Was wrapped in a sheet by her brother; gnawed a hole in the sheet and saw a sight that would come back to haunt her.

Preston Tanner. His wife was too hot for his own good.

Margaret Moore. She got around. A femme fatale with two grown "nephews" thought to be her sons by two different fellas. Called herself an "unmarried widow."

Henry Hargis. Possibly a son of Margaret Moore. Possibly murdered by eccentric possible half-brother James Moore.

James Moore. Argued with possible half-brother Henry Hargis over an inheritance. Prone to staring hypnotically

at the ground as if waiting for something—or someone—
to come out of it. Said he didn't know anything about body
found buried beneath his cabin.

Frederic Moore and Rosa Lyons. Brother/sister team; possibly murderers, definitely up to something sinister.

Howard Sampson. In love with Preston Tanner's wife.
Accused murderer.

Andrew Sampson. Father of Howard. Accused murderer.
Not welcome in Booger Hole.

It transpires that the tale of the Booger Hole murders is impen-
etrably convoluted and muddled by the varying names some
folks were known by, the community's predilection for living
off what little grid there was back in those days, and the fact
that newspapers proved unreliable narrators when it came to
Booger Hole. (Perhaps they were just so gleeful to be printing
the words "Booger Hole" that they didn't worry too much about
getting the facts straight.) The names of folks involved in one
case were often switched out for names of folks from another
case, depending on which paper you read. Now, if we get into
the whole "who murdered whom in Booger Hole" thing, we'll
be here all day, so for our purposes, which are of the witch type,
we'll mostly stick here to the murder of the alleged witch, Miss
Lacy Ann Boggs (with guest appearances by some of the other
characters)—the case that was the centerpiece of what became
known as the Booger Hole Murders.

Booger Hole's Very Bad Beginnings

Booger Hole, lying somewhere in the vicinity of Big Otter,
West Virginia, was a land of rolling hills, rocky gorges, creeks

that were sometimes tainted with blood, and dense woods and thickets that hid dark secrets. The Hole was founded by pioneer types who were fervently self-sufficient and who not only weren't scared of being all alone out in the backwoods of wherever-it-was West Virginia, but even preferred it that way. Because truth be told, sometimes folks were up to things that would be best kept to themselves. During the Civil War, bushwhackers of the worst kind claimed the area, seeing the chaos of war as an opportunity to rob, rape, and murder. After the Civil War, Booger Hole never quite recovered, and the combination of rough-hewn pioneer-cum-outlaws, mixed in with the bloodthirsty taste for vengeance left from the war, made for a deadly brew. To be quite fair, the Hole wasn't alone in its bad reputation; the entire county and surrounding areas were putrescent with rumors of incest, murdered infants, blood feuds, lynchings, and pretty much any unsavory doing anyone could think of.

Amid the shady criminal element, which was admittedly considerable, there were also plenty of good, hard-working folks. One of the more forward-thinking residents of the general vicinity financed a schoolhouse for the often-illiterate offspring of Booger Hole's residents, who, along with their parents, promptly pretended not to see it. Eventually all pretense of education was abandoned, and so was the schoolhouse itself. There was more than one abandoned place in Booger Hole, and anyone with any sense of self-preservation knew those were just the places to avoid. At any given time, so the stories go, one might expect to encounter anything from moonshiners to trysting dirt farmers to throat-slashers to spooks and witches— possibly all at the same time—if one wandered very far afield.

Booger Hole: Not Welcoming to Witches

If there was one thing Booger Holers (okay, *Boogers*) didn't like—besides schoolteachers, revenuers, and officers of the law—it was outsiders. Case in point: the man known as "the Peddler," who had apparently not gotten the memo about the Hole's dislike of non-Holers and stopped by sometime around the turn of the century. He had been going from house to house (or shack to shack, as the case may be), peddling, one assumes, his wares, when he unceremoniously vanished between point A and point B, with the inevitable whispers of foul play quickly ensuing.

It probably stood to reason that when Lacy Boggs, an elderly widow from neighboring Roane County, came to town in 1899 looking for a place to settle, folks commenced whispering. For starters, Lacy was a relation of the fellow who had built the old unwanted schoolhouse, and since it wasn't being used for anything else, he let Annie go ahead and move on in. There she dwelled in the decrepit old place, so run down it didn't even have glass in the windows. For Lacy, it was a fixer-upper dream house. She tacked some old quilts up over the broken-out windows, put in a big garden, and installed her rocking chair in a cozy spot in front of a window. For an old gal, she was pretty badass; she wasn't at all spooked by the fact that, sometime before she moved in, somebody had supposedly been murdered there. The alleged murder-ee, Joseph Clark, had last been seen overnighting (sleeping one off?) in the abandoned schoolhouse, and he vanished under mysterious circumstances—trail-of-blood-type mysterious circumstances. The trail of blood in question had started at the schoolhouse and led toward the creek, but stopped abruptly just short of the water.

At any rate, Lacy's fearless independent streak didn't sit 'ʾ so well with some in Booger Hole. The fact that this feisty old woman had the nerve to pick up and move to a new town in her dotage—why, it was enough to make folks think she had been run out of town for being a witch or something! Actually, according to Lacy's kinfolk back home, she *had* been run out of town for being a witch. At least that was the rumor. It didn't take long until it became a generally accepted Booger Hole fact: old Lacy Boggs was a witch.

Belief in witches was common enough in the hills of West Virginia, as folk magic was still practiced, especially for healing. Belief in "haints," or ghosts, and all manner of superstition held sway. Patrick W. Gainer, a professor and folklorist, traveled to the backwoods of West Virginia over the course of fifty years, talking to old-timers and collecting stories, which he compiled in *Witches, Ghosts, and Signs: Folklore of the Southern Appalachian*. He wrote that "almost without exception" the folks who told him these weird tales thoroughly believed them. One of the stories Gainer heard firsthand was about a witch—our heroine—whom he called "The Witch of Booger Hole."

Revenge Riding

Old Man Cottrell was the Booger Holer most vexed and ⤵ bewitched by Lacy Boggs. His complaint: Lacy Boggs was "riding" him at night until he thought he'd die. Being ridden by a witch usually entails having the witch visit you in the night while you're asleep, place you into a state resembling sleep paralysis (probably sleep paralysis), climb on top of you, and sort of physically commandeer your body as a conveyance on her unsavory errands of the night, or possibly just for a thrill ride. It's described as a draining, painful experience, although in Cottrell's case apparently being "ridden" was a whole lot more literal. We're talking saddle and bridle literal. When Gainer was gathering his West Virginia stories, he spoke with a woman identified only as "the grand-daughter-in-law" of Lacy Boggs, and she knew all about the strange affair: she had been there. She even confirmed the night-riding incident—sort of. She told Gainer that a neighbor man (presumably Cottrell) had asked to borrow "Grandma's" mare, old Fannie, to do some plowing. Lacy reluctantly acquiesced, with the stipulation that he not work the old horse too hard. When the neighbor returned the horse in a worn-out condition, she was livid, hollering, "You ruined my mare!" She decided to teach the horse-abuser a lesson. She told him, "You worked her too hard, she looks mighty peaked! Now I'm a-gonna ride you every night til you're just as peaked as old Fannie!"

Did the granddaughter-in-law believe it? Well, she wouldn't necessarily rule it out: "Some folks around said Grandma was a witch and that she could do strange things. I don't think Grandma ever witched anyone, but then again, she mighta done it." Fair enough. Granddaughter-in-law also said the man had been mighty sorry he hadn't minded Lacy Boggs. He claimed that the witch had indeed followed through on her threat and pulled a classic witch stunt: she had shown up in his bedroom in the night and made certain he got a taste of his own medicine. "She had put a bridle on him and rode him all over Pine Knob. He'd wake up in the morning all tired out with burrs in his hair and his mouth sore from the bridle bit."

These equestrian antics had gone on until the man was ⸝ "almost crazy." But Lacy had more horse-related witchery up her sleeves. The old lady had her suspicions about what had happened to Henry Hargis, one of the Hole's most notoriously missing persons. Henry was a Holer who had vanished after coming into the large fortune of $300; neither Hargis nor his cash had been seen since 1893. The granddaughter-in-law said,

> Grandma thought she knew one of the men who had killed Henry Hargis, so they say she put a spell on this man's horse so that he couldn't ketch it. The horse had always been tame, but now every time the man would come near it, it would kick and bite. He had an idea that Grandma had put a spell on his horse so he went to her and begged her to take the spell off his horse. She said "All right I'll take the spell off your horse if you tell me where Henry Hargis is buried." Well, he finally told her.

The talk of witching was one thing, but an outsider knowing too much about the dark deeds of certain Booger Holers was another matter entirely. If she knew where Hargis was buried, she might have a pretty good idea of who had done him in; apparently Booger Holers could be counted on to keep their murder victims close. Pretty soon, a new rumor started going round, and it was a bad one: the witch was going to be lynched.

Lacy Boggs wasn't lynched, but she was sure enough murdered. One night, as she sat in her rocking chair smoking her corncob pipe, and, according to some, peeling an apple and regaling a little granddaughter with wild Indian tales from her youth on the frontier (talk about multitasking), someone nudged aside the old quilt that hung over a window, poked a shotgun barrel inside, and fired.

Cottrell, having made a big fuss over the whole being ridden by Boggs in the night thing, was a natural suspect, and so was his son, who claimed Boggs had started riding him at night, too. The Law hauled the Cottrells in, and their trials made for some unlikely court testimony. Deputy United States Marshal Dan Cunningham recalled the trials in his 1928 memoirs:

> The two Cottrells swore that Mrs. (Lacy) Annie Boggs was a witch, said she would come to their cabin in the night carrying a bridle and saddle. She would put the bridle and saddle on one of them and ride him all over the neighborhood and out as far as Blue Knob where there were chestnuts, burrs, and briars, then she would ride him back home, unbridle him and unsaddle him and bridle and saddle the other one.

The Cottrells had been happy to testify in court to their claims about Lacy bewitching and riding them, but they insisted they hadn't had anything to do with her killing. The pair was eventually set free, as there was no evidence that they had done the old lady in. But there were others in Booger Hole who had reason to want Lacy Boggs dead. Just before her murder, Lacy, in front of a roomful of Booger Holers, had announced that she "could light her pipe and before it burned out go to the place where Henry Hargis was buried." This, of course, was bad news for Hargis's killer, and since folks in Booger Hole tended to help one another out quite a bit, also bad news for any accomplices in the case. It took several years, but sure enough a whole

group of Holers were eventually arrested for having a part in ⳑ
the killing of Lacy Ann Boggs; almost simultaneously, one John
Lyons and his brother-in-law, James Moore (who was also possibly half-brother to Hargis), were arrested for the murder of
Henry Hargis.

Disturbing new evidence had come to light about the murder of Hargis. James Moore's sister, Caroline, testified that one
night as a little girl she had seen her brother and his accomplice
John Lyons bury Hargis—*inside* the Moore cabin. Caroline said
her brother and Lyons had wrapped her up in a sheet to keep
her from witnessing their criminal activities, forgetting that
wrapping someone up in a sheet has the inherent effect of making her even more curious about what you're doing, while also
making her not want to die of suffocation. Thus, little Caroline
had "gnawed" a hole in the sheet ("Gnawed Hole in Sheet and
Saw Brother Commit Crime" was a resulting headline) just in
time to see a Henry Hargis–sized figure being dumped into a
shallow grave under the cabin floor. She had tried to tell folks
afterward, she said, but nobody would listen to her; it was very
likely she had been warned to keep quiet.

Sure enough, the remains of Henry Hargis, or at least what
remained of his remains, were uncovered beneath the kitchen
hearth of the Moores' home: bits of bone, tufts of hair, and a
pair of cufflinks bearing his initials. This simultaneously solved
the disappearance of Hargis, called into question the stereotype
that all Booger Hole men were bad dressers, and at least partly
accounted for the bad smell that would waft over the Hole when
Mrs. Moore would slow-cook venison stew.

The Booger Hole saga, with its bloody trail, midnight ⳡ
burial, the shrouding of a little girl in a sheet and silencing

of her story, and the execution of an old lady who knew too much, proved again that there were things in the world a whole lot more dangerous than witches. Yet with all these macabre and terrible goings-on, the Booger Hole murders were framed around the character of Witch Boggs, demonstrating that even in the early twentieth century belief in witchcraft lingered in the psyche of America—and that a witch trumped a Boogie Man any day.

CHAPTER 14

The York Hex Murder: A Twentieth-Century Witch Hunt Gone Wrong

I got the witch.

—John Blymyer, 1929 court testimony

The baleful braying of an unhappy mule pierced the crisp November air in Rehmeyer's Hollow in York County, Pennsylvania. The animal's cries became relentless enough that they brought Oscar Gladfelter over to his neighbor's farm to find out what was going on. There, in Nelson Rehmeyer's barn, he found the distressed mule, apparently unfed for several days. Gladfelter was concerned. It seemed odd that Rehmeyer would neglect his animal; it just wasn't like the hard-working farmer. Something unsettling hung in the air as Gladfelter approached the farmhouse; it could have been a tinge of smoke, or perhaps it was the unnatural quiet at the home where there should have been signs of life. He climbed onto the familiar porch and knocked on the door. The silence inside remained unbroken. Gladfelter tried the doorknob and opened the old farmhouse door onto a scene of horror.

Down and Out in York County

In twentieth-century America, there were always the tried and true motives for murder: greed, jealousy, and, of course, the occasional grisly work of a random drifter following some dark urge. But in the 1920s, a surprising motive for murder crept out of the shadows and took a horrified Pennsylvania community by surprise. It was witchcraft. Americans were *pretty* sure they were safe from the stereotypical witches of colonial days, those sinister hags who liked to murder babies, turn themselves into malicious cats or hogs, and appear in midnight bedrooms to torment sleepers just for kicks. *Those* witches had been relegated to storybooks and All Hallows Eve merriment. But that didn't mean that *all* folks had given up on the idea—or even the practice—of spellcasting. As a matter of fact, witchcraft was at the heart of one of the most high-profile murder cases of the 1920s.

The central character in this strange case was a troubled young man named John Blymyer. Blymyer had been down on his luck, and not just in the way a guy born poor and raised in a rural community, with little education and a life of manual labor stretching before him like an unending punitive sentence, could expect to be down on his luck. Blymyer had spent his entire life on shaky ground. The child of hard-working German immigrants, John had developed opnema as an infant. Opnema was a colloquialism democratically used for both livestock and babies that was described as a wasting disease wherein the baby—or cow—would begin uncontrollably losing weight, sometimes until death resulted. It was essentially malnutrition, and, between the poverty and lack of education rampant in rural Pennsylvania, the malady was not uncommon. This childhood malnutrition could have been a contributing factor to the lifelong physical and mental disabilities that awaited Blymyer.

Neighbors described little John Blymyer as an awkward sort, sickly and short of friends. He didn't last long in school, and then jobs didn't last long for him, either. This gave him more time to obsess over his avocation, for there was one constant in John Blymyer's life, and it was a bit of a strange one: pow-wowing, a.k.a. faith healing, a.k.a. *witchcraft*. Today we might call it folk medicine. In Blymyer's community, it wasn't unusual; the rural southern Pennsylvania area had been settled by German immigrants who brought their own special brand of magic with them, magic that was a quirky combination of Christianity and sorcery. Though pow-wowing incorporated incantations, which were similar to Christian prayers, it often involved other things. Things like, oh, a potato or a lock of hair or, well . . . *blood*.

Practitioners of pow-wowing were known as pow-wow artists, witches, wizards, conjurers, and a host of other honorariums of dubious implication. Pow-wowers didn't mind answering to "doctor," but the practice didn't limit itself to medical issues; through pow-wowing, lost objects could be located, men could be protected in battle, and fire could be stopped in its tracks.

Since they were being used by human beings, we couldn't expect the powers of the pow-wow artists to be used only for good, and this is where the concept of "putting a hex" on someone comes in. "Hexing" is just another way of saying "putting a spell" on someone, and it seems those who believed in hexing suspected they had been hexed a lot more often than they actually were hexed. Seriously—pow-wow artists just had too many ailing babies and wormy livestock to tend to; who had time for recreational hexing? But hexing, like bewitching, got blamed for an awful lot of hard luck, and hard luck was the one thing folks like John Blymyer had in spades.

The Long Lost Friend

There was a tangible object at the heart of the magic of many pow-wow artists: a magical spell book. Though folk healing was usually passed down through practice and word of mouth within families and communities, actually possessing one of these spell books was believed to enhance the power of the pow-wow artist. In John Blymyer's story, there was one particular spell book that would spell big trouble.

As one might reasonably expect, the book in question was of mysterious origin, but it certainly *sounded* innocuous enough: it was called *The Long Lost Friend*. The book was compiled by an immigrant named John George Hohman, who set sail from Germany in 1802 and settled among the Pennsylvania Dutch, where he set up a publishing business. Hohman first printed a version of *The Long Lost Friend* in 1820, but the book's magical roots stretched way back into the old country, and, according to tradition, possibly even back to ancient times. It's not hard to see the Christian influence in the pow-wows in *The Long Lost Friend*, although they tend to be a bit more colorful than typical prayers, and they are often pretty specific in topic. For instance, there's this handy charm, which is said to help with a common, everyday problem:

> A good remedy for worms, to be used for men, as well as for cattle:
> Mary, God's mother, traversed the land,
> Holding three worms close in her hand;
> One was white, the other was black, the third was red.
> This must be repeated three times, at the same time stroking the person or animal with the hand; and at the end of each application strike the back of the person or the animal, to wit: at the first application once, at the second application twice, and at the third application three times; and then set the worms a certain time, but not less than three minutes.

This charm is also good to use if you want to convince someone you have obsessive-compulsive disorder in addition to worms.

Sometimes, pow-wows were more like recipes, like this one for catching fish: "Take rose seed and mustard seed, and the foot of a weasel, and hang these in a net, and the fish will certainly collect there." Presumably one would first use a spell to get the foot from the weasel; we couldn't find that one. But here's another one to "bond a dog to a person":

> Try to draw some of your blood, and let the dog eat it along with his food, and he will stay with you. Or scrape the four corners of your table while you are eating, and continue to eat with the same knife after having scraped the corners of the table. Let the dog eat those scrapings, and he will stay with you.

Typically, you could probably expect the dog to stay with you without the addition of the blood to the food, but either way.

There were several variations of the spell book used by the pow-wowers, but they generally incorporated the same charms as those described in *The Long Lost Friend*. In the mountains of Maryland in the 1800s, where some of the Pennsylvania Dutch eventually relocated, a folk healer known as Wizard Zittle carried a German version from which he practiced, and he published *his* own English version: *Friend in Need: Sympathetic Knowledge*. That book begins cryptically:

> The arts contained in this book are taken from an ancient manuscript, which was found in the possession of an old hermit who dwelt as wizards do a hundred years in a cave, in the valleys of Gran Buenos, and in that vicinity accomplished many marvelous things, and among others, banished a ferocious dragoness, with her litter, consisting of four young ones who frequented the forest.

Well, that all seems plausible enough, and who doesn't like a mother of dragons? After the big, dragon-heavy buildup, *Friend in Need: Sympathetic Knowledge* goes on to offer more practical spells, like this one said to stop bleeding, which most likely wasn't written with bagel-slicing lacerations in mind, though it would probably be applicable just the same:

> As soon as a person is cut, breathe on the cut three times; pray the Lord's Prayer three times; and say the Three Highest Names three times. The blood will stop.

And then there's this one to cure a sty, which, unlike most of the other charms, has a reassuring emphasis on sterilization:

> Dip a clean thumb in alcohol. Close your sty eye. Repeat as follows: sty blister sty, I rub you with my clean thumb that you must remove and purify. The Three Highest: Father, Son, and Holy Ghost. Rinse eyelid with water. Do 3 times.

The spells were of impressive variety. For those living in bad neighborhoods, there are spells claiming to stop bullets and catch horse thieves. There are also spells for curing opnema, or the "go-backs"—the condition that the infant John Blymyer had almost died from. There is also a handy spell for curing "thislo," for which there seems to be no modern counterpart; maybe the pow-wowers actually wiped that one off the face of the earth. But it might be fun to try the cure and see if something that's been ailing you finally goes away.

Folks in Blymyer's world knew well the powers of charms such as these, and many even credited the magic with saving family members, livestock, and crops. But despite its helpful reputation, *The Long Lost Friend* would be the pivotal prop in the unimaginable tragedy that would soon ensue in the otherwise unremarkable York County.

A Spell of Bad Luck

John Blymyer was the odd boy out as a child, but not necessarily because he started practicing pow-wowing as an eight-year-old. Pow-wowing was common enough in the rural county, and the practice was said to go back several generations in the Blymyer family. But John did have some issues; he was troubled by strange visions from a very early age, for starters. He also had a tendency toward sickliness and seldom attended school, which didn't particularly help him overcome the label "slow-witted" that he seemed to have been knighted with. On top of all that, his peers made great fun of his appearance: he was thin of frame and large of nose. John dropped out of school at thirteen to work in a cigar factory. All in all, he was *not* having a good time.

John did occasionally perform pow-wow services in York County; it was the one thing he felt he was good at. He charged no fee—it was considered bad luck to take money for pow-wowing—and he was considered competent enough in the art. The highlight of his pow-wowing career came when he used a charm to calm a rabid dog, an event that was, fortunately, witnessed by a number of witnesses. They said a snarling, foaming-at-the-mouth beast had approached John and a group of his co-workers. John quickly deployed the appropriate incantation, and not only did the charm get the aggressive dog to chill out, it also actually *cured* its rabies! As the froth disappeared from its muzzle, Blymyer patted the dog on the head; it was last seen trotting off behind him as he walked home. But apparently rabid dogs weren't enough of a problem in York to make John's peers want to hang out with him on a regular basis.

Several years later, the long-lonely Blymyer may have thought things were looking up when he found a gal willing to marry him, but the couple's first baby, a little girl, died in infancy, and then their second baby, another girl, died too. Blymyer was let go from his job at a local factory, and then his wife announced he was being let go from his marriage as well; John Blymyer's hard-luck life had become a Groundhog Day of loss. He began having trouble sleeping and eating, and he also fretted over what he saw as his waning pow-wow powers. No matter what pow-wows or spells he tried on himself, he just couldn't turn his luck around. He began telling folks that he was certain someone had hexed him. He would lock himself in his room for long periods of time, where he could be heard talking to himself—or someone that only he could see. Blymyer's soon to be ex-father-in-law decided the thin, jittery young man had lost his mind, and he managed to get Blymyer committed to an institution. But the troubled young man had no faith in traditional medicine or hospitals, so he casually walked away from the institution one day (nobody seemed to notice).

Blymyer visited some of the other area pow-wowers for advice; although pow-wowers could sometimes be competitive, when they themselves had problems they couldn't solve, they, like others in the community, turned to other pow-wowers. These local wizards all confirmed John's fears: someone had put a hex on him. And that someone, of course, could only be another person with pow-wow powers. John Blymyer was now certain that a witch had it in for him.

It was during this period that, for once in his life, Blymyer had friends of a sort; he had found himself a pair of compatriots who shared his predicament. They were two local boys, seventeen-year-old Wilbert Hess and fourteen-year-old John Curry; both believed they, too, had been hexed. The Hess family had once run a thriving farm, but now all they had left were failing crops and that time-honored hallmark of bewitchment, sick hogs. Ma and Pa Hess were about at the end of their rope, and often told Wilbert the whole family had been hexed.

John Curry, meanwhile, was suffering through the jinxed life of an abused child from a poverty-stricken home, where nobody seemed to notice or care whether he was home or not. As the trio commiserated and bonded over their sad state of affairs, Blymyer grew uncharacteristically proactive. He was going to find the rat fink of a pow-wower who was putting evil hexes on people, and by golly, he was going to make him stop.

Blymyer kept making the circuit to various local pow-wowers, who continued to confirm that he had been hexed, though none of them knew who was doing the hexing. At last the desperate Blymyer found himself at the home of an especially powerful lady pow-wower. She was known as the River Witch, a.k.a. Nellie Noll, and she quickly determined exactly where Blymyer's particularly pernicious strain of bad luck had come from. The name she gave was a familiar one to the young man: Nelson D. Rehmeyer, lifelong denizen of nearby Rehmeyer Hollow and respected pow-wow artist.

White Witch Problems

Like Blymyer, Rehmeyer had been brought up steeped in the Pennsylvania Dutch pow-wow tradition, only with more education and less starvation. But the two witches did have more in common than pow-wowing and their oddly rhyming names. Blymyer had worked on the farm of the older witch in the past, digging potatoes. Now, said the River Witch, Rehmeyer had hexed him, and hexed him good. (If Blymyer asked why, exactly, the other man did this, it is not recorded.) But not to worry; she had just the prescription to break the spell: Blymyer must cut off a lock of Witch Rehmeyer's hair and bury it six feet beneath the hardening November ground. By some accounts, ‥ the River Witch also told Blymyer that he should liberate a certain book that Nelson Rehmeyer was known to possess and bury it as well, although according to other accounts he was supposed to burn it. The book, of course, was Rehmeyer's copy of *The Long Lost Friend.*

What would you do if you were raised on pow-wowing, witchcraft, and faith healing, and you believed that someone had put a hex on you, and that you had to get a lock of his hair or your bad luck would continue forever? In that hard-to-imagine circumstance, perhaps you would first pay a visit to the pow-wower in question and just kind of scope out the situation; at least that's the reason Blymyer gave for enlisting fourteen-year-old John Curry to accompany him on a visit to Rehmeyer's Hollow on the rainy night of November 26, 1928.

Although Rehmeyer is often described as a "recluse," he apparently had quite a bit of game. The fellows found him not at home that night, and stopped by the house of the farmer's estranged wife, just up the road, to see if perhaps he was there. The Rehmeyers had remained quite friendly in spite of—or perhaps because of—their separation, and that night Mrs. Rehmeyer informed the young men that Nelson was out with a lady-friend. The guys returned to the farm and spent some time creeping around in the dark outside the modest but neat farmhouse in the cold rain. Hidden in the darkness, the pair finally spied the farmer return and watched him enter the house; moments later, they knocked on the farmhouse door. They soon found themselves in the cozy, lamp-lit parlor chatting with Rehmeyer, who had apparently had quite a pleasant evening and was in a genial mood. Casually, Blymyer inquired as to whether Rehmeyer did indeed own a copy of *The Long Lost Friend*, as they had heard. He owned that he did. *Cha-ching!* Blymyer began to think he might see a light at the end of his dark tunnel of misfortune.

In one of the more surreal aspects of the crime, the young men and the older farmer had such an enjoyable evening, and their fraternization went on for so long that the farmer invited his visitors to stay the night. The pair accepted and settled in to spend the night in the parlor. Blymyer had difficulty sleeping, though; as he lay there in the darkness, he attempted to use some on-the-fly mind power to will Rehmeyer into rising from his bed, fetching his spell book, and handing it and a piece of his hair over like an agreeable sleepwalker. But the older witch did not stir. Blymyer drifted into a fitful sleep.

Blymyer and Curry awoke the next morning to find Rehmeyer setting the kitchen table for a home-cooked farm breakfast that they happily, and—unused to such hospitality— perhaps a bit suspiciously, devoured. Then they left. What had they learned from their visit? That Rehmeyer was a really nice guy who would have had no reason to hex several random people? Nope. According to testimony, what Blymyer learned from the previous night's reconnaissance was that Nelson Rehmeyer was a whole lot bigger than he had remembered. The old guy also looked to be a heck of a lot stronger than one would expect from a man of his age. As he planned a return visit, Blymyer knew he would need a third person to help subdue Rehmeyer long enough to secure the needed bounty, and he knew that third person would be his pal Wilbert Hess. Also: he was going to need some really strong rope.

A Friend in Need

Blymyer brought his best anti-witch game when he went to the
Hess home to ask Wilbert to come with him back to Rehmeyer's
Hollow. As Wilbert, his brother Clayton, and his parents watched,
Blymyer whipped out a Bible and read some witch-related verses,
but he was preaching to the choir. The Hess family may not have
had much formal education among them, but they were all well
schooled in the ways of pow-wowing and witches. So when
Blymyer finally informed them that the entire family had been
bewitched by Nelson Rehmeyer, he didn't really need to try very
hard to convince them. Nonetheless, he skillfully spun his web,
dramatically recounting his visit to the River Witch and explaining
what needed to happen in order for the spell to be broken. Wilbert,
Blymyer frankly stated, would be needed to come along with him
and John Curry to the Hollow to help restrain old Rehmeyer.

It sounded like a lot of trouble to Wilbert, not to mention not very neighborly. Plus, he really hadn't been feeling too
well. Even as he hesitated, Ma Hess spoke up. The possibility
of changing the family's sour luck sounded pretty good to her.
She told Wilbert to go along and help. "All right, Ma," the boy
said resignedly; then he sighed and followed his gaunt, haunt-
ed-looking friend out the door. John Blymyer, Wilbert Hess,
and John Curry made their way to Rehmeyer's Hollow under
a full moon. The next day was Thanksgiving, but none of them
were thinking about food.

Getting the Witch

John Blymyer's second visit to the Rehmeyer farmhouse that
November would not be so neighborly; he arrived at the hollow

❦ wound up for a fight. For him, it was a matter of life or death. For Wilbert Hess, it was a family obligation. And for young John Curry, it was a weird, welcome adventure. Later, when asked on the stand why he had gone along with Blymyer on his visit to Rehmeyer's Hollow, he would answer, "I wanted to see some of this witchcraft performed."

Nelson Rehmeyer must have been disappointed to see the young men return that night, so aggressive and confrontational, after his hospitality the night before. But he probably wasn't frightened, not at first. He was used to fending for himself in the hollow, and he was well aware of his own strength. When Blymyer demanded the hair and the pow-wow book, Rehmeyer felt no compunction about telling him to get lost. Later, Blymyer would insist that he and the boys had only tied Rehmeyer up and started beating him *after* he had refused to cooperate. If he'd only given them the book and let them take a piece of his hair, everything would have been just hunky-dory. But regardless of the intent, the facts remain that the trio executed what was basically a home invasion, and then they executed the man who just that morning had generously prepared a hot (and probably really good) breakfast for two of them.

The crime scene told the terrible story, and courtroom testimony filled in the blanks. The farmhouse kitchen had been the setting of the horror. What was left of Nelson Rehmeyer's body was mixed in with the remains of an old mattress and a blanket, forming a charred nightmare of bone, blood, and ash on the floor. Scorched bits of rope ornamented the farmer's body, suggesting he had been tied up, and one of his legs had burned away right through the floor, leaving a hole looking down into dark, smoldering nothingness. Pieces of a broken wooden chair lay here and there like random afterthoughts of mayhem.

Investigators were struck by the eerie dissonance of the crime scene: the body had burned, but the house had not. Then they realized that before the murderers fled the scene, in the hope of having it burn to the ground, they had closed the house up tight; but this action had effectively kept out any air that might have spread the fire. Meanwhile, in a macabre handiwork of nature, the victim's own body fluids had helped snuff out the impromptu funeral pyre.

The police began their search for the killers in the right place. One quick visit to Rehmeyer's estranged wife's place up the road later, and they had the identities of their suspects: the odd young men who had visited Mrs. Rehmeyer the night before looking for the farmer. Now the police were looking for Blymyer and Curry, whom they soon found and arrested, and when the pair implicated Hess, they were ready to prosecute. Trials would begin with the New Year, 1929.

The York Hex Murder Trial

While prosecutors tried to frame the murder as a robbery gone wrong—which in a way it was—and to leave witchcraft out of it altogether, they were unable to do so. Witchcraft was at the dark heart of the crime, and as soon as Wilbert Hess's brother Clayton took the stand as the witness to whom Blymyer had first confessed, the gig was up. The confession, Clayton said on the witness stand, had consisted of four words: "I got the witch."

The press immediately came down with witch fever and descended on the newly christened York Witchcraft Trial in swarms. "Witches Ride Broomsticks in Hex Trial" and other attention-getting headlines greeted eager readers. Newspapers all over the world reported the sensational details that emerged from the courtroom each day, details that went something like this: according to John Blymyer, Rehmeyer had resisted, forcing Blymyer to smash him in the head with a wooden chair. As planned, Blymyer and his accomplices tied Rehmeyer to another kitchen chair with pre-cut pieces of the length of rope bought at a local hardware store earlier that day. Wilbert Hess smashed a block of wood into the head of the restrained farmer; then Blymyer took the block from him and smashed it even harder into the old witch's head. Their stories conflicted as to which had executed the blow that killed Rehmeyer; each blamed the other. John Curry admitted that he had poured lamp oil over the body of their victim so Blymyer could light him on fire.

Though they believed the house would go up in flames and destroy any evidence of their crime, Rehmeyer had remained an oddly self-contained fire and burned himself out expeditiously. The young men confessed that they had also taken a small amount of money from Rehmeyer, but no one had snipped any of his hair. This was because, Blymyer explained, the hex was already good and broken by the farmer's death, and besides, all the witch's hair was going to end up buried anyway, along with the rest of his remains. Done and done.

Newspapers were far from evenhanded in their descriptions of the three accused murderers and their seemingly lowbred families. One reporter described Wilbert Hess as a "shifty eyed superstitious youth of eighteen with a head full of superstitious ideas" and went on to advise readers that "this tall gangling youth that was raised in an atmosphere of witchcraft and medieval traditions will reveal to the jury the twisted mental psychology that made him a willing fool in the slaying of Rehmeyer." Oh, and P.S., the paper added, Hess's mother was "matronly-looking." Blymyer, another article noted, was "ferrety"; meanwhile, young John Curry, who had helped set Rehmeyer's body on fire, was said to be "apple-cheeked."

During his trial, Blymyer seemed uncharacteristically calm. He told reporters that before the hex was lifted he hadn't been able to eat or sleep—had literally been wasting away— "but ever since we killed Rehmeyer I have felt fine—better in fact than at any other time in my life." His parents were called in to testify, and, as he watched disinterestedly, the origins of John Blymyer's issues became a bit clearer. On the witness stand his father had great difficulty in recalling the number of children in the family; he finally settled on six. His mother testified that, yes, indeedy, her son was hexed all right; he had been most of his life. As a matter of fact, she added, in addition to the pow-wow-ing they had had done on him in his infancy for the wasting disease, she and his father had had their boy pow-wowed, oh, about fifteen times give or take before he was even ten years old. But, she added with a resigned sigh, "Somebody's got Johnny hexed. But you can't tell who. There's so many witches around." John Blymyer yawned. After not sleeping for so long, he finally felt safe enough to begin to relax.

John Curry took the stand and confirmed that Blymyer's intention had been to get "the witch-lock" (i.e., a piece of the old farmer's hair). The boy betrayed his youth with tears, and guilelessly confessed to all his terrible actions on the night of the crime. A newspaper reported that it was a "rosy-cheeked, slick-haired lad" who had entered the courtroom that day, but that his smile had soon disappeared; the heading placed above the article read, "Talk of Electric Chair, Dead Men and Goblins Saddens Prisoner."

All three defendants were convicted; Blymyer received life in prison. The reluctant Hess made out better; he got a generous ten to twenty years. After his sentence was read, it appeared Hess felt that some display of good manners was called for but wasn't quite sure how to proceed; finally, he approached the jury box and shook the hand of each juror before being taken from the courtroom. Blymyer said he believed his own sentence was "a little stiff," but he could live with it. "I never was happier. I can eat and sleep now and I feel fine. There's no spell over me anymore."

⁴ It was the sentence of John Curry that caused controversy. The "apple-cheeked" fourteen-year-old was sentenced to life in prison, a conviction that made many uncomfortable. After all, if it hadn't been for Blymyer, the boy would have been out somewhere looking for a place to sleep, or at the army recruiter's lying about his age to try to enlist in the army, or at home being beaten by his stepfather, or any one of the other activities that were part of his cheerless routine.

Hex in Peace

In a way, if you weren't looking at the case from a vehemently thirst-for-vengeance vantage point, the criminal justice system somehow actually did well by the three underprivileged and formerly marginalized young men. Ultimately, none of the trio would do his full sentence, and it seems they all did quite well in prison—perhaps better than they would have made out in life had the Hex Murder tragedy not happened, or, to put it frankly,

had they not murdered Nelson Rehmeyer. Early on, Hess and
Curry told reporters that they had been converted during
church services and revivals conducted in the jail by the nice,
fun-spoiling members of the Women's Christian Temperance
Union; they said they now "felt secure," newspapers reported.
They would stay out of trouble from then on; they were, apparently, repentant.

Many people who knew Curry and Hess in their post-
prison lives described the men as gentle and kind. A gifted artist,
Curry served as a cartographer in WWII and played a significant
role in the creation of maps that would be integral during the
Invasion of Normandy. Later, as a civilian, he painted portraits
for local families. Hess went back to his family's farm, which had,
ironically, turned around since the year of the Hex Murder. He
eventually married, volunteered as a church caretaker for many
years, and retired from a factory job in about 1970.

And what of Blymyer? After his conviction, he was shipped
off to the notorious Eastern State Penitentiary in Philadelphia.
He didn't complain much; he seemed to find incarceration a
small price to pay for being cured of the bewitchment that had
bedeviled him as long as he could remember. Blymyer was
reputedly a quiet prisoner, although once, while attempting to
get his sentence commuted, he made the somewhat-ambiguous
statement that "There is no evidence that I hexed anyone while
in prison." John Blymyer was released from prison in 1953. The
world heard nothing more of him until his death in the 1970s;
he had spent the intervening years in peaceful anonymity,
working as janitor and a night watchman.

The one guy who wouldn't get a chance for a second act
was, of course, Nelson Rehmeyer—aside from the dubious

second life given to him in the newspapers, in which he was referred to as a "voodooist," "the old witch," and a "practitioner of the black arts." In reality, Nelson Rehmeyer's life had not revolved around old superstitions; as a matter of fact, he was a complex man, self-educated, well-read, and known to be active in the socialist party in Pennsylvania.

Rehmeyer's pow-wowing skills, as well as his tragic book, were probably passed down in his German family. The old farmer was said to genuinely like helping others in whatever way he could, and sometimes, for whatever reason, it seemed as if the old charms really *did* work. For instance, a long time ago, there had been that frightened, poverty-stricken couple who had sent for him, begging him to help their baby. There was no money for a doctor, and besides, they believed strongly in pow-wow magic—they had seen it work before. Rehmeyer had answered their plea, and found the infant to be a pitifully weak, wailing little thing. Looking on the failing baby and its sad surroundings it was easy to think that, even if he survived, there would be no bright future for this poor wretched soul. But Rehmeyer had done his pow-wow work there, and later he heard that the baby had begun gaining weight and survived. In fact, the child's parents would credit this man, this pow-wow artist named Nelson Rehmeyer, with saving their son's life. And just who was this child, born in the hills of York County and saved by Nelson Rehmeyer thirty-three years before his own death? He was none other than John Blymyer.

PART V

Witch Awards

CHAPTER 15

Outstanding Moments in American Witchcraft

W hen you read about American history, you inevitably come across things that make you pause, do a double take, and think, "Did they really do that?" When examining the history of witchcraft in America, as we have seen, one will have quite a few such moments. There are so many, in fact, that we couldn't possibly fit them into one volume. But there were some moments in American witchcraft so amazing, so amusing, or so poignant that they deserve an award—so we're going to give them one. We present you with the Witch Awards for Outstanding Moments in American Witchcraft. And the winners are . . .

Worst Witch Recipe

Yes, even worse than a "witch cake." In Georgia, old-time witches had an especially distasteful recipe: mix together some dried scorpions, toads, and snakes, and add . . . *ground-up puppies.* Yes, that last ingredient is puppies. When your victim consumes this dish, the spell will cause the critters to reanimate inside his body and consume him from the inside out. Or he might just die from disgust. Either way.

Most Rarefied Witch Skill

One of the charges against accused Connecticut witch Elizabeth Godwin, who was arrested several times for witchcraft in the 1650s, was that she inexplicably knew that another woman, Mrs. Atwater, had figs in her pocket, when another lady present was unable to smell the figs at all.

Weird Thing That Came Up in a Witch Trial That We'd Just As Soon Not Know About

In the 1655 trial of Connecticut couple Nicholas Bayley and his wife, Goody Bayley, some real TMI testimony was given by a long-suffering neighbor. Observing the Bayleys' dog getting amorous with a pig (!), the neighbor told Bayley that he should kill his dog, and Goodwife Bayley responded, "What would you have the poor creature do? If he has not a bitch, he must have something."

Most Kanye Witch Trial Moment

If the Salem witch trial testimony of one James Darling is to be believed, twenty-seven-year-old laborer Job Tookey had some serious swagger when it came to evil. Darling testified that his acquaintance Tookey had boasted to him that "he was not the Devil's servant—the Devil was *his* servant." Bam!

Grouchiest Witch

She was Wilmot Read, wife of a fisherman, and she was infamous for having a foul mouth. Despite her cozy nickname of "Mammy" Read, she had been accused of witchcraft and generally avoided because of her well-known, all-around nastiness long before she was arrested and tried at Salem. Before Roseanne Barr uttered her classic "Now I know why animals eat their young" line, or Bernie Mac told his nephew, "I'm gonna bust your head til the white meat shows," Mammy Read blazed the trail with her trademark rejoinder of telling people she hoped a "bloody cleaver" would be found in their baby's cradle.

Best Unintentional Irony in a Witchcraft Case

In 1704, the Colony of Virginia tried Grace Sherwood for witchcraft, but her "witch ducking" test experienced a weather delay. Court records from that year noted that the accused witch's "ducking" was postponed, "the weather being very rainy & bad so that it possibly might endanger her health." Grace ultimately failed her ducking test but eventually went free anyway.

Lamest Witch Get-Together

William Barker's confession stands as one of the most detailed narratives of the activities of the witches of Salem. The forty-something Barker, who had been arrested and brought to Salem from his home in nearby Andover after being accused of witchcraft, was examined and confessed that same day. Besides revealing the witches' mission statement, which conveniently confirmed Cotton Mather's theory that the devil had specifically targeted America because its citizens were so special and so pious, he also gave a complete blow-by-blow of what had to be the lamest witch soiree of all time; dinner parties at Cotton Mather's house were probably wilder. Testimonies of many other accused witches also mention this get-together. It's hard to read without having the line "today is the day the teddy bears have their picnic!" begin playing in your head.

William Barker testified that he was taken to a get-to-gether of about one hundred witches, which was held right on the village green next to the minister's house, the minister being, apparently, quite a sound sleeper. The devil himself was there and approached the star-struck William with The Book. Sign it and I'll pay off all your debts, and you'll totally live "comfortably," the devil told him, and the words were barely out of the profane one's mouth when William had done the deed. The devil then gave a speech in which he revealed to the witches some of the details of his terrible plan: under his reign there would be no churches, everyone would live as equals, and there would be no judgment, punishment, or shame. If William could have, he probably would have signed The Book a second time. Then it was time to enjoy some light refreshments—bread and wine—and hobnob a bit with his fellow witches, some of whom he recognized as neighbors. Details filled in by the testimony and statements of other accused witches included the facts that the wine had come from Boston; that someone else had brought along some cheese; that they had sat on green grass by a brook and drank cold water from it; and that many of the witches rode in on "poles."

Dirtiest Trick Pulled by a Witch:
The Case of the Vanishing Beer

Many mysterious things were purported to have happened in seventeenth-century Salem, and witches got blamed for all of them—including this peculiar incident, reported by William Baker in his testimony against accused witch Rachel Clinton. Baker was working as a servant in the home of Master Rust. On the day in question, a "barrel of strong beer" had been brewed. The following night the mistress of the house went downstairs to check on the beer only to discover the entire barrel, though still sealed, was now completely empty and the floor around it was completely dry. Who was to blame for such a tragic, inexplicable event? Why, a witch, naturally! Weird witch aside: what exactly was the evidence that connected Rachel Clinton to this dirty witch trick? Someone said they had seen her walk back and forth in front of Master Rust's home the day before.

Best "Are You Still Beating Your Wife?"
Line of Questioning

You know how in movies and TV shows set in courtrooms, lawyers are always shouting, "Objection, Your Honor. Counsel is leading the witness!"? Well, that never happened at the Salem witch trials, mostly because the accused witches had no lawyers. As a result, there were some almost unbelievable exchanges when defendants took the stand. The questioning of Bridget Bishop, however, endures as the most stellar example of no-win witch questioning. We'll join the trial already in progress; Bridget has just been asked by Judge Hathorne to talk about how she bewitched the girls of Salem:

Bridget: I know nothing of it. I am innocent to a Witch. I know not what a Witch is.

Hathorne: How do you know then that you are not a Witch?

On June 10, 1692, Bridget Bishop became the first person to be hanged for witchcraft in Salem.

Most Poignant Account of a Witch Trial

Captain Nathaniel Cary could also get an award for best husband to an accused witch, although his actions may have been partly based on feeling guilty for nearly getting his wife executed in the first place. You see, Nathaniel Cary, a shipmaster from Charlestown, Massachusetts, was a sensible man; when he heard that the afflicted girls in Salem had accused his wife, forty-two-year-old Elizabeth Cary, of being a witch, he did what he thought the reasonable thing to do was: he took his wife on a quick visit to nearby Salem to speak with the accusers in person and just get the whole silly misunderstanding cleared up. Nathaniel had grossly underestimated Salem, where reason was not in play. In the course of a day, his wife went from courtroom spectator to jailed witch (which could really be its own separate award for the fastest role reversal in American witch history, but we only have so much space).

Later, Nathaniel wrote an account of what happened to his wife at Salem, and it stands as a remarkably human glimpse into what it was like to be accused of witchcraft and to have a loved one accused of witchcraft. The account is one of the most painful to read of all the writings to come out of Salem. Cary says,

> Being brought before the justices, her chief accusers were two girls; my wife declared to the justices that she never had any knowledge of them before that day. She was forced to stand with her arms stretched out. I did request that I might hold one of her hands, but it was denied me. Then she desired me to wipe the tears from her eyes, and the sweat from her face which I did, then she desired she might lean herself on me saying she should faint. Judge Hathorne replied, she had strength enough to torment those persons, and she should have strength enough to stand.

Nathaniel took his life into his hands by challenging the court on what he called the "cruel proceedings," and he further annoyed the judges by announcing that God would have vengeance on them. God "deliver us from the hands of unmerciful men," he prayed in court. The court ignored him, and Elizabeth Cary was committed to jail, where things only got worse:

> The jailor put irons on her legs (having received such a command) the weight of them was about eight pounds; these irons and her other afflictions, soon brought her into convulsion fits, so that I thought she would have died that night. I sent to entreat that the irons might be taken off, but all entreaties were in vain if it would have saved her life, so that in this condition she must continue. I did easily perceive which way the rest would go.

Nathaniel petitioned for his wife's release; as a matter of fact, he did everything possible to save her, even getting arrested himself at one point. And he did save her. Realizing that if she were tried for witchcraft in Salem she would very likely be convicted and hanged, Nathaniel orchestrated her escape from jail. The couple was assisted by many while they were on the lam, including the governor of New York. They returned to their home after the witch craze ended.

Most Sorry Witch Trial Judge

On a winter's day in 1696, a young Boston boy read aloud a Bible verse, Matthew 12:7: "And if you had known what this means, I desire mercy and not sacrifice, you would not have condemned the guiltless." From that moment on, life would never be the same for his father, a former judge in the witch trials at Salem.

Samuel Sewall was an England-born, Harvard-educated merchant who had married well and was living a pretty good life—until the governor appointed him as a judge in the upcoming witch trials in 1692. Samuel was not without political aspirations, so the position wasn't unwelcome. Plus, like most of his contemporaries, he believed in witchcraft. But he most definitely did not anticipate that by the time all was said and done, more than twenty people would be dead as a result of the proceedings at Salem.

There were signs that Sewall felt some uneasiness of conscience not long after the witch craze ended. In a diary notation a year after the trials, he mentions that he had apologized to former accused witch John Alden that day for the hardships that trial had caused him. Sewall had come to feel that he was being punished for his part in the witch trials. While the tragedies and travails that visited Sewall and his family were really no worse than those one might expect in the 1600s, they were portentous to a religious man with a guilty conscience. Within a few years of the witch trials, the Sewalls had lost a young daughter to disease, and Mrs. Sewall had delivered a stillborn son; various household calamities, mostly in the forms of storm damage and fire, had struck the family's new house. Then, in December 1696, his three-year-old daughter, Sarah, sickened; on December 23, he wrote in his diary, "About break of day she gives up the ghost in Nurse Cowell's arms. Neither I nor my wife were by, Nurse not having expected so sudden a change, and having promised to call us." He then heartrendingly added, "I thought of Christ's words *could you not watch with me one hour!* And fain would have sat up with her." The next day, his young son, reading aloud from his Bible, happened to hit on the verse that concluded with the words "you would not have condemned the guiltless." An emotional Sewall wrote in his diary that night, "The verse did awfully bring to mind the Salem Tragedy."

On January 14, 1697, something unexpected appears in Samuel Sewall's diary. He wrote a long notation that day that began: "Copy of the bill I put up on fast day, giving it to (Rev.) Mr. Willard to read as he passed by." At church that morning, Samuel had gotten to his feet and stood as the long statement was read to the townspeople, bowing his head at its conclusion. What Rev. Willard read was Samuel Sewall's apology for his participation in the Salem witch trials. He "desires to take the shame and blame of it," the reverend read to the stunned listeners. The document begged forgiveness from his fellow citizens, but most especially, Sewall wanted God to know that he real-ized he had made a grave error by participating in the persecu-tions at Salem, and he was really, really, really sorry for it. Sewall wasn't simply sorry for his participation in the witch hunt; he was terrified for his mortal soul, as well as for the well-being of his family. If there was one thing he knew, it was that God was vengeful.

One might have thought that this humiliating public apol-ogy would be enough to show repentance, but Samuel Sewall wasn't taking any chances. About the time of his apology he began wearing his own version of a hair shirt; each day he would don the rough sackcloth garment, where it would stay hidden beneath his clothing all day, his constant reminder of his sin, and hopefully, God's reminder that he was, as he said, really, really sorry for it. Sewall continued to wear the punish-ing garment for the rest of his life.

Despite already being an outcast among some of his peers because of his opinions on the witch trials, Sewall went on to further alienate himself in colonial Massachusetts by going against another popular opinion. In 1700, the former judge wrote and published *The Selling of Joseph*, the first American anti-slavery tract.

Most Out-of-Control Witch Trial

At their best, witch trials were exercises in absurdity. But when diminutive sixty-seven-year-old Susannah Martin was brought before the Salem court on May 2, 1692, the berobed magis-trates seemed to lose all control of the proceedings. As usual, the afflicted girls, Mercy Lewis, Abigail Williams, and Ann

Putnam, were present, and the man known as John Indian, husband of Tituba, who had been implicated early in the witch craze, was also there. The first line of the courtroom transcript of Susannah's examination reads, "As soon as she came in many had fits. In short order, Abigail Williams called out, it is Goody Martin she hath hurt me often!" Mercy Lewis pointed at Susannah and "fell into a little fit." Then Ann Putnam threw a glove at her. What happened next didn't sit well with the court at all: Susannah Martin laughed. When the magistrate asked the accused witch why she laughed, she responded, "Well I may at such folly." The exchange continued:

Magistrate: What ails these people?
Susannah: I do not know.
Magistrate: But what do you think?
Susannah: I do not desire to spend my judgment upon it.
Magistrate: Do you not think they are bewitched?
Susannah: No. I do not think that they are.

As the testimony continued, with Susannah laughing at the antics of the bewitched and calling them liars, the witnesses grew ever more frustrated and frantic. John Indian fell into a "violent fit"—a common enough thing for women and girls, but quite unusual for a man at a witch trial. He cried out in agony, saying that Susannah was biting him, even as she stood in front of the courtroom several yards away. One girl said she could see a spectral Susannah sitting up in the ceiling beams of the courtroom, and another said that "the black man" was standing next to the accused woman, whispering in her ear. Mercy Lewis shouted out a comment about Susannah's entrance in court being delayed that day and added nastily, "You can come fast enough in the night!" This elicited a paternal "No, no sweetheart" from the magistrate. Next, John Indian announced that he was going to kill Susannah on the spot, but as he approached her, he was flung violently down to the floor by an unseen force.

Unfortunately, the court had the last laugh; in addition to the charges already made against her, they entered depositions from the bewitched girls against Susannah for the very fits she had sent them into in court that day. Susannah Martin, a widow and mother of eight, was hanged less than two months later.

Best Timing: Abigail Falkner

It said "From Salem Prison," but it may as well have said "From Hell."

For most accused witches, the only words of theirs that survive are the curses they supposedly sputtered at neighbors they had had a disagreement with, or their courtroom denials as transcribed by their persecutors. But in the first half of the twentieth century, a document emerged from a musty trunk in a dark corner of a New England attic that turned out to be written in the hand of Abigail Falkner in 1692, when she was pregnant and waiting for the execution of her death sentence for witchcraft in Salem. For a short time, the petition was in the hands of an antique dealer, who made "photostatic" copies of the document to be archived; the original document itself was then sold to a private collector. Recently, this poignant relic from the Salem witch trials, touched by few but its tortured author, emerged again, this time from the archives of a ꝼ private collector in Maryland. Worn, weathered, and stained, the letter is still striking in the neatness of the hand and the care with which it seems to have been written—and no wonder. Abigail Falkner was writing for her life. Her petition begins like this:

> The humble petition of Abigail Falkner unto his excellence Sr. William Phips, Knight and Governor of his Majesty's dominions in America: humbly showeth that your poor and humble petitioner having been this four months in Salem Prison and condemned to die having no other evidences against me but ye spectre evidences.

ꝸ The petition was written from her cell in Salem Prison, and it was a plea for her life and for the lives of her now-helpless family: a husband who suffered from "fits" (apparently not the witch-related kind) and six children. Abigail's execution had been temporarily delayed due to her current pregnancy. The Puritans weren't savages—they could bide their time for a few months and wait until *after* she gave birth to hang her for witchcraft; it's not like they didn't have other witches to hang. Well, actually, they might have hanged her anyway, with the way things were going in Salem, but there was an old English law still in effect stipulating that a pregnant female felon couldn't be executed until after she gave birth. Abigail had been languishing in the damp, freezing prison, barely fed and barely sleeping, for months, when she made the last ditch effort to save herself and her family by writing a letter to Governor William Phips in December 1692. The beleaguered Phips was not a huge fan of how the witch trials were going, and even as

graves were being dug for yet another round of hangings early ⚘
in 1693, he began issuing reprieves. Eventually all the accused
witches were released, including Abigail. If Abigail Falkner
hadn't been pregnant she would most likely have been hanged
in 1692. And if she hadn't sent her affecting letter just when
Phips was getting fed up with the witch trials, more of the convicted witches who were languishing in prison may have been
executed as well.

On March 20, 1693, Abigail gave birth at her home to a
baby boy, her seventh child, whom she named Ammiruhama,
Hebrew for "My people have received mercy." Abigail died in
1729; her long-ailing husband outlived her by three years. After
his mother's death, Ammi and his wife, Hannah, named their
next daughter Abigail.

And finally, our last award:

Most Embarrassed Descendant

Ever been so embarrassed by your relatives that you just ↖
wanted to change your name? One of America's greatest writers, Nathaniel Hawthorne—or, to use his real name, Nathaniel
Hathorne—can totally identify. Hawthorne was the great-
great-grandson of John Hathorne, the Salem witch trial judge
who was notorious not only for his persecution of alleged
witches, but also for his ultra-nastiness to Quakers. And John
Hathorne's father, William Hathorne, did his share of witch
and Quaker tormenting, too. Despite publicly acknowledging
that these unlikeable guys were his ancestors, Nathaniel felt
compelled to at least do *something* to disassociate himself from

their reprehensible behavior. That was why, in 1830, Nathaniel added the "w" that spoke volumes to his last name. Still, the writer felt haunted by what he considered to be the family curse; in the introduction to his most famous work, *The Scarlet Letter*, he wrote,

> [William Hathorne] had all the Puritanic traits, both good and evil. He was likewise a bitter persecutor, as witness the Quakers, who have remembered him in their histories, and relate an incident of his hard severity towards a woman of their sect, which will last longer, it is to be feared, than any record of his better deeds, although these were many.

Hawthorne doesn't speculate on how many "better deeds" it would take to make up for the incident of "hard severity," which was the public whipping of Quaker Ann Coleman that William had ordered, but continues,

> His son [John Hathorne], too, inherited the persecuting spirit, and made himself so conspicuous in the martyrdom of the witches, that their blood may fairly be said to have left a stain upon him. So deep a stain, indeed, that his old dry bones, in the Charter Street burial-ground, must still retain it, if they have not crumbled utterly to dust! I know not whether these ancestors of mine bethought themselves to repent, and ask pardon of Heaven for their cruelties; or whether they are now groaning under the heavy consequences of them,

in another state of being. At all events, I, the present writer, as their representative, hereby take shame upon myself for their sakes.

Hawthorne, thanks to his judgmental Puritanical ancestors, knew a thing or two about the concept of bearing a "scarlet letter," even if it was a psychic one. So it seems that at least one good thing came out of the witch persecutions: one of the greatest American novels.

The Reign of the Blair Witch: How a Made-Up Witch Took On a Life of Her Own and Terrorized a Town

I don't often encounter other people when I go hiking in the woods near my home in rural Maryland; when I do, they're usually mountain bikers who whiz by me with barely a "Hey." So on a summer afternoon when I come upon two little boys of about five or six, a mom, an athletic set of grandparents, and two big happy dogs, all splashing in a creek (the one I always timorously ford by jumping from rock to rock and where I had recently seen the tail of a snake poking out from beneath a branch in the water, causing me to take a fifteen-minute detour), it is an unexpected but fun sight. We exchange friendly greetings, and then the grandfather, who seems to be the spokesperson for the group, gestures to the two grinning dark-haired boys and says something surprising: "They're looking for witches."

I think I must have misunderstood him. I look over at the boys and see that they're nodding in enthusiastic agreement at what the older man had said.

"Um, *what* did you say they're looking for?"

"They said they wanted to come to the woods to look for witches." More nods.

I had been spending the summer immersed in writing this ♦ book—on witches—but this was pretty much the last thing I'd expected to hear had brought two bright-eyed little boys into the woods on a summer afternoon. Bears, maybe. Tadpoles, sure. Squirrels, weird bugs, cool rocks, heck, even Bigfoot wouldn't have struck me as odd. But . . . *witches*? Really?

"I'm actually writing a book about witches," I admit, still feeling a bit disoriented.

"Good—do you know where any are around here?" Granddad seems oddly unsurprised by what seems to me a pretty weird coincidence.

I gather my wits and say that the scariest thing I'd seen in these particular woods was that snake in the creek the week before. The family seems pretty unconcerned about the snake, given that they're all still standing in the creek.

I try to ask the boys what made them come looking for witches of all things, but the family is all talking at once, the dogs are being frisky and getting ready to bolt, and I don't want to seem weird by hanging around too long; but when I hike on I'm still disconcerted. *Little boys want to go into the woods on a summer day to look for witches?* True, this strikes me as incredibly awesome, but also kind of unaccountable. Hmm . . . woods and witches . . .

Well, it just so happens that Burkittsville, the fabled home of the Blair Witch in the film *The Blair Witch Project*, is only about ten miles from where I live. And a whole lot of people had gotten really excited about the Blair Witch—so excited that they had stormed the town of Burkittsville looking for her.

Burkittsville, Maryland, Summer of 1999

Scary things were happening in the tiny Maryland town of Burkittsville in the late 1990s. A woman came up from doing laundry in her basement and found a strange man wandering around her living room. He didn't want to leave. The friendly "Welcome to Burkittsville" sign disappeared, and when it was replaced, it disappeared again. Strangers rang doorbells in the middle of the night, snapped photos of local children, and accosted residents on their porches demanding to know why there were no public restrooms in the town so itty-bitty there also wasn't a single store or gas station. Meanwhile, out in the town cemetery, black-clad teenagers were . . . well, they were *looking suspicious*. And someone—no one's pointing any fingers, black-clad teenagers—actually *left a candle burning* in the cemetery; a pretty dangerous scenario, one resident pointed out, what with the dry summer and all.

This is a true witch story. It is a fact that ever since 1999, a witch has caused quite a disturbance in Burkittsville. This was the year a strange and compelling film called *The Blair Witch Project* careened from out of nowhere and became a phenomenon. Since then, people have come from far and wide to the rural town of Burkittsville in search of the nightmarish entity known as—da da da—the Blair Witch.

In case you've been held hostage in the crawlspace of an isolated cabin in the woods for the last fifteen years, *The Blair Witch Project* is nicely summed up by the words that appear on the screen in the beginning of the movie:

In October of 1994, three student filmmakers disappeared in the woods near Burkittsville, Maryland while shooting a documentary. A year later their footage was found.

If you want to get picky about some of the details of the film then, yeah, okay, there's no Black Hills Forest, which is the name of the woods the students got lost in according to the movie—at least not in Maryland. And Burkittsville was not built on the site of a town formerly called Blair like the movie says. (Although it *was* originally named something else: the decidedly un-spooky "Harley's Post Office.") And those murders the movie mentions? Never happened. Not a single bloody one of them. And the witch? One hundred percent made up.

As a matter of fact, she and the gruesome legend surrounding her were both totally invented by filmmakers Eduardo Sánchez and Daniel Myrick. There never was a Blair Witch. But try telling that to the denizens of the Internet who recount the legend as pure fact, and yes, they'd *love* to argue the point with you. Try telling that to the folks who head for Burkittsville like Richard Dreyfuss heads for Devil's Tower National Monument in *Close Encounters of the Third Kind*. The nonexistence of the witch is also little consolation to the 152 (give or take) residents of the little burg, who were said to have practically chased producers out of town with pitchforks when they came to discuss filming another Blair Witch movie there.

How did this seemingly inexplicable thing happen? What would make people believe in something that common sense should tell them can't be real? How did a made-up witch come to life and terrorize the tiny town of Burkittsville?

"A Witch Was the Only Option"

"When we made it we couldn't have anticipated all this happening. We were broke filmmakers no one had heard of; we didn't have any reason to think anyone would even see this," Eduardo Sánchez says, sipping a Diet Coke in a restaurant near his Maryland home. Sánchez, NBA-tall and boyish behind a bushy beard, is a humble guy, generous with his time and kind to fans—pretty cool considering he is one half of the team that made a film that enjoyed one of the biggest opening weekends of all time, grossed $248 million, and was given four stars by legendary film critic Roger Ebert.

It seemed to happen overnight, but in fact it was a several-year process: Sánchez and Myrick, fellow Florida film school grads, had made their low-budget horror movie in 1997, filming mostly in Seneca Creek State Park in Montgomery County, Maryland, but of course filming that tiny (but oh-so-impactful) bit in Burkittsville.

Sánchez says that it was his and Myrick's inexperience and lack of funds that ultimately made *The Blair Witch Project* possible: "We really didn't know what we were doing. But since we had nothing to lose, we could afford to take chances." Making the movie independently gave the young filmmakers creative control over the film. "There was no one to tell us 'you can't do that,'" Sánchez says. "The whole thing wouldn't have happened if we were working for a studio. Studios don't want something that doesn't follow the rules. So doing it on our own, there was no pressure." He admits, though, "It was a crazy idea and a lot of luck."

It may have been a crazy idea that involved a lot of luck, but it also took a lot of creativity, hard work, and, of course, a *witch*. So just what made the guys decide to make the fear factor of their film a witch, anyway? "We wanted it to be something that could fit into a historical context, and be something that really could have happened," Sánchez says. "And, you know, ⸭ there must have been all kinds of stuff like this in the colonies: murders and people disappearing, scary stuff like that. So we wanted something that could seem more *real* than a monster or that kind of thing. It seemed to us like it had to be either a witch or a wizard, and wizards just don't have that scary context. A witch was really the only option."

In early 1999, the filmmakers got their project into the iconic Sundance Film Festival. There, after a well-hyped midnight showing, some viewers walked out of the theater clutching their hearts. Others claimed to be dizzy. Others came out confused—was it real or not? Execs from Artisan came out of the screening totally on board. They wanted the Blair Witch, and within hours they had her; a deal was signed that morning. The rest, as they say, is history—in this case, film history. *The Blair Witch Project* would be released in theaters in a remarkably short time—less than six months. But the witch's reputation would precede her.

The Pitch-the-Witch Project

There was a strange new force at work in 1999—a force that ⸭ folks had yet to realize the power of, but one that would help propel the Blair Witch to the top of the box office: the Internet. Before the film even made it to Sundance, Sánchez had set up a website—one that certainly *seemed* to be the website for a documentary about an unsolved missing persons case—that just happened to involve a witch. And before "going viral" was even a thing, the story of the Blair Witch shrieked across the country, mostly from college campus to college campus in the beginning; then suddenly it was everywhere. The Blair Witch seemed to capture the darkest parts of America's imagination, and she just wouldn't let go.

The filmmakers had gone to a lot of trouble in the creation of the back story of the Blair Witch—the lore that comprised the story of the witch, a.k.a. Elly Kedward, and the lingering effects of the terrible curse she had put on the town that would become Burkittsville. "Just before we released the film we made a fake documentary called *Curse of the Blair Witch* and released it a few weeks ahead of the movie," Sánchez remembers. "The documentary was well made and we made sure the legend we created made sense. It gave it a good solid foundation. The story was something that was certainly not probable, but it seemed *possible*."

It was also something a whole lot of people wanted to see more of. *The Blair Witch Project*'s opening weekend broke records, and during the week of August 16, 1999, the film got the cover of both *Time* and *Newsweek*, with *Time*'s cover featuring Sánchez and Myrick and their "Rags to Witches" story.

But the filmmakers and Artisan had done a little *too* good of a job of making it all seem real. Despite the fact that the "missing students" in the film were listed as actors in the film's credits, and despite the fact that the filmmakers and actors were giving interviews left and right, many people either chose to believe, or couldn't help believing, that the movie consisted of real footage of three people being terrorized by a real witch in the woods.

In addition to acclaim for its creators and the spawning of what would become known as the found-footage genre of film making, the movie had another unforeseen effect. The

once-obscure barely-a-town of Burkittsville, Maryland, shown
for only moments in the movie, suddenly became the center
of worldwide interest, all for something it didn't really have:
a witch.

M.I.A. in Burkittsville

Why *Burkittsville*? The folks living there certainly asked themselves that question many times in 1999. Sánchez's answer is a
simple one: "Really it was just that it was the most picturesque
town we could find. It had a cemetery and a church, and it was
just a small, perfect setting."

It's true that Burkittsville is picturesque. There's a church,
all right, and of course that iconic cemetery; there's also a wee
post office, and, aside from the homes, not much else. Oh
wait, it does have something else, and no, I'm not going say "a
witch." The teensy town of Burkittsville has a very savvy mayor.
I wanted to meet her and chat in person about the Blair Witch,
and the mayor graciously agreed to talk to me. So, on a hot
summer afternoon, I headed to Burkittsville.

I arrive twenty minutes early for a meeting with
Burkittsville's mayor, Debby Burgoyne, and wander up to the
cemetery—the one Heather is seen standing in early in *The
Blair Witch Project,* talking about dead children and things
being "etched in stone." The cemetery is perched on top of a
hill, like the best cemeteries are, with a gorgeous view of rolling Maryland countryside. From its heights I can also take in
the town, and I quickly notice that, while Burkittsville is picturesque as heck all right, it's also kind of, well, *dead.* The multi-
story houses, many of them in the Victorian or Federal period

style, cozily hug the brick sidewalks, but not a soul haunts a front porch on this pretty summer afternoon; as a matter of fact, no one seems to be home in Burkittsville.

In September 1862, the Battle of South Mountain brought real horrors to the village of Burkittsville as nearby fighting bled into town, and houses filled with wounded and dying soldiers. The desecration of human life, the blood, the suffering, the fear—it all topped anything the Blair Witch could have imagined in her fondest daydreams.

In today's Burkittsville, the boom of cannon has been replaced by the deep bass rumble of American-made pick-ups; in the cemetery the sound seems to come from all around you, like a phantom parade of twin cabs, or those creepy noises coming from everywhere outside the lost campers' tent. But aside from the trucks, Burkittsville is peaceful and pretty, no place for a witch at all. And here in the cemetery the dead seem to be sleeping peacefully; the only motion, which you might catch out of the corner of your eye and be briefly unsettled by, are the wispy stirrings of tiny American flags fluttering calmly on a few of the graves.

But maybe there *is* something to this witch thing, because my meet-up time with the mayor comes and goes, and no one appears. I find some shade and sit on a small brick wall outside the back entrance of the church where we're supposed to meet. I pull out my phone and double-check my email. Yep, I'm at the right place. I'm pre-annoyed with myself about how, when the mayor shows up and apologizes for being late, I just know I'll be unable to refrain from saying, "I thought the Blair Witch got you, ha-ha!" When she's twenty minutes late, I call her contact number. She doesn't answer, but her voicemail is jocular: "You almost reached Mayor Debby Burgoyne!" Yes, I guess I almost did. I leave her a message saying I hope I'm waiting in the right place, even though I know I am, and that I'll be sticking around a little while longer in case she's still on her way.

I watch fat clouds pose against the classic blue sky above the cemetery. My phone screen remains black. I can almost imagine that I've gone back in time. I hop off the wall and wander a little ways down the street; a sign in front of the church advertises an upcoming ghost story program. So apparently the deal is there are no witches in Burkittsville, but there *are* ghosts. I call it a day.

Driving out of town I pass a lone little girl marching along the brick sidewalk, a grin on her face and a bag of candy in her fist. She's the first person I've seen on the street. Just outside town I pass a house with a Confederate flag hanging from its porch; funny, I don't remember noticing that on my way in. I manage to drive almost ten miles before I realize I'm heading in the wrong direction, so I have to turn around and pass the same damn flag again. The little girl is nowhere to be seen.

Three hours later Mayor Debby calls me. "I blew it. I'm so sorry!" She says that for some reason she had been certain all day that it was Wednesday—not Thursday, our scheduled meeting day. In the weird timelessness of Burkittsville, I can believe it. The mayor is so sweet and so apologetic that I practically apologize to her for being there on the right day. We reschedule.

The following Tuesday we pull into the parking lot facing the cemetery at almost exactly the same time, and Debby lets us into the South Mountain Heritage Museum in the back of the church where I had waited for her the week before.

♦ She snaps on the light and suddenly we're surrounded by artifacts of old-time Burkittsville: a general store/post office mock-up that seems so authentic you expect to see ol' Postmaster Harley himself pop up from behind a counter. Weathered documents and first edition books of local history are laid out reverently in slightly dusty cases. From the walls, faces of early town residents stare down at us from inside heavy dark frames, a bit severe maybe, but not a witch among them. We get comfortable at the cozy table in the middle of the room. Suspended directly above us from the high ceiling is the oddest light fixture I've ever seen—what appears to be a large wooden lectern hanging upside down, with a light attached to it. It's all very . . . *Burkittsville.*

The Mayor Witch

⋈ The mayor of Burkittsville is a free-spirited one-time hippy. Refugees from the DC suburbs, Debby and her family have called the pocket-sized town home for nearly twenty years. Currently in her third term, Debby wasn't the mayor in 1999, but she and her family were well ensconced in Burkittsville by then. The proximity to the Appalachian Trail, which wends through nearby Gathland State Park, was one thing that had originally drawn the family to the area. But it was what Burkittsville *didn't* have that Debby found most appealing. "It was one of the few places where you really didn't have to lock your doors," she said. "You still had that freedom." Unfortunately, things weren't fated to stay that way.

In the summer of 1999, people started saying strange things to Debby. She heard from a worried friend in another state who wanted to know if everyone was okay; she had heard that weird things were going on in Burkittsville. The strangest stories were going around, and an unexpected word kept cropping up again and again: *witch*. And there was more: supposedly, a number of little kids had been murdered in Burkittsville at some point in the past, and now more people were missing. Then it got even weirder.

On July 11, 1999, the Sci-Fi (now SyFy) network broadcast the documentary Sánchez and company had made, *Curse of the Blair Witch*. Viewers were alarmed. It seemed three young college students had vanished in the woods outside Burkittsville in 1994 after going on a film-making expedition following a local legend. The legend, the program said, was that of the Blair Witch.

The Blair Witch, viewers learned, was the ghost of an old woman who had been suspected of being a witch and had been cast out of town and left to die a horrible death. She had put a curse on the town—because, apparently, she actually *was* a witch—and since then, her angry spirit would periodically invade the bodies of unfortunate people and make them do terrible things—things like committing gruesome murders.

According to the documentary, locals were certain the Blair Witch was behind the disappearance of Heather, Josh, and Mike, the young film students who had gone into the woods to make a movie about the legend. Their disappearance had remained unsolved, maybe even *hushed up*, but there had been a recent development: a backpack had been found in the woods, and inside were the video cameras and tapes left behind by the lost students. The Sci-Fi program was effectively constructed, weaving local history, interviews with teachers and relatives of the missing students, and news footage about the case. It was also chock-full of creepy details involving things like disemboweling and dead children, and the implication was that the missing students had met the same gruesome fate.

But most disturbing of all was the footage from the found cameras. It was clear that the students had been menaced by something very evil in the woods for days before their disappearance. The footage showed the trio begin optimistically, full of good humor, then gradually become progressively lost, frightened, and then, as they said, *hunted*.

The *Curse of the Blair Witch* was one hundred percent fiction. Credits at the end of the documentary included the names of the lost film students along with other cast members. It listed the filming locations—none of which matched the locations purportedly shown in the documentary. And the old photographs supposedly from Burkittsville were attributed to a historical society in, of all places, Florida. To an observant or skeptical person, it was obvious that the "documentary" was fictional. But few viewers were skeptical the night of July 11.

After the theatrical debut of *The Blair Witch Project* on July 30, 1999, things in Burkittsville quickly devolved into a "this is why we can't have nice horror movies" situation. What the people who made the pilgrimage expected to find in Burkittsville was unclear. But they tore the town apart looking for it.

"We were blind-sided," says Debby today of what ensued after the movie debuted. Bumper-to-bumper traffic jammed the quaintly bricked Main Street. Visitors expected souvenir shops, and, finding none, helped themselves to whatever they could pick up in people's yards. Families watching television in their living rooms were startled by the faces of strangers peering in their windows. Residents couldn't leave their homes without having their pictures taken and being accosted by people asking about the Blair Witch. And that leaving-the-doors-unlocked thing? Forget it.

When Debby found a strange man wandering around her living room one day not long after the movie's release, he seemed unconcerned about Debby's arrival and continued poking around, casually commenting, "It almost looks like somebody lives here."

"Somebody does," Debby informed him. "People live in *all* of the houses here."

"Oh," the stranger replied, "I guess that explains why so many of the doors were locked."

Debby got asked by visitors so many times where they could find the Blair Witch that she would sometimes entertain herself by answering, "I'm her."

One visitor in particular worked Debby's last nerve until she just about went all-out Blair Witch. The woman emerged from a luxury vehicle with out-of-state tags "dressed to the nines, full make-up, hair, everything," Debby says. She planted herself on the sidewalk in front of Debby's house as Debby and her little daughter attempted to walk to their front door. The woman began berating Debby for making her child live in Burkittsville. "How dare you!" the woman roared, coming closer. "You people shouldn't be allowed to have children in this town! Don't you even care that children are being murdered? Don't you care about your daughter?"

Debby looked down at her wide-eyed daughter, then back at the self-righteously enraged woman. "Ma'am, you're mistaken," Debby told her, tugging the girl closer. "This isn't my daughter. *This is my lunch.*" And with that she hustled the little girl inside the house, leaving the shocked woman gasping on the sidewalk.

A low point for Debby was when she answered her door to find a pregnant woman on the porch, begging to use her bathroom. Burkittsville has no public facilities, and Debby took pity and let her in. After the woman left, Debby discovered she had stolen a treasured antique bottle her daughter had dug out of their backyard.

During the worst of it, the town of Burkittsville was cast into a dark place. Someone was digging up dirt from the graveyard and selling it online. And then it was discovered that two known pedophiles were taking advantage of the free-for-all situation in the town, lurking around almost continually, seizing every opportunity to photograph little girls. "It was horrendous," Debby remembers. Police eventually intervened, but these were alarming times for the folks of Burkittsville.

But Debby says now that the real villain in the scenario wasn't the filmmakers or even the Blair Witch herself. It was Artisan, the film company that bought *The Blair Witch Project* from its creators.

Some Burkittsville residents had found a small way to get something out of their big witch-induced inconveniences: in response to the demand for non-existent Blair Witch memorabilia (and probably also to discourage people from just taking stuff), they took to selling whatever they could think of as impromptu souvenirs. Some folks sold rocks from their yards, and some put together little bundles of sticks in homage to the Blair Witch's somewhat-crude installation art projects. One particularly crafty little old lady designed and produced Blair Witch–themed t-shirts.

In short order, all of these industrious residents found some very un-neighborly cease and desist letters from Artisan in their mailboxes. The film company might have unleashed the Blair Witch in Burkittsville, but any money the old gal generated was expected to go right back to Hollywood.

It probably wasn't witchcraft, but it may have been karma: despite the runaway hit status of its witch movie, Artisan wound up deeply in debt. In December 2003, it was bought by Lionsgate and effectively ceased to exist.

Debby says she knows of one Burkittsville resident who paid off her truck by selling rocks from her yard, so there's that.

Life has moved on in Burkittsville, where things have quieted down quite a bit despite the fact that the spirit of the Blair Witch seems to have taken up permanent residency. Case in point: some of Debby's mayor duties continue to include things like fielding middle-of-the-night phone calls from a man in the Midwest who accuses her of being part of a conspiracy to cover up the Blair Witch murders.

Believe it or not, to this day Debby says she still hasn't seen *The Blair Witch Project*. Another film she surprisingly hasn't seen is *The Blair Witch Project 2: Book of Shadows*—the universally panned sequel to the original that was *not* made by Sánchez and Myrick—in which she and several other town residents briefly appear. Their agreement to appear in the film seemed almost as unlikely as there actually being a witch in Burkittsville; when producers originally came to town to discuss the project, a local councilman was so rude the group left in disgust, leading to sensationalized national coverage of how they had supposedly been run out of town.

As mayor, Debby encourages the idea of growth in her town. Some of Burkittsville's antiquated status is unwanted; Debby says prohibitive county regulations keep anyone in town from opening so much as an antique shop, and she and her team are working to change that.

And, believe it or not, the mayor says she would even be open to a *Blair Witch 3* movie being filmed in Burkittsville—provided it's made by the original filmmakers. Debby says she likes Ed Sánchez, because "he's a nice guy." When the "Welcome to Burkittsville" sign disappeared, Sánchez had paid for a new one "out of his own pocket," she says. When that sign also disappeared, he paid for another. And there's a bit of a strange coincidence that might also account for the little soft spot Debby seems to harbor for the Blair Witch: she grew up on the edge of Seneca Creek State Park, the locale where most of *The Blair Witch Project* was actually filmed. She used to play in the woods portrayed in the film as the domain of the Blair Witch.

Today Mayor Debby's in a unique position to give advice to any other town that might find itself unexpectedly thrust into the limelight. "I'd tell them to just go with it," she says. "Try to work with the people. You might as well enjoy it as much as you can, because you can't stop it."

By the way, there is one thing Debby admits Burkittsville should have done during the worst of the Blair Witch mayhem. She's still really bothered by the thought of those candles left burning unattended in the cemetery. "We should have hired a night watchman for the graveyard," she said.

Projecting Witches

"What's that?" Debby says distractedly as I ask her yet another question. She must be getting tired of all the witch talk, and I don't blame her. I've been badgering her with witch questions for well over an hour. It seems to be growing darker in the South Mountain Heritage Museum. Then Debby asks me if I know about Spook Hill. I do.

Lots of towns boast a Spook Hill—one of those places along the roadway where, it's said, if you stop and put your car in neutral, it will be pushed uphill by an invisible force— namely, ghosts. The Burkittsville version of this involves leftover Civil War soldiers—Confederate ghosts to be specific—who, hanging around in the misty afterlife, somehow mistake a stopped car for a cannon every single time and can be counted on to rush to help push the heavy "weapon" up the hill. If you plan ahead and put baby powder or flour on the hood of your car, you might even find handprints from the phantom soldiers.

"I've heard about a Spook Hill being somewhere around Burkittsville, but I never knew exactly where it was," I admit.

"Do you want to go there right now?"

Do I ever! A few minutes later we're idling in Debby's car just past the "Welcome to Burkittsville" sign (which, like many other things, is much smaller in person). At the base of a hill lined with trees the Mayor checks to make sure no vehicles are coming behind us, then shifts the car into neutral. I expect a barely perceptible "maybe I'm imagining it" caliber of movement, but we are instantly being propelled backward as if her foot is on the accelerator. *Sweet!* I know there are complicated physics/optical illusion factors in play, but *still*. Suspension of disbelief can be a thrilling thing.

After we bid a fond adieu to the Confederate ghosts, Debby takes me on a little tour of the town, pointing out the location of a one-time fur trading post, a spot where she says an Indian massacre once occurred, and her house. Tiny town, huge history. Also: very obliging ghosts. But no witch—unless you count the Mayor Witch.

True to form, I turn the wrong way when I pull out of the parking lot. This time, however, I realize I'm going in the wrong direction much sooner and turn around before I reach the Confederate flag house, heading instead in the direction of the dead Confederates. You just can't get away from those guys. Just outside of town I check to make sure no one is coming up behind me, then shift my car into neutral. Immediately, it heads backward, pulling me toward Burkittsville. I grin and shift back into drive.

In my more contemplative (or possibly goofier) moments, I've wondered if perhaps America's fascination with *The Blair Witch Project* was a case of collective precognition. Was the film's "witch" an embodiment of unseen, unwelcome forces that were gathering in the nation, that sense of unease that would soon segue into dread, before blossoming into full-blown terror as America was sucker punched by terrorism, divisive wars, and financial disaster? We would lose things we didn't even know we could lose to malignant forces we were barely beginning to sense in 1999.

But I really want to know why Eduardo Sánchez, the legend's creator, thinks it is that people persist in believing the Blair Witch, so I ask him. "Well, there are people who deliberately

spread misinformation on the Internet just for their own amuse-
ment, trying to get reactions out of people," he explains. "And
a lot of people just haven't heard enough of the story. They've
just heard parts of the story and think it's real. Some people just
want to believe it. They really want to live in that world."

He also has some ideas about why we're so darned fasci-
nated by witches: "I think it's something to do with the idea of
women having power. If you look at our history, men have been
suppressing women from the beginning of time, and a witch is
someone who has powers. A witch is a superhero really. And
women are supposed to be nice, and nurturing, and so the idea
that witches are sinister—it's just so fascinating to people. It also
has to do with the Christian faith, which has always been very
male-centered. In history, witches were tied to satanic activity
and demons." Sánchez also has a pretty good idea of what it is
about witches living in the woods that is especially spellbinding:
"The idea of a witch living in the middle of the woods makes
you wonder, *what is she up to in there?*"

Apparently, we can think of all kinds of things she could be
up to in there. "Sometimes things are scary because your brain
fills in the blanks with scary things," says Sánchez.

As he said back at that lunch, when talking about why
Americans kinda-sorta still believe in witches, in America
"there's a history and a pre-history. There *could be* anything."
He makes an encompassing gesture. "That's the beauty of
mythology: you can create your own reality. You can use your
imagination."

Plus, judging by how long-standing and pervasive the
worldwide belief in witches has been, it seems as though
humans are hardwired for it, and the so-called "New World" has

certainly been no different. From the unlucky women blamed for bad weather during early voyages across the Atlantic, to the children whose communities got them so worked up about witchcraft that they believed themselves bewitched, to the ladies who found ways to make a living or even become wealthy and powerful by their purported witch-like abilities—witches have manifested their influence over America throughout its history. And even today we delight in carting out the stereotypical old hag and seeing what new and awesome situations we can put her into, à la the sinisterly vindictive Blair Witch.

There's still just enough Blair Witch taint remaining on Burkittsville to give the town a sort of mystery. We might *know* it's just a story, yet we *feel* that somewhere way out on the farthest frontier of possibility there's just the very slightest chance that there's some truth to it, that crazy Blair Witch legend. We like being pulled into this world, where these terrible, dark possibilities dwell.

Or maybe we like to go looking for the Blair Witch because we know we're not going to find her.

Acknowledgments

I would like to express my sincere and enthusiastic thanks to the following people; each and every one of you contributed to my work in some way. So, many loud and boisterous thanks to:

Betty H. Moore and the Hampton Historical Society, Eduardo Sánchez, Douglas Bast and the Boonsboro Museum of History, Debby Burgoyne (and the awesome little community of Burkittsville), Doris Keck the best ILL person ever, Sharon Martin for many, many checkouts, library people everywhere, Tony Lyons, my editor Olga Greco, who gave me very welcome encouragement and very, very helpful suggestions, Mannie Gentile, Tim Rowland, my son Robinson Fair for always being willing to have a conversation with me about weird stuff and for always knowing so much, Zombie Cat (may he rest in peace), all the folks who have worked so hard transcribing the surviving witchcraft documents over the years and those who still work on this daunting task, all the writers who have compiled thoughtful and exhaustive accounts of witchcraft and the historians who curate that history, and all the fantastic little boys and girls who still look for witches in the woods.

Selected Bibliography

Burr, George Lincoln, ed. *Narratives of the Witchcraft Cases, 1648-1706*. Mineola, N.Y.: Dover Publications, 2012.

Calef, Robert. *More Wonders of the Invisible World*. Bainbridge, N.Y.: York Mail-Print, 1972.

Davies, Owen. *America Bewitched: the Story of Witchcraft after Salem*. New York: Oxford University Press, 2013.

Demos, John Putnam. *Entertaining Satan*. New York: Oxford University Press, 1983.

Doesticks, Q.K. Philander. *The Witches of New York*. Philadelphia: T.B. Peterson and Brothers. 1858.

Dow, Joseph. *History of the Town of Hampton, New Hampshire*. Salem, Mass.: Salem Press Publishing and Printing Company, 1894.

Eddy, Mary Baker. *Science and Health with Key to the Scriptures*. Boston: Christian Science Publishing Society, 1918.

"The Failure of the Shawnee Prophet's Witch-Hunt," by Alfred A. Cave, University of Toledo. *Ethnohistory* 42:3 (Summer 1995).

Games, Alison. *Witchcraft in Early North America*. Lanham, MD: Rowman & Littlefield Publishers, Inc., 2010

Heyrman, Christine Leigh. *Commerce and Culture the Maritime Communities of Colonial Massachusetts 1690-1750*. New York: W.W. Norton & Company 1984.

Hill, Marilynn Wood. *Their Sisters' Keepers: Prostitution in New York City, 1830-1870*. Berkley: University of California Press, 1993.

Karlsen, Carol F. *The Devil in the Shape of a Woman: Witchcraft in Colonial New England.* New York: W.W. Norton & Company Inc., 1987.

Mather, Cotton. *Cotton Mather on Witchcraft: Being the Wonders of the Invisible World.* New York: Dorset Press, 1991.

Mather, Cotton. *Diary of Cotton Mather, 1681-1724.* Google Books. Accessed July 4, 2015. https://books.google.com/books/about/Diary_of_Cotton_Mather_1681_1724.html?id=6uwSAAAAYAAJ.

Milmine, Georgine. *The Life of Mary Baker Eddy and the History of Christian Science.* New York: Doubleday Page & Company, 1909.

Roach, Marilynne K. *The Salem Witch Trials: A Day-by-Day Chronicle of a Community Under Siege.* Lanham, MD: Taylor Trade Publishing, 2004.

Sewall, Samuel. *The Diary of Samuel Sewall 1674-1729.* New York: Farrar, Strauss & Giroux, 1973.

Silverman, Kenneth. *The Life and Times of Cotton Mather.* New York: Columbia University Press, 1985.

Tucker, Ruth. *Another Gospel.* Grand Rapids: Zondervan, 1989.

Upham, Charles W. *Salem Witchcraft and Cotton Mather. A Reply.* Minneola, N.Y.: Dover, 2010.

"Witchcraft in North Carolina" by Tom Pete Cross. The University of North Carolina. *Studies in Philology.* Volume XVI July, 1919 Number 3.

University of Virginia *Salem Witchcraft* website at: http://etext.lib.virginia.edu/salem/witchcraft

https://archive.org/stream/witchcraftinnort00crosuoft/witchcraftinnort00crosuoft_djvu.txt

"Witchcraft in the American Colonies, 1647-62." By Frederick Drake. *American Quarterly* 20 (1968).

Index